# J. FRANK DOBIE

# J. FRAN

CHARLES N. PROTHRO TEXANA SERIES

Steven L. Davis

UNIVERSITY OF TEXAS PRESS AUSTIN

Copyright © 2009 by the University of Texas Press
All rights reserved

First edition, 2009

Requests for permission to reproduce material from
this work should be sent to:
    Permissions
    University of Texas Press
    P.O. Box 7819
    Austin, TX 78713-7819
    utpress.utexas.edu/index.php/rp-form

♾ The paper used in this book meets the minimum requirements
of ANSI/NISO Z39.48-1992 (R1997) (Permanence of Paper).

Library of Congress Cataloging-in-Publication Data

Davis, Steven L.
    J. Frank Dobie : a liberated mind / Steven L. Davis. — 1st ed.
        p. cm. — (Charles N. Prothro Texana series)
    Includes bibliographical references and index.
    ISBN 978-1-477-31232-2 (cloth : alk. paper)
    1. Dobie, J. Frank (James Frank), 1888–1964. 2. Folklorists—
United States—Biography. 3. Authors, American—20th century—
Biography. I. Title.
    GR55.D58D39 2009
    398'.092—dc22                          2009017763

*for Georgia*

# CONTENTS

*Acknowledgments*   ix

A LIBERATED MIND   3

PART 1: REBEL OF THE LOST CAUSE   9
   Chapter 1: Along the Ramirenia   11
   Chapter 2: The Education of a Brush Countryman, 1904–1912   19
   Chapter 3: From Texas to New York, 1913–1914   30
   Chapter 4: Fighting Conformity, Courting Bertha, 1914–1916   37
   Chapter 5: The Great War, 1915–1919   43

PART 2: THE RISING STAR   51
   Chapter 6: A Rangeland Epiphany, 1920–1921   53
   Chapter 7: The Making of a Folklorist, 1921–1923   59
   Chapter 8: The Rising Star, 1923–1926   63
   Chapter 9: Voices of the Southwest, 1926–1930   68
   Chapter 10: Regionalism Goes National, 1929–1930   75

PART 3: MR. TEXAS   83
   Chapter 11: Dobie in Bloom, 1930–1934   85
   Chapter 12: Into Mexico, 1933–1935   100

*viii*

Chapter 13: The Flavor of Texas, 1936   109
Chapter 14: The Austin Liberals, 1936–1938   124
Chapter 15: *Apache Gold* vs. *Pale Horse*, 1937–1939   131

PART 4: TEXAS NEEDS BRAINS   137
Chapter 16: The Longhorns, 1939–1941   139
Chapter 17: True Patriotism and the Singing
        Governor, 1940–1941   143
Chapter 18: The Liberal Hero, 1941–1943   150
Chapter 19: A Contemporary of Himself, 1943–1946   155
Chapter 20: A Texan in England, 1943–1946   163
Chapter 21: Texas Needs Brains, 1946–1947   173

PART 5: ELDER STATESMAN   181
Chapter 22: Coyote Wisdom, 1948–1953   183
Chapter 23: Elder Statesman, 1951–1958   190
Chapter 24: Literary Dictator, 1952–1960   197
Chapter 25: End of an Era, 1955–1959   206

PART 6: TWILIGHT   219
Chapter 26: One Touch of Nature, Plus, 1960–1962   221
Chapter 27: Sunset, 1962–1964   230
Chapter 28: Dobie's Legacy   234

*Notes*   *243*
*Selected Bibliography*   *269*
*Index*   *279*

# ACKNOWLEDGMENTS

**J.** FRANK DOBIE mentored and encouraged numerous younger writers during his lifetime. Though I came along too late to benefit from Dobie's counsel, I've had the good fortune to be influenced by Bill Wittliff, who was himself inspired by Dobie. It was Bill who, along with his wife Sally, founded the Southwestern Writers Collection at Texas State University–San Marcos in 1986. They established the collection with a gift of J. Frank Dobie papers, which Bill rescued just before the material was to be dispersed at an estate sale. It was Bill, too, who encouraged me to write this biography of J. Frank Dobie, and who provided me boundless support throughout my venture. I'm indebted to him for this and many other kindnesses.

I found in working on this book that invoking the Dobie name often leads to gracious assistance, and I've received support from many fine people. At Texas State University–San Marcos, I've had the pleasure of working for Connie Todd, the Curator of the Wittliff Collections, whom I'm privileged to consider a friend. Also at the Southwestern Writers Collection/Wittliff Collections I've benefited from the friendship and support of several staff members: Amy Cochran, Carla Ellard, Beverly Fondren, Mary E. Garcia, Michele Miller, Joel Minor, Katie Salzmann, Karen Sigler, and Joe Sumbera.

*x*     I'm very grateful to the Albert B. Alkek Library and Texas State University–San Marcos for providing me with seven weeks of professional development leave in the summer of 2007 in order to work on this book. Thanks in particular to the library staff who first proposed the program, and also to Joan Heath, Assistant Vice President–Alkek Library; Carl Van Wyatt, Vice President for Information Technology; and Denise Trauth, President of Texas State University–San Marcos, for supporting the staff's professional development.

The early drafts of this book received welcome corrections, critiques, and advice from a number of astute readers: Francis Edward Abernethy, Mark Busby, Georgia Ruiz Davis, Dudley Dobie, Jr., Don Graham, Susanna R. Hill, Joel Minor, Bud Shrake, Connie Todd, and Bill Wittliff. Thanks to their suggestions, this book is much stronger, though of course none of these readers are responsible for its remaining flaws.

Many other people contributed information, advice, and support throughout this project. Among them are Gwynedd Cannan, Mary Comparetto, Joe Davis, Truman Davis, Dick Holland, Don Hurd, Carol MacKay, Elizabeth Burdine and the family of Bill Malone, Theresa May, Larry McMurtry, Bill Minutaglio, Rollo Newsom, Alan Paredes, Vincent Paredes, Audrey Slate, Marc Simmons, Marcelle Dobie Smith, Sheryl Smith-Rodgers, Cathy Supple, Don Wilkinson, and Marc Wilkinson. Thanks to Dudley Dobie, Jr., for giving me a tour of the Dobie house, and to Polk Shelton, Jr., for recounting his run-in with Dobie. A special thank you also to Bob Barton and Dorothy "Dot" Moore for their early support and encouragement, which has sustained me for years.

For the cover art I'm most grateful to Olivia Hogue Mariño, who agreed that the beautiful portrait painted by her father, Alexandre Hogue, in 1931 would make a terrific cover. Thanks, too, to Susie Kalil for sharing her insights on Hogue's painting, and to Marc Carlson, Director of Special Collections at McFarlin Library, Tulsa University, for coordinating the painting's digitization.

This work has benefited from the assistance lent by staff members at several archival repositories. In particular I'd like to acknowledge the help I received from Richard Workman at the Harry H. Ransom Humanities Research Center at the University of Texas at Austin; Kathryn Stallings at the A. Frank Smith, Jr. Library Center, Southwestern University in Georgetown, Texas; Jim Bradshaw at the Haley Memorial Library & History Center in Midland; Laura Eggert at the Lyndon Baines Johnson Library in Austin; Beth Alvarez at the University of Maryland, College Park Library; John Anderson at the Texas State Library & Archives Commission; Thomas Kreneck at the Bell Library, Texas A&M University–Corpus Christi; Claudia Rivers and Yvette N. Delgado at the Special Collections Department, University of Texas at El Paso University Library.

In addition to the wealth of archival material, my research was greatly aided by Al Lowman's generous donation of a very extensive collection of Dobie-related publications to Texas State University–San Marcos. Thank you, Al.

Researchers such as myself have greatly benefited from new technologies. We still have to scroll through our share of microfilm, but, increasingly, the contents of old newspapers, magazines, and scholarly journals are becoming available via computer, often with the aid of keyword searches. The Albert B. Alkek Library at Texas State University–San Marcos has a reputation as an excellent academic library, and researchers such as myself are grateful to its fine staff for making these new technologies available in a very efficient manner.

As the endnotes and bibliography will attest, I've also benefited from the previous work of many scholars and writers. Among those who have been the most helpful are Francis Edward Abernethy, Mark Busby, Don Graham, Joe Frantz, James McNutt, Américo Paredes, Nolan Porterfield, Paul Stone, and Lon Tinkle.

Finally, a deep thank you to my wonderful wife, Georgia Ruiz Davis, and to my awesome kids, Natalie and Lucia, for all their love and support.

# J. FRANK DOBIE

Dobie in his study, ca. 1940s. Southwestern Writers Collection/
The Wittliff Collections, Texas State University–San Marcos.

# A Liberated Mind

THE WHITE HOUSE, APRIL 25, 1964. 12:10 P.M.

Lyndon B. Johnson: Hello.

Harry S. Truman: This is Harry Truman talking.

Johnson: Yes sir, Mr. President, how are you? Lyndon Johnson [here].

Truman: Well, my goodness alive.

Johnson: I'm mighty glad to hear your voice.

Truman: I thought I ought to report that I appeared. I thought maybe if it was convenient to you after lunch I'd like to come over and pay a call to you.

Johnson: Well, I've got a good old friend of mine . . . why don't you come and have lunch with me?

Truman: Oh, my goodness alive.

Johnson: Come over here . . . you can walk over here. I'm going to have a little press conference . . . I'm going to let them come in and tell them they can go for the weekend. But if you want to come over, say 12:45 or 1:00, why we'll say howdy to the boys and then you and I and Dr. Frank Dobie, an old friend of mine that you've met down in Texas two or three times with Rayburn, he's here, and we'll just have a quiet little luncheon. You come and eat with us. I'll give you a snort or two, but I won't put you on the helicopter.

Truman: [laughter]

Johnson: I won't put you on the helicopter.

Truman: [laughter] . . . all right . . . you know I always obey the President, especially when it's you.

Johnson: Thank you, Mr. President.

Truman: I'll be over.

Johnson: Wonderful to see you.

**J.** FRANK DOBIE was not quite a "doctor," as Johnson described him. Although a longtime professor at the University of Texas at Austin, the independent-minded Dobie had always resisted the stuffiness and pedantry of academia. Indeed, he led a lifelong rebellion against his own profession, working to bring scholarship out of the ivory tower and down to earth, where it could be shared among the people. He had long ago forsworn getting his doctoral degree, famously observing, "The average Ph.D. thesis is nothing but a transference of bones from one graveyard to another."[1]

4    It had not been easy for Johnson to bring the ailing seventy-five-year-old to Washington. When the president's staff extended the invitation, Dobie turned them down, citing his poor health. Then Johnson placed a direct call. The president didn't tape that conversation, but he did record a subsequent phone call to journalist Marshall McNeil. "I called old man Dobie this morning," Johnson said, "and told him I'd send Lady Bird's plane and bring him to Dallas and I'd buy his tickets . . . and I'd get him up here and he'd stay at the White House and, goddammit, he'd have to come up and do it." Johnson added, "He said he didn't know whether he'd make it, but said 'I'm like a horse that's down in his bottom.'"[2]

Dobie spent three days in the president's company, sitting in with Johnson during meetings with California Governor Pat Brown and United Auto Workers Union President Walter Reuther. He also joined Johnson and Truman for lunch and a press conference. After Dobie's return home to Austin, Johnson announced that he was awarding him the Presidential Medal of Freedom, the nation's highest civilian honor. Dobie would live just long enough to see the medal.

After his death, an old friend of Dobie's, Kate O'Connor, reached for her copy of his book *The Longhorns*, which had been published some twenty years earlier. Dobie had written portions of it on the O'Connor Ranch and had dedicated a chapter to her. He had warmly inscribed this particular copy to the O'Connor family. She opened the book and wrote, "J. Frank Dobie died in Austin Texas Friday Sep 18-1964—unloved and unmourned—because he defected to the enemy—communism."[3]

Dobie was hated and loved, sometimes by the same people. A University of Texas regent who sought to remove Dobie from his teaching post observed, "[He is] beloved by all of us and I don't know anybody who isn't his friend." Yet the regent added, "I tell you frankly you can either fire him or keep him, you can't control him." One of Dobie's sternest critics, a Mexican American scholar named Américo Paredes, later told an interviewer, "I found him to be a very loveable old . . . fraud." Paredes produced the most scathing literary portrait of Dobie in existence, yet he also sang a song in the old man's honor after his death. Dobie's long-suffering wife, Bertha, who was often left alone while he set out on adventures, once observed, "I should say that in Frank, pig, charging bull and mule together make a half, and that the other half is *humanity at its very finest*." Although Dobie received the Presidential Medal of Freedom, the U.S. government also secretly investigated him as a subversive threat, according to recently declassified FBI documents.[4]

James Frank Dobie came to prominence in the 1920s as the savior of Texas's rural past, hailed by his many admirers for capturing the region's folk history, which was quickly disappearing ahead of the nation's rapid industrial expansion. He was the first Texas writer to achieve significant national attention, and he parlayed his success into building an image for himself as "Mr. Texas." As a highly quotable, often controversial figure, Dobie was a publicist's dream. A stocky man of medium height, he exuded vigor and charm. The stubborn set of his jaw and his blazing blue eyes were offset by a wide, contagious grin and cackling laughter. He had a thick thatch of prematurely gray hair and bushy dark eyebrows. He puffed thoughtfully on an ever-present pipe and outfitted himself in crumpled khakis, tucking his pants into his boots, rancher style. Resting on his head was a Stetson hat. Dobie looked and sounded like he had just come from the ranch, but then he could quote Shakespeare with ease.

Many people viewed Dobie as Texas's ambassador to the world and he relished his status, working vigorously to influence the state's cultural development in the directions he thought it should go. He grew up in Texas during an era when the state was emphatically Old South, when farmers outnumbered ranchers and cotton was king. Yet Dobie focused his attention on cowboys, cattle ranching, and the early Spanish Mexican presence, helping Texas reinvent itself as part of the New Southwest.

At the University of Texas, Dobie challenged his colleagues to broaden their conceptions of education beyond the traditional emphasis on classical and European civilizations. A great university, he argued, should be *of* the state it is in, and he criticized those who have "no more sympathy for the life of the Southwest than they have for life in Patagonia." Despite encountering significant opposition, Dobie helped pioneer the concept of "regional studies" in academia. The point of studying one's own region, Dobie noted, is that, "If people are to enjoy their own lives, they must be aware of the significances of their own environments."[5]

Dobie also helped dismantle the traditional "Great Man" approach to history, in which historians explained the past by focusing on the military and political exploits of a few powerful individuals. Dobie's own aim was to capture stories that "express a social background" by revealing "the mind, the metaphor, and the *mores* of the common people."[6] It took the historical profession a few decades to catch up with Dobie and other renegades like him, but many scholars eventually recognized that social history—examining the lives of everyday people—provides a more compelling portrait of our shared past.

Prior to Dobie's time, academics were expected to publish narrow treatises, primarily for the benefit of other scholars. Many academics abhorred the thought of being understood by common readers. Dobie's ability to convey scholarly ideas through accessible prose is one of his enduring achievements. He inspired many future scholars—although by no means a majority—to aim for clarity in their writing.

However, Dobie's own legacy as a writer remains uneven and, like the man himself, is full of contradictions. Highly praised during his lifetime, he has been attacked by legions of critics since his death. His rallying cry was always "authenticity," yet he approached his native region with a romanticism that unwittingly contributed to the same "Wild West" stereotypes he railed against. Although he claimed deep friendships with Texas Mexican vaqueros, his view of race relations was complicated by his fealty to Anglo American culture, and Chicano scholars have since accused him of jingoism. He consistently demanded the highest level of achievement in other writers, and yet his own prose sometimes reads, as one critic complained, "as if it had bored him to write it."[7]

Despite his flaws as a writer, Dobie succeeded in capturing vital aspects of Texas's past that would have otherwise been lost. His books helped nourish future generations of authors—such as Larry McMurtry—who freely adapted his tales into their work. Dobie also mentored dozens of younger writers—men, women, Mexican Americans, and African Americans—who went on to significant accomplishments of their own.

Dobie grew up worshipping the nineteenth century's open range, and he absorbed many of the mythologies—and prejudices—of those times. He believed that Anglos were entitled to expand their control over territory previously held by other ethnic groups. He lionized frontiersmen such as Jim Bowie, whom he once described as "brave, bloody, rough, romantic, real, enigmatical . . . who fought for nebulous treasure as hardily as for a nation's liberty."[8]

Dobie's provincial pride led him to engage in chauvinistic boosterism, and he made such claims as, "In one Texas town there is more color of legend and history than can be found in the whole state of Iowa."[9] When Texas braggadocio reached new heights during the state's 1936 centennial celebration, Dobie took the opportunity to enshrine his reputation as "Mr. Texas."

Dobie also expressed "violently anti-New Deal" opinions during the 1930s, as his fierce devotion to freedom led him to oppose any governmen-

Dobie wearing a tie with a paisano (roadrunner), his totem animal, ca. 1950s. Southwestern Writers Collection/The Wittliff Collections, Texas State University–San Marcos.

tal constraints. He was ill equipped to understand the causes of the Great Depression, nor did he accurately gauge its severity, and he was among those who believed that Franklin Roosevelt threatened to turn proud, individualistic people into "a nation of sap-suckers."[10]

But change was on the horizon for Dobie, thanks to his principled belief in free-range thinking. Even though he seemed to embody conservative Texas's traditional values, he was never an easy man to pin down. In the 1920s he single-handedly integrated the Texas Folklore Society, installing a Mexican American woman named Jovita González as the organization's president. In the 1930s he inducted J. Mason Brewer, an African American writer, promoting his work and career with equal fervor.

As the United States began to pull out of the Great Depression, conservative political opposition to Roosevelt mounted into hysteria, and Dobie began to realize that abusive corporations, rather than the federal government, posed the larger threat to individual liberty. Attacks by right-wing businessmen on academic freedom at the University of Texas made the battle personal for him, and at the age of fifty-three, Dobie came out fighting as a political liberal.

8      The transformation was remarkable. The person who once symbolized Texas provincialism began criticizing "Texas bragging that goes no deeper than the imitation felt of a big hat."[11] With his customary gusto, Dobie fought for labor, free speech, and civil rights. By 1946 he was calling for the complete integration of the University of Texas. Many old friends thought he had lost his mind, and many fans felt betrayed.

Dobie never backed away from his convictions, and he continued to broaden his mind and sharpen his writing as he grew older. He ultimately realized the limitations of political activity, concluding that personal "enlightenment is the only answer." In his later years Dobie became viewed as a "sage of the sagebrush," sharing his hard-won insights with others in the hope of inspiring a wiser and more tolerant humanity. By the end of his life, Dobie overcame many—though not all—of his early limitations. The epitaph he penned for his own tombstone sums up his life's journey: "I have come to value liberated minds as the supreme good of life on earth."[12]

*Rebel of the Lost Cause*

# Along the Ramirenia

I N NOVEMBER 1528 a group of Spanish conquistadors washed ashore at what is now Galveston Island. These were the last remnants of a once-proud expedition, originally six hundred strong, that had set sail from Cuba half a year earlier, intent on conquering Florida and finding vast riches of gold. They had run into misfortune from the very beginning, suffering disease and starvation while coming under attack from hostile Indians. Finally, in desperation, they built makeshift wooden rafts and floated down the Gulf Coast, hoping to eventually find their countrymen in Mexico.

The few dozen castaways named their landing place the Island of Misfortune. Most died, and some resorted to cannibalism. Only four survived, and they would live among various Indian groups for eight years before they saw their countrymen again.

Their leader, Álvar Núñez Cabeza de Vaca, later wrote an account of the experience. He provided much valuable information about preconquest Native Americans, and he chronicled his personal transformation from an arrogant conquistador into a passionate defender of Indian human rights. Cabeza de Vaca argued eloquently against the Spanish policy of enslaving Indians, and of one Indian group along the Texas coast he observed, "These people love their children more and treat them better than any other people on earth."[1] He also suggested that many of the so-called "savages" he encountered would make better Christians than the Christians themselves.

Cabeza de Vaca's book, *La relación*, first appeared in 1542 and has captivated readers ever since. His book is not only one of the world's great adventure stories, it is also the first written work on the region that became Texas and the Southwest.

After several years of living among the coastal Indians, Cabeza de Vaca and his companions journeyed south, toward Mexico. Before long they came to a harsh, nearly impenetrable land of cacti and tangled thickets of thorned brush. In contrast to the well-marked trading trails they had used farther north, no paths were cut through this isolated region. Food was scarce, and few Native Americans made permanent homes here. Those who did, Cabeza de Vaca observed, had to dig for roots in order to survive. The only reliable staple was the prickly pear cactus.

The men sometimes went days without food, and their feet bled profusely from the thorns and cacti. The vegetation was not tall enough to provide shade, and yet the dense brush grew too high to see the way ahead. Navigating their way through this thorny labyrinth, Cabeza de Vaca got separated from his companions. Five days later, miraculously, he found them again. They were amazed, as they assumed that he had been killed by one of the ubiquitous rattlesnakes.

Cabeza de Vaca's travels eventually carried him thousands of miles, and he saw numerous areas where future Spanish settlements might prosper. Indeed, his book touched off something of a land rush, as Spanish Mexican explorers and settlers converged on New Spain's northern territories. Yet nothing in Cabeza de Vaca's account inspired anyone to visit the rugged, thorn-choked land he had described near the beginning of his journey—an area that in later years would become known as the South Texas Brush Country.

It wasn't until the mid-1700s, more than two hundred years later, that Spanish Mexican colonists began arriving in this region. The settlers brought along tough, long-horned cattle that could survive in the harsh environment, thus pioneering the great Texas tradition of cattle ranching. The men who took care of the cattle, the vaqueros, became the progenitors of the American cowboy.

J. Frank Dobie was born to this land in 1888, on a Brush Country ranch owned by his family. Their acreage was just south of the Nueces River, the modest waterway that had once marked the international boundary between Texas and Mexico. Dobie was "out of the old rock," as he liked to say. The Dobie clan, originally from Scotland, came to Texas from Virginia in the 1830s.

The Dobie ranch was part of a much larger spread that had once belonged to two brothers, José Antonio and José Victoriano Ramirez, who had been granted the land by the King of Spain in the 1700s. The Ramirezes founded a cattle ranch and built a fortified compound to protect against Indian attacks. But they were no match for a party of raiding Comanches that struck in 1813, killing almost everyone and forcing the survivors to abandon the settlement.

The Ramirez grant remained part of Mexico until 1848, when the U.S.-Mexican War pushed the border two hundred miles farther south, to the Rio Grande. The Dobie family arrived to this newly annexed area soon afterwards. The Nueces Strip, as the Brush Country land between the Nueces River and the Rio Grande became known, was famous for its lawlessness. Indian raids were a continuing threat into the 1870s and plenty of Anglo outlaws also roamed the territory. Most of the violence, however, resulted from clashes between the newly arriving Anglos and the established Mexicanos.

The U.S. government had pledged to honor preexisting Spanish and Mexican land grants, but Anglos systematically expanded their control, often through questionable methods. Mexicanos were subjected to forced land sales and, occasionally, physical intimidation. Texas Rangers, who Mexicanos considered to be employees of Richard King's ranch, often carried out these acts of aggression. The relentless expansion of the King Ranch received much criticism. In 1878, an anonymous newspaper commentator observed that King's neighbors seemed to "mysteriously vanish whilst his territory extends over entire counties."[2]

Some Mexicanos actively resisted this Anglo encroachment, and sporadic raids became a part of life along "the Bloody Border." In 1859, just as the Dobies were getting settled, a South Texas landowner named Juan Cortina led an armed uprising against the Anglos. In his widely circulated proclamation, Cortina asserted that Mexicanos had "been robbed of [their] property, incarcerated, chased, murdered, and hunted like wild beasts. . . ." He declared a new country, "The Republic of the Rio Grande," and he called for "Death to the Gringos!"[3] Cortina recruited vaqueros from area ranches and he defeated the Texas Rangers in a string of battles. Only the arrival of the U.S. Army quelled the insurrection. Many Mexicanos, naturally, considered Cortina a great hero. Anglos, however, saw him as a bandit.

Dobie's family received small tastes of this border violence. There were times, Dobie wrote, when "Mexican bandits were raiding up into Texas from below the Rio Grande, sometimes killing." The men from the Dobie ranch would go out in pursuit, while Dobie's grandmother "alone with her little ones at night would stay awake near a rifle."[4]

Dobie was the first of six children and he grew up immersed in the passions of Anglo Texan history. He heard thrilling tales of the battle against enemy Mexicans at San Jacinto, his grandfather's fight against the enemy Yankees in the War Between the States, and the ever-present threats posed by Mexican bandits.

Most fascinating to Dobie, however, were the stories of the open range. He heard about his father and uncles driving vast herds of half-wild longhorns all the way up the trail to Kansas, crossing swollen streams, fighting through dust storms, heading off stampedes, and keeping an eye out for hostile Indians.

The railroad arrived in South Texas shortly before Dobie's birth, and this new technological advancement quickly brought an end to the trail drives. The tough, noble longhorns were no longer necessary, and ranchers began turning to fat, docile breeds that could be easily packed into railroad cars and shipped north to meatpacking plants. Barbed wire was fencing off the open range, and the great frontier was dying out.

Hearing all the stories about the iconic events that happened before his birth convinced Dobie of one essential truth: he had been born too late, and he had just missed out on the last great era of human adventure.

★ ★

The Dobie ranch was situated in one of the prettier parts of the Brush Country, in Live Oak County, where rolling hills give rise to scattered strands of live oak trees, which appear majestic amidst the thornscrub. Ramirenia Creek winds through the caliche hillsides, making its way towards the Nueces River. During Dobie's youth wildlife was still abundant, although the once-common alligators had been hunted out. The thick brush remained a prime habitat for rattlesnakes, and the Dobie family kept the area around their ranch house cleared of all vegetation, "a pioneer tradition that guarded against snakes."[5]

Dobie's father, Dick, had been a good fiddle player as a young man and was much in favor at country dances. Folks called him "Dancing Dick of Sore Toe." But after getting married, he "became rigidly religious, quit dancing, disposed of his fiddle, never to play one again, and stopped smoking."[6] Throughout the rest of his life, Dick Dobie maintained a reputation as a scrupulously Christian man of steady temperament. He provided well for his family, although his children regretted that they never saw his more ebullient side.

Dobie's mother, Ella Byler Dobie, was an energetic, strong-willed woman who outworked everyone. She was the first person awake and the last to bed, cooking meals, maintaining the household, and raising the children. She averaged about four to five hours of sleep each night. A former schoolteacher, she taught Dobie to read at an early age. She, too, was of Scottish descent, and she took great pride in her family's heritage. She had a favorite saying for her eldest child: "Never forget whose son you are."[7]

Most Texas households at the time had only one book—the Bible. But Ella Dobie had broader aims for her children. Dobie recalled, "My mother had pasted on the inside of her wardrobe door a printed list of maybe 20 of the best books—out of two or three centuries—fitting for young people to read. In the course of Christmases we got them all."[8] Dobie loved reading, but he could never get enough books at the ranch to keep him happy.

His mother made certain that no tales of the "Wild West" entered their home. Even Andy Adams, a family friend who had written the definitive trail drive account *Log of a Cowboy*, was not considered suitable for inclusion in the Dobie family library. In this regard, Ella Dobie conformed to propriety by discriminating between "literature"—which was exalted—and plain "storytelling"—which was considered plebeian. Her son, however, would eventually rebel against such distinctions, breaking down the artificial barriers.

Every night, Dobie's family gathered around a kerosene lamp so that Dick Dobie could read aloud from the Bible. Yet even from an early age Frank had little interest in those stories. To him, it was the world outside that was alive, and he possessed "an almost animistic relationship with nature." He explored every acre of the ranch, observing "the green on mesquites in early spring so tender that it emanated into the sky" and "the mustang grapevines draping trees along Ramirenia Creek." He heard "the bobwhites' cherio in the morning, the bullbats' zoom at twilight [and] the coyotes serenading from every side after dark." Dobie recalled later, "I did not know it at the time, but I began listening to this piece of land talk while I was the merest child."[9]

The Dobie kids loved to explore what they called Fort Ramirez, which was, in actuality, the ruins of the previous settlement. "Some of the rock walls were still standing when I was a boy," Dobie wrote, "and a person on top of them had a grand view of the S-winding Ramirenia Creek."[10]

America was rapidly industrializing during Dobie's childhood, as great factories arose in the Northeast and Midwest, mass-producing standardized products and drawing millions of new immigrants into teeming urban centers. Railroads, telephones, and electricity were knitting the country closer together, but the Dobie ranch remained largely immune to social change.

The children attended a one-room schoolhouse and the family made occasional horse-drawn trips to the nearby towns of Alice or Beeville for supplies. Such journeys often took a day or more along the narrow pathways cut through the brush. The family often camped out along the way, only rarely encountering another person. In those years, Dobie recalled, "Alice was more distant in travel time from our ranch than New York now is from San Antonio."[11]

Religion was central to their lives. Dobie's father helped build two Methodist churches in the area, and he "insisted on observing [the Sabbath] with puritanical sternness." He abstained from working on Sundays and forbade his boys from doing any chores. Yet, as Dobie later observed, the women and Mexican servants were expected to "cook or help cook, haul water in barrels, bring up wood, stake the horses, and do other chores." Church became an all-day affair, with morning and afternoon services, interrupted only by a picnic lunch and plenty of hymn singing.[12]

"So far as religion goes," Dobie recalled, "the prayers gave me nothing enduring. To tell the truth, they generally bored me."[13] Far more interesting was ranching. Dobie was comfortable on horseback by the time he learned to walk, and as he grew older he joined in the work, spending long days in the saddle. "I grew up among men who had spent their lives on the ground," he recalled, "often sleeping upon it, eating upon it, riding horseback over it, gazing beyond it." Before he was a teenager, he was branding cattle, moving them between pastures, and doctoring those infected with screwworm. He learned from his father and the vaqueros how to quiet nervous cattle by singing to them. Rather than the cowboy songs of popular lore, Dobie's father soothed them by singing Methodist hymns.[14]

The Brush Country suffered severe droughts during Dobie's childhood, and cattle on neighboring ranches often died of thirst. The Dobies were fortunate to have a good well on their property, but even then the cattle often went hungry in the drought-ravaged landscape. At times the vaqueros had to burn the spines off prickly pear cactus in order to feed the livestock. Dobie also observed cattle fighting each other at the first smell of water, and he "heard them bawling all night long and all day long for water."[15]

Dobie's firsthand experience with the gritty reality of cattle ranching imbued him with authenticity, and he consistently railed against romantic notions of cowboy life. Popular compositions such as "Home on the Range" were tripe, Dobie observed, because any rancher knows that a land "where the skies are not cloudy all day" is a place where the cattle are dying from drought.

One aspect of the Dobie ranch that made an impression on him from the beginning was the fact that its workforce was overwhelmingly Mexican American. "I cannot remember my first association with Mexicans," Dobie later wrote, "for I was born and reared in a part of Texas . . . where Mexicans were, and still are, more numerous than people of English-speaking ancestry."[16]

Entire families lived and worked on the Dobie ranch, just as earlier generations had worked for Spanish Mexican ranch owners. The class structure was highly stratified. The vaqueros who worked with the cattle enjoyed some measure of respect, but most other Mexicanos were relegated to *peón* (laborer) status. Dobie's father was the *patrón* (boss), and he provided food, lodging, rudimentary medical care, and small bits of money in exchange for a lifetime's service.

At Christmas Dobie's father gave each of the ranch families a new blanket, and their children received candy and apples. Mortality rates were high, particularly for infants, and whenever one died, Dobie's father "would be called upon to make the coffin, sawing it out of pine boards and lining it with cotton sheeting."[17]

Growing up as the eldest son of the patrón, Dobie became accustomed to being treated with great deference by the resident Mexicanos. He, in turn, admired many of their qualities, in particular what he saw as their deep attachment to the land and their "uncomplaining loyalty."[18]

"Among the best friends I have are some old Texas vaqueros that I grew up riding with," Dobie later wrote. His closest companion was Genardo del Bosque, whose "intelligence, energy, cow sense and responsibility would have made him a first-class manager of a big outfit."[19] Genardo came from a family that had once owned land in Texas, and he likely held conflicted feelings about serving the family. Dobie, however, saw only devotion in his father's employee.

As a teenager, Dobie's fondest hope was to quit school and ride full-time with Genardo and the other vaqueros, but his parents put a stop to that idea. Barriers were being put into place between Dobie and the ranch Mexicanos. Like many Texas Anglos, the Dobies considered Mexicanos culturally inferior, and they passed along their beliefs to their eldest son.

Despite the fact that the Dobie family used many words adapted from the original Spanish, such as ranch, corral, lariat, lasso, and stampede, Dobie's parents strongly dissuaded him from learning any Spanish other than a few "boss" words. He also was told in unsparing terms that he should never consort with a woman of Mexican descent. His family did allow Mexican American children on the ranch to attend the one-room schoolhouse, but the few who did, Dobie recalled, "were ostracized by the English-speaking children both in the schoolroom and on the playground."[20]

As one scholar later noted, Dobie's upbringing conditioned him "to regard Mexicans in a highly paternalistic fashion, secure in the [belief] of his own ethnic and cultural superiority."[21] Overcoming these early prejudices would involve a lifetime's work.

# The Education of a Brush Countryman
## 1904–1912

ICK AND ELLA DOBIE raised their children during an age when the possibilities for improvement seemed limitless, but were measured in generations, rather than years. Dobie's father "hoped that his sons would find something better in life than ranching." Although neither parent had ever been to college, they made it clear from the beginning that they expected their children to do so. "Without being much concerned about intellectual values, they felt deeply that somehow a college education would elevate us to a higher plane of living," Dobie recalled. He was "indifferent to the idea; at that time, in our environment, college was as remote as the pyramids of Egypt."[1]

In order to get into college, Dobie needed to attend a high school, and so in 1904 the family sent him to Alice, Texas, to live with his maternal grandparents. Alice was a thriving Brush Country town founded in 1888—the same year Dobie was born—as a rail junction to ship cattle to northern cities. Many of the cattle came from the nearby King Ranch, and Alice, in fact, was named for Richard King's daughter.

The city boasted three newspapers and several bustling businesses along its main avenue. No water or sewage system existed, but residents were proud of the brand-new rail line that ran two hundred miles south to Mexico, rendering the old stagecoach journey obsolete. Long-distance telephone service had just been established and automobiles had ceased to be a startling sight.

Dobie was a shy young man and he missed the close-knit ranch. Yet he eagerly took advantage of the opportunity to explore a larger world, and he was quite taken with his Grandpa Dubose, a Civil War veteran whose beard was "stained by leakage from the corncob pipe constantly in his mouth." Dubose hated Yankees, subscribed to the *Confederate Veteran*, and "was rather pleased with himself for never having taken the oath of allegiance to the United States," Dobie wrote. Dubose refused to celebrate the Fourth of July, and in this regard, Dobie noted, he "had company all over the South until the Confederate graveyards filled up."[2]

Dubose was a man of some prominence, and he "knew all the ranchmen, horse traders, sheriffs, and rangers of the country." Through him Dobie got to meet many of the leading Brush Country folk. Dubose served as Justice of the Peace in Alice and he made a little extra money by marrying "Mexicans who could not afford a priest." He was not regarded as a particular friend of the Mexican American community, however. An oft-cited testimony about him reported Dubose's response to a Mexican man's death: "Make[s] no difference, plenty more."[3]

Dubose was the opposite of Dobie's father in that he rigorously avoided church affairs. "Some people considered him an irredeemable sinner," Dobie recalled. "He was as cold as a well-digger's rump toward some of the preachers whom Grandma had for supper on Sunday dinner." Dobie, who had already begun to develop a few inklings of doubt about organized religion, saw his grandfather as a positive role model.[4]

The Dubose home was extraordinarily well stocked with books, and Dobie realized that there must be some connection between his grandfather's independent attitude and the great number of books he possessed. Dubose "never advised me on my conduct," Dobie recalled, other than "urging me to get an education."[5] Obligingly, Dobie immersed himself in a library that offered him Dickens, Twain, and Longfellow.

In school, Dobie remained quiet and distant from the other pupils, although he distinguished himself by making very good grades. During his two years of high school, he received only one writing assignment. Dobie's topic was "War," and the teacher was impressed enough by his paper to read it out loud in front of the class.

As graduation approached, he was chosen to speak at the ceremony. Despite his academic successes, Dobie's personality remained a work in progress. As he rose to give his speech, he recalled, "My legs were shaking like cottonwood leaves in a breeze . . . and my mouth was dry." After stumbling badly through his presentation, Dobie "sat down in misery and despondency."[6] Such were the humble beginnings of a man who would later become one of Texas's most sought-after public speakers.

In the fall of 1906, the bowlegged eighteen-year-old left his native Brush Country, arriving by train in Georgetown, Texas, home of Southwestern University. This was a Methodist school best known as a "breeding ground for preachers," and there was some hope in the Dobie family that he might follow that calling. While waiting to register for classes, he sat alone, ill at ease, wearing new shoes that pinched his pigeon-toed feet. He looked out a window and wished for all the world that he could be back at the ranch, riding his favorite horse, Buck.[7]

A distinguished-looking gentleman stopped by and introduced himself. This was R. S. Hyer, the president of the university. Hyer made conversation by asking Dobie if he enjoyed reading. The young man nodded, then Hyer "said something that made a profound and enduring impression on my mind," Dobie recalled. "He said that he had long made it a practice to read one book a week."[8]

For Dobie, who loved reading but dreaded being labeled a bookworm, this proved to be a serendipitous introduction to campus, and he resolved to follow Hyer's example. Once classes began, Dobie soon became a prize student of Albert Pegues, a charismatic English professor. Dobie recalled, "No other teacher I came under, least of all in graduate work, so enlarged and enriched life for me, so started up growths inside me." It was Pegues who introduced Dobie to the English Romantic poets, a group of literary rebels opposed to the industrial age. These poets celebrated nature, cherished instinct over science and individualism over conformity. Although none of them had ever been anywhere near the Brush Country, they spoke directly to Dobie's soul, and he became entranced. He began taking long walks along Georgetown's San Gabriel River, reading and reciting from the works of Wordsworth, Keats, Byron, and Shelley. "I was at my most essential self" during these moments, Dobie recalled. He began to dream of becoming a writer.[9]

Socially, Dobie became exposed to a much wider world at Southwestern. He was initially shocked by the relative sophistication of other students on campus, who used swear words, drank alcohol, and freely consorted with members of the opposite sex. He, in contrast, was bound by a saying of his father's, who maintained that he would rather see one of his daughters dead "than dancing in the arms of a man." This, Dobie wrote, "had a strong effect on me. I came to believe that the delights of the flesh were sinful and to feel shameful towards all implications of sex." Dobie later started work on an autobiographical essay about these years. He titled it, "When I was a Prig."[10]

Dobie gradually enlarged his circle of acquaintances. His best feature was his sunny, open smile, which came more easily as he grew more comfortable around others. He went out on a few dates and he regularly attended "recitals, concerts, glee-club programs." He became an officer in the Alamo Literary Society and he "eagerly took part" in the debates, although his knees continued to tremble whenever he stood up to speak in public.[11]

Dobie worked part-time as a reporter for the *Williamson County Sun* and he also wrote for the school newspaper, the *Megaphone*. In his junior year he got caught up in a cause "that aroused his innate democratic sympathy, his dislike of hierarchy and elitism, and his propensity for taking the side of the underdog." He was a leader of the nonaligned students, the Barbs (barbarians), who were feuding with the fraternities. Dobie used his position on the *Megaphone* to wage a campaign against the Greeks, calling for their expulsion from campus because of their "snobbery." Tensions became so inflamed that President Hyer suspended publication of the paper. Dobie was removed from his post, and Hyer suggested that he pay more attention to his grades, which had declined precipitously during the affair.[12]

In addition to his rhetorical blasts in the student newspaper, Dobie also contributed to *Southwestern University Magazine*. He published pieces of standard literary criticism, written in the accepted style of the day. Other essays showcased his devotion to his Southern heritage, clearly an influence from his Grandpa Dubose. Dobie had already purchased a colored print of "Robert E. Lee and His Generals" while in Georgetown, and he felt much "sentimentality over the Lost Cause." In one essay, he contrasted "the courtliness, the refinement, the culture of the Virginia gentleman"— Robert E. Lee—against Abraham Lincoln, whom Dobie described as an "Illinois backwoodsman, who came out of the depths." Robert E. Lee stood in Dobie's mind as "the immortal personification of all that is manly and aesthetic and pure and tender—the ideal soldier, gentleman and Christian of the world."[13]

Nothing in this formal, highly stylized prose distinguished Dobie from the thousands of other young university students across the country enmeshed in academic writing. Yet Dobie also undertook something different, even distinctive, as he began to create engaging tales from his native

Dobie's college portrait, 1910. Southwestern Writers Collection/The Wittliff Collections, Texas State University–San Marcos.

Bertha McKee's college portrait, 1910. Southwestern Writers Collection/The Wittliff Collections, Texas State University–San Marcos.

Brush Country. One of his stories was titled "Don Julian," and it told of a dying vaquero who complained about the closing of the open range: "I have seen a land of free men and great herds changed into a land of 'gringos' and plow mules." Although the old vaquero did not speak in the elevated language of an English Romantic poet, his instincts were exactly the same. Don Julian said, "Once I was free and happy; once I rode as far and as fast as the wind; once I was young, and this country was young and glad, too. Then the great iron horse came snorting down from the north . . . ."[14]

Dobie's most intriguing story was "The Buried Lariat," which told of a boyhood friend, Jack, who inherited an old document purporting to reveal the location of a buried Spanish treasure. Jack consulted a fortune-teller who assured him that he was on the path to great wealth. He enlisted Dobie and another friend, and the group set out on a quest for the treasure. They found the likely location and then discovered a critical clue—a buried lariat—but as they kept digging in ever-widening circles the treasure never appeared. After another day of digging, Dobie and the other friend began to express doubts. Not Jack, however, and as the story ended it appeared that he would continue the search even if it took him the rest of his life.

Thus unfolds Dobie's first-ever tale of buried treasure, a work in the literary genre that would make him famous two decades later. These were precisely the sorts of "tales" his mother did not approve of, nor did this type of work merit attention from the academic profession. Dobie's stories were printed merely as entertaining asides. But looking back at hundred-year-old issues of the *Southwestern University Magazine*, it becomes clear that Dobie's stories were the journal's most enduring achievements. The tales are not only far more compelling than the grim columns of deadening academic analysis, but they also provide keen nuggets of Texas's social history.

\* \*

As a senior, Dobie was elected editor of the college yearbook, and in that capacity he became friendly with Bertha McKee, a yearbook staffer who was one of the outstanding students on campus. She was intelligent, well mannered, beautiful, and aloof. She was also somewhat frail, having barely survived a childhood illness. Like Dobie, Bertha was primarily interested in literature, and she confessed to him that she had wanted to be a writer ever since she was eight years old. As they worked together they discovered that they were very compatible, and they soon became a steady couple.

Bertha and Dobie talked about their possible futures as writers, knowing that the odds were stacked against them. Texas was a poor, backward-looking state that had progressed little beyond the frontier age. Most of its population was rural, cotton was the primary cash crop, and over half the state's farmers were sharecroppers. In an environment such as this, the cultural arts were a luxury that few Texans took advantage of.

Still, some literary activity was occurring. O. Henry, who had once lived in Texas but was now in New York, had become America's leading short story writer, and some of his stories were set in Texas. More significantly, some native writers were capturing pieces of Texas history in their fiction. In 1899, Mollie E. Moore Davis published what many scholars consider to be the first serious Western, *The Wire Cutters*, which describes cowboy life and the fence-cutting wars that signaled the end of the open range. Another Texan, Andy Adams, became so dismayed by a sensationalistic account of cowboy life (Owen Wister's *The Virginian*) that he wrote his own book, *The Log of a Cowboy*, as a rebuttal. Many still consider Adams's book, which appeared in 1903, to be the most authentic depiction of a trail drive ever published.

Far more common, however, were the sensationalistic "dime novel" treatments of Texas, almost all of which were written by outsiders. The Alamo was often a favorite subject for such fiction, and so many books about the Texas shrine appeared during the late nineteenth century that the American writer Stephen Crane could ironically observe, "Statistics show that 69,710 writers have begun at the Alamo."[15]

Dobie and Bertha both despised the dime novels, and each lamented the fact that so little of Texas's true-life history had ever been used in fiction. They saw great potential in creating authentic writing about their home state, and yet both were aware of a tremendous obstacle—despite the modest successes of Davis and Adams, professional writers from Texas were unheard of.

Bertha was studying to be a teacher, but Dobie had put off his own career choice for as long as possible. He told Bertha that he dreamed of starting a magazine about Texas, to be read by Texans, but there was no practical way to put that plan into action. He recalled later, "I had not yet settled on a career, had not resolutely applied myself to anything, had merely drifted, reading what I wanted to read, neglecting courses that required application of will. . . . I had found the drifting so pleasant that I did not want to leave college, college town, college friends."[16]

As he weighed his options, his love of reading and writing offered a path to the future. "Without any consideration of a professional career," he recalled, "I drifted into teaching solely because I had fallen in love with English poetry and wanted to continue and communicate that love."[17]

He enrolled in the required education courses so that he could become certified to teach, and he quickly became dismayed by the pedantry. "Any moron who slept through the classes could have got the credit," Dobie wrote later. "I learned, in nine months, to open the schoolroom windows if it was warm and to close them if it was cold." This was a big letdown after studying world-class literature. The education curriculum, Dobie maintained, "spurred nothing in me and added not a whit to my fitness to teach anything or anybody."[18]

At graduation, Bertha was the class valedictorian and commencement speaker. She obtained a teaching position in a small town in the Texas Panhandle. Dobie applied for a job in nearby Amarillo. The superintendent seemed interested in hiring him and sent a questionnaire inquiring about his southern ancestry and church affiliation. "I could have answered in a way to influence people," Dobie recalled, "but did not propose to suffocate intellectually."[19] He turned down the opportunity to be near his sweetheart. Instead, he accepted a job as a teacher in Alpine, out in the wide expanses of the Big Bend region of West Texas. Since he would be the only male faculty member, he was also named principal of the small school. He promised to keep in touch with Bertha by correspondence.

An ambitious young man, Dobie understood that teachers received only modest salaries, barely a living wage. He planned to supplement his income with writing. Yet there was no longer an outlet for him. Editors in New York did not read *Southwestern University Magazine*, and even if they had, few would have been interested in his tales about the South Texas Brush Country.

Dobie knew that for a Texas-based writer, the surest path to developing experience and contacts was to work as a newspaper reporter. So the summer before beginning his teaching career, he took a reporting job with the *San Antonio Express*. He earned only fifteen dollars per week—an amount so paltry that even schoolteachers were rich by comparison. But he thoroughly enjoyed knowing that people were paying for the privilege of reading his words.

As the summer wound down, the *Express* offered him a dollar-a-week raise to stay, which still amounted to only half his teaching salary. He seriously considered the idea, but in the end his practical side won out and he reported for duty in West Texas.

Alpine was a cattlemen's town, set in a wide mountain valley that had only recently been reached by the railroad. It retained many vestiges of the Wild West, and it was about as close to the frontier as one could get. Dobie took an upstairs room in a boarding house off the main street. One nice benefit of Alpine was that he was so far away from home that he no longer had to go to Sunday services. "This year marked the end of my regular church attendance," Dobie wrote, "soon to become regular nonattendance."[20]

The students at Dobie's high school were products of rural Texas cattle country and were not exactly at the forefront of educational innovation. Dobie began diligently introducing them to the pleasures of English poetry—a less exalted experience than he had imagined it would be. He claimed later that his pupils "were for the most part as intelligent as university professors." In truth, however, few were interested in intellectual matters. Dobie also ran into a little trouble with some parents after telling their children about Darwin's theory of evolution. Dobie's mother became very upset when he sent her a letter about the controversy. She wrote to him, "Oh! My son it is bad enough to fill your own mind with poison but for God's sake and my sake don't try to shake any child's faith in God and God's word."[21]

For Dobie, the best thing about Alpine was its closeness to the frontier, which meant that fresh memories still lingered close to the surface. He began meeting some old-timers who told him colorful stories about Big Bend characters. Through them Dobie learned of Alice Stillwell Henderson, who ran a ranch "without any man to boss her" and by herself pursued cross-border raiders into Mexico, successfully retrieving her stolen horses. Dobie loved the tales, and the storytelling sessions also helped him overcome his shyness, as he saw that simply being a good listener gained him trust and affection.[22]

In Alpine he also met and befriended John Young, a mostly retired cattleman from the Brush Country who told him dashing stories about trail drives and battles with Indians and Mexicans. These were the same sorts of tales Dobie had grown up hearing from family members, only Young had been more adventurous and so his stories were even more fascinating. Eighteen years later Young would become the subject of Dobie's first book.

While Dobie was in Alpine the Mexican Revolution erupted across the border. Many young Americans—and a few old ones, such as the famed writer Ambrose Bierce—scrambled to join the action. Some fought as soldiers; others went as reporters. The Revolution promised the grand adventure that Dobie and others of his generation had been waiting for. A classmate from Southwestern had already gone to Mexico and invited Dobie to join him. Dobie wrote later that he felt "a strong inclination" to take up the fight against "the old dictator Don Porfirio Díaz," but, for reasons that remain unknown, he stayed in Texas.[23]

Part of Dobie's hesitancy may have come from the fact that Díaz was deposed relatively quickly, and the opposition quickly splintered. What began as a noble cause quickly disintegrated into chaos. The Revolution would continue to tear Mexico apart for the next decade, killing over a million people—including, presumably, Ambrose Bierce, who disappeared while accompanying Pancho Villa's army. Bierce had been prepared to meet his death, however. In one of his last letters he wrote, "If you hear of my being stood up against a Mexican stone wall and shot to rags please know that I think that a pretty good way to depart this life. It beats old age, disease, or falling down the cellar stairs. To be a gringo in Mexico—ah, that is euthanasia."[24]

★ ★

As his year of school teaching drew to a close, Dobie tired of Alpine's extreme isolation, and he missed the camaraderie and intellectual stimulation of Georgetown. He kept up an active correspondence with college friends, including Bertha. He also maintained his connection to the university by keeping in touch with faculty members and publishing literary criticism in the campus magazine. In one such article, which certainly drew praise from the school's religious administrators, Dobie criticized William Gilmore Simms, a now forgotten novelist, for "speaking a thousand 'damns' and 'hells' and other curse words." Such realism in writing, Dobie opined, is "too dark and terrible to be tolerated. . . . The novel, even a realistic novel, should aim to make the ideal real."[25]

Near the end of the school year, Southwestern University president R. S. Hyer offered Dobie a job, which he quickly accepted. Back in Georgetown, he taught at the college's preparatory high school. In the fall of 1911, he learned that Bertha was coming to town for a visit. This would be the first time they had seen each other since graduation. She arrived looking radiant and announced that she had been accepted into graduate school at the University of Chicago.

Dobie was forming a plan of his own. He decided that he would also go to graduate school so he could obtain a Ph.D. He wanted to teach at a university instead of high school. In this way, he could share his love for English poetry and literature, just as Professor Pegues had done for him at Southwestern. The Ph.D. would also give him more prestige, an important factor as he surveyed his real ambition—to become a writer.

The faculty at Southwestern believed strongly in Dobie's potential, and with their assistance he focused on writing literary criticism—the accepted method for gaining academic credentials. As he considered various graduate programs, he decided against joining the beautiful, intelligent Bertha in Chicago. Instead, he applied to Columbia University, a prestigious Ivy League school. It was no coincidence that Columbia was located in New York City—the publishing capital of America.

# From Texas to New York
## 1913–1914

**T**HE DOBIE FAMILY sold off some of the cattle earmarked for their eldest son, and armed with that stake, twenty-four-year-old J. Frank Dobie arrived in New York City in January 1913. Five million people lived in the city, more than in the entire state of Texas. Tenement buildings overflowed with new immigrants, skyscrapers dominated the horizon, and the subways were littered with advertisements. Dobie saw faces "grown hard or indifferent," and he considered New York a "great monstrosity of human society." In a letter to his mother, he sardonically observed, "The NY subway is a great preserver of one's aesthetic tastes—it prevents one from having to look at the city."[1]

New York was America's main port of entry, and almost half the city's population was foreign-born. The waves of immigrants supplied the cheap labor necessary to maintain America's rapid industrial expansion, but a nativist movement arose in protest, and immigration was fast becoming a political issue.

Columbia University seemed far removed from such matters, at least on the surface. Founded in 1754 by King George II of England, it gained a reputation for educational innovation and created one of the country's first graduate programs. The year before Dobie's arrival Columbia launched a new school of journalism, founded by Joseph Pulitzer.

The university boasted a number of internationally famous scholars. Among them was Franz Boas, a German-born professor widely credited as the founder of modern anthropology. In his studies of so-called "primitive" tribes, Boas came to the groundbreaking conclusion that these non-Europeans were simply different, rather than inferior. He argued that all humans were generally capable of equal achievements, and that differences between groups of people were largely cultural, rather than genetic. In his book *The Mind of Primitive Man*, published two years before Dobie's arrival, Boas overturned conventional thinking by arguing that no racial group is genetically "pure." Such academic work influenced the immigration debates, as Boas's studies seemed to disprove the nativists' fears that new arrivals from southern and eastern Europe would turn the United States into a "mongrel" nation.

Dobie was firmly in the nativist camp. He had trouble adapting to New York's diverse cultures, particularly the new immigrants from southern and eastern Europe. In letters back home he complained about "the human refuse of Europe" coming into the country and "killing our genius, our individuality, our right to self-expression." Among those who bothered him were the Jews, whom Dobie admitted to having developed a "deep-seated" prejudice against.[2]

"I had a strong tendency to want all people to look like the people I came from, to act like the people I was used to in Texas, and to think and feel as I thought and felt," Dobie admitted later, adding, "I hate to admit to such smugness and insularity."[3]

At Columbia, he attended lectures alongside African American students—something he had been warned about back in Texas. He claimed later that "this was the beginning of my conversion to the idea that Negroes have as much right to an education as anybody else." But at the time Dobie was much less conciliatory. He adamantly supported segregation, and he denounced a newspaper reporter who criticized southern treatment of Negroes as a "fool." When asked by a northern cousin to justify segregation, Dobie erupted, "We just wanted to, by God."[4]

The professors at Columbia were often very formal in their presentations, and kept a stiff distance from students. This was quite a change from the friendships Dobie had cultivated among the faculty at Southwestern. Dobie also saw that many of the literature professors at Columbia were less interested in celebrating great literature than in analyzing it, often through a series of elaborate theoretical constructs that struck Dobie as foolishly pedantic. The critiques seemed designed to prove the superiority of the critic over the artist.

As far as Dobie was concerned, such scholarship sapped the life from literature. He was expected to obediently produce essays on such subjects as "Platonism in the Renaissance Age," but he had little interest in such abstractions. "I admire intelligences that create systems of thought," he wrote later, "but I cannot follow them, except by an effort that I am unwilling to exert."[5]

Columbia offered him many opportunities, but as the scholar Paul Stone observed, Dobie "bypassed not only whole fields of creative and intellectual wealth, but the giants standing in them as well."[6] Columbia was one of the first universities to teach American literature as a separate course, and Dobie took a class from the professor, William Porterfield Trent, who had a national reputation as an expert in the field. Dobie wrote later, however, that he didn't remember anything the professor said.

The most intriguing opportunity Dobie missed was in folklore, a new field being pioneered in America at universities such as Harvard and Columbia. Franz Boas, professor of anthropology at Columbia, was a leading figure in the folklore movement and served as editor of the *Journal of American Folklore*. The year before Dobie arrived, Boas put together a special issue on Mexican folklore and wrote the lead article himself. His journal also published articles on Southwestern folklore and Texas folk songs.

Considering that Dobie had already expressed an interest in writing about his native region, one might think that he would be keen to investigate such developments. Yet there is no record that he ever made contact with Boas at Columbia. Part of Dobie's problem was that he understood so little that he didn't even know what the word "folklore" meant at the time. It was also the case that Boas was a scientist, and he favored a fact-based, analytical approach to folklore. Dobie may not have known much, but his instincts were already set in opposition to those who saw "mastery of facts" as "the supreme virtue of a scholar."[7]

One reason Dobie had such difficulty adapting to Columbia was that, for the first time, he was competing against students who seemed to outclass him. Many came from privileged backgrounds and underwent a rigorous classical education during the very same years that Dobie was holed up in a one-room schoolhouse with his brothers and sisters. Dobie failed one of the courses at Columbia and he was keenly aware of his academic shortcomings. In his journal he recorded a pensive entry: "Suppose that ten years ago I had been placed under the care of wise tutors and that my natal love for the beautiful and eloquent had been directed . . . with the idea of some day turning me out a real scholar. What is there in life?"[8]

Cut off from his native landscape and the social connections that nurtured him, Dobie lost his bravado and entered a "languid, almost swooning emotional state." He reached out to Bertha, who became his lifeline while he was in New York. He kept in close touch with her, writing at least once or twice a week. In class, he was often timid, but with Bertha, he could be his natural self. The two debated intellectual matters, and they exchanged personal confidences. He loved playing up his iconoclasm for her, on one occasion writing that he was proud of his sins, adding, "what a wicked devil I am."[9]

Dobie began to spend less time on campus, and more in the city, enjoying the shows on Broadway, which cost less than a dollar to attend. Dobie had read Shakespeare's plays, "but only now in the theater did they begin to accumulate connotations." The actors in such performances made far greater impressions on him than Columbia's professors. Their dramatic reinterpretations of familiar material stirred up a new thought in him: "Any tale belongs to whoever can best tell it."[10]

★ ★

As he struggled at the university, Dobie's other plan, to find a New York publisher for his writing, also ran into trouble. As the commercial center of American publishing, New York drew many successful writers, and Dobie longed to join their ranks. He wrote several short stories and submitted them to New York–based magazines, including *McClure's* and *Scribner's*. None of his work was accepted for publication, and none of the efforts survive today. Dobie received little encouragement, and his diary from that time records him feeling "wasted, sick in body and heart" as he noted the latest rejections among New York publishers.[11]

Yet the city itself became a literary hotspot during Dobie's time there, as a group of young writers—Dobie's own generation—assembled in New York and helped develop a new trend in American literature—modernism.

Modernism was an artistic reaction to the new industrial order, which promised endless waves of technological and scientific advancement. Artists converged on the idea that "the new" represented the pinnacle of human achievement. Tradition was disposed of, and radical experimentation became the rage, with style becoming as important as substance. Modernism was often unsettling and intentionally provocative, and it took its cues from Darwin, Freud, and Einstein, all of whom liberated writers from the shackles of religious certainty. Writers were also influenced by anthropology, where Franz Boas's studies of "primitive" cultures advanced notions of cultural relativity. No longer was European culture assumed to be the infallible standard for humanity.

These new ideas were shaking up the world, and artists became more than cultural commentators—they were also revolutionaries. Stravinsky's "The Rite of Spring" provoked a riot when it premiered in Paris in 1913, and Picasso's experiments in cubism—initially decried by purists—transformed modern art. T. S. Eliot, a leading modernist poet who was born the same year as Dobie, became famous for "The Waste Land."

Closely tied to modernism was political radicalism. In the United States, writers dismayed by capitalism's excesses—Upton Sinclair's *The Jungle*, published in 1906, was emblematic of these feelings—increasingly turned to socialism and communism. Not all of these politically oriented writers utilized the avant-garde techniques associated with modernism. Instead, they preferred to employ social realism in order to more easily arouse the masses.

In New York, many of these voices, both political and artistic, were gathering at the Greenwich Village apartment of wealthy socialite Mabel Dodge, who began holding weekly salon discussions in 1912. Several writers in their midtwenties—the same age as Dobie—joined the scene. One was John Reed, a journalist who would soon gain national attention for his writing about the Mexican Revolution. Reed went on to even greater fame covering the Bolshevik Revolution in Russia. Also present was Sinclair Lewis, who later became the first American writer to win a Nobel Prize. Dramatist Eugene O'Neill, born the same year as Dobie, also joined the gatherings. He, too, became a future Nobel laureate. Several prominent political figures were also on hand, including birth control activist Margaret Sanger and famous anarchist Emma Goldman.

Dobie never made it to Mabel Dodge's apartment, but he did get a chance to see one of Emma Goldman's speeches while he was in New York. "I didn't get any ideas" from her, he wrote later, "only glimpses of another world and a feeling of vitality. In those days I had few ideas about anything."[12]

The New York writers represented the future of American literature, and Dobie could not have been further removed from them in outlook or

temperament. His only sense of politics was passed down from the nineteenth century, and it consisted of the strong belief that people should be
left free from any government interference. His views on literature were
"still puritanical, at least in regard to contemporary writing." He would
later write Bertha that it was impossible for him to be a writer in New York
because "I [am not] so far gone in succumbence to Banality to follow the
unnumbered herd of sociology—fiction and pornographic—play writers
who have made *pediculous* that city with themselves. I should go where the
winds blow strong, the blood is red, and the world is new . . . ."[13]

Dobie liked to consider himself a rebel, but he was a rebel only in the
conservative sense, in that he resisted modern society's degradation of traditional values. He wanted to turn culture backwards, and the modernists
were relentlessly pushing it ahead.

Many aspiring writers who came to New York found entry-level jobs in
the publishing industry or in one of New York's hundreds of newspapers
and magazines. They also congregated at key places. Dobie found no job,
published no writing, nor did he become part of a writers' circle. Nor was
he able to develop a relationship with a mentor who could help advance his
career. His experience in New York made him painfully aware of how far
removed he was from the currents of modern American writing, scholarship, and publishing.

As the magnitude of his failure became evident, he lashed out in bitterness. He wrote to a cousin back home, "God ought to destroy New York
like he did Sodom and Gomorrah. It is enough to make a man an infidel to
see such a super-Hell existing in the summertime."[14]

He complained about life in the city to Bertha, and then he added, "I
don't know why I should ever have started off on such a matter, anyhow.
If I were somewhere where I could listen to the silence a while and look at
the stars and all such animosity would die within me."[15]

Dobie came to rely on Bertha more heavily while he was adrift in New
York, and his letters to her became more frequent as the pair's emotional
bond deepened. He often began a letter to her first thing in the morning,
then went about his day's activities, returning at night to continue writing.
Their letters gradually became more tender, evolving into a formal courtship. She sent him a flower by mail and he enclosed one in return, writing,
"And now it is night and I am lonely but not bitter, and I wonder in my
heart how you are tonight and what you are doing and thinking of. I never
in my life wanted to see you more than I do now." In another letter he

wrote, "Goodnight, Bertha, and may the salubrity of the morning's down [sic] be upon you."[16]

After three semesters at Columbia, Dobie decided that he'd had enough. "I finally passed enough classes" to earn a master's degree, he wrote to a friend.[17] He could have stayed on and obtained a Ph.D., but he was aware that, in Texas at least, a master's was enough to get him a college teaching job. He was anxious to get home, not only to begin his new career, but because he wanted to make Bertha his wife.

# Fighting Conformity, Courting Bertha
## 1914–1916

**D**OBIE RETURNED TO TEXAS in the summer of 1914 to good news—he would start in the fall as a beginning English instructor at the University of Texas at Austin. Bertha was already teaching English at a small college in East Texas. They arranged to meet at a reunion in Georgetown—the first time they had seen each other in almost two years. The visit went well, and Dobie wrote to her soon afterwards, "I believe I can win you now."

While waiting for the fall semester to begin, Dobie again took a summer job reporting, this time with the *Galveston Daily Tribune*. He loved getting published, and when he overheard people talk favorably about one of his stories he described the praise as "music to my ears." Once again, he was tempted to give up teaching in favor of reporting.[1]

It did not help matters when a friend joked that teaching would turn him into a "sissy." Dobie, in fact, already worried about that. He wondered if he might be better off returning to cattle ranching after all, and he wrote to ask Bertha for advice. She was quick to assure him that, while he was "sensitive," he was also "the most manly man" she knew.[2]

He and Bertha wrote each other daily, and romance bloomed in their correspondence. Bertha wrote to tell him, "Whatever my tongue might be saying, my heart was beating your name." He addressed a letter to her,

"To my whole life," and he wrote, "Oh, Bertha, I can't live without you . . . don't you know that I love you, love you, love you with every atom of my being?"[3]

Their lack of worldliness was evident in their ignorance regarding sexual matters. Bertha and Dobie could only rarely arrange to meet in person, and during one such visit they spent an evening exchanging tender kisses. Afterwards, Bertha made a "sobbing admission" to a friend, worried sick that she had become pregnant.[4] Frank, for his part, understood that he hadn't impregnated her. But he wasn't exactly certain what he *had* accomplished, either.

In September 1914, as the Great War spread across Europe, Dobie and Bertha announced their engagement. Dobie's salary at the university was one hundred dollars a month, the same amount he had been making four years earlier at Alpine High School. He had amassed considerable debt while furthering his education, and he and Bertha understood that, for financial reasons, marriage would not be practical for a couple of years yet. Dobie hoped to eventually supplement his income with writing and cattle ranching. Bertha was willing to endure a few lean years at the beginning of their relationship, because, as she wrote to him, "You will win ultimately, that I know."[5]

With the prospect of marriage, Bertha informed Dobie that she would not be a typical wife, as she was more at home in the library than in the kitchen. Dobie, obviously delighted, wrote back, "Bertha, believe me when I tell you that I am glad you love a poem better than you love a dress and that you can criticize a novel better than you can cook a cobbler." But he hastened to assure her that she was even more important to him than his beloved books. "I would rather touch your hand than possess all the libraries in the world," he wrote to her.[6]

Dobie had hoped to teach English poetry at UT, but he was soon disabused of that notion. With only a master's degree, he was relegated to freshman composition, and he found the academic environment at UT even stuffier and more regimented than Columbia. The chair of the English department, Dr. Morgan Callaway, was a noted specialist in grammar and had written entire books on such subjects as *The Absolute Participle in Anglo-Saxon* and *The Temporal Subjunctive in Old English*. Callaway informed Dobie that "he had not yet found himself wrong in an opinion" and he apparently believed, according to Dobie, that "young instructors could do no better than to reverence him."[7]

Dobie tried to do the straight scholarship. He wrote critical essays and he began thinking about doing a book on the seventeenth-century British writer James Howell. He contacted a New York publisher about the idea and received an encouraging response, but he soon abandoned the project. Although he had intellectual inclinations, he had no passion for formal academic work.

"I want to be independent and original," he wrote to Bertha, but he had few ideas how to proceed.[8] He was persuaded by other faculty members at UT to join the newly formed Texas Folklore Society, but he didn't take part in its activities, even though other young instructors at the university were making inroads into folklore. One colleague, Walter Prescott Webb, who taught in the history department, had already made a research trip to Beeville, Texas, just a few miles from the Dobie ranch. There Webb collected a number of tales and folk songs, which he published in 1915 in Franz Boas's *Journal of American Folklore*. If Dobie was aware of this activity, there is no evidence of it.

Dobie spent his time composing short stories and writing essays that he considered "iconoclastic." None survive today. In one letter, he informed Bertha of his interest in "the world of Mexican lore," and his intention to seek out all he "could gather, and shall gather."[9] However, he apparently undertook no further work in this regard.

Bertha, who did him the favor of reading some of his manuscripts, agreed that his talent lay in literature, not scholarship. She wrote to him, "I do think that you can write, if only you have sufficient staying power. . . . Once you create something worthy, you will see how cordially [the academic world] will recognize your creation . . . ."[10] Everything Dobie submitted for publication, however, was rejected, and his frustration mounted.

He was also troubled by the fact that the undergraduates were little different from the high school students he had taught in Alpine. He had entertained grand dreams of sharing the best of the English language, and he spent much class time reading poetry out loud, hoping to inspire students. However, he found few kindred spirits. His students' disinterest became evident one afternoon when they rushed to a window to watch a cockfight taking place outside. Disgusted, Dobie dismissed the class and stalked out.[11]

Students viewed him as a tough grader, and he once boasted to a colleague, "I have fought for standards, failing more than fifty percent of some of my classes." His judgments could be scathing. On one young man's paper, Dobie dispensed with the usual niceties about the need to work harder. Instead, he simply noted that the student, who came from a rural area, "should be home plowing."[12]

Dobie wrote to his mother about his life at the university: "I am in a wild revolt against existing conditions, against the restrictions of my profession, against the commonplaceness around me."[13] His iconoclasm was becoming more evident. Even though he failed to get published, he did manage to get his name into the newspaper by paying "my respects to the editorial page," as he wrote to Bertha.[14]

He also described for Bertha how he "read to a class or two an absurdly constructed sentence" from one of the *Austin American*'s editorials. Dobie's action soon came to the attention of the paper, which responded with a short, unsigned commentary that noted, "It is just as well to remember that the cowboy word for lousy calf is 'doby.' Fortunately no real man is named that."[15]

★ ★

During the summer intercession in 1915, Dobie applied for a reporting job at several newspapers, but none would hire him. Still in debt and with no foreseeable improvement in his fortunes, Dobie began a major "speculation in cattle."[16] The war in Europe had spurred a demand for meat, and business was booming. His uncle, Jim Dobie, a successful rancher, offered to co-sign his bank note, and Dobie went into debt for sixty-four hundred dollars—the equivalent of nearly six years' teaching salary. He leased two thousand acres next to his family's ranch and put about one hundred and thirty cows on it.

The reality of the business was not quite the stuff of dreams. Twenty of his cattle died within a few months from tick fever. Persistent drought kept the survivors too thin to sell. The cowboy life was also taking its toll on his body. One morning a "fighting cow" made a run at Dobie's horse, jabbing it with her horn. His horse began bucking, and, as Dobie wrote to Bertha, "I was thrown and somehow wrenched my back."[17] Fortunately, his old friend, the ranch hand Genardo del Bosque, was nearby. Genardo got some mules and a wagon to haul Dobie back home. It was several days before he could walk again.

Dobie returned to UT to teach in the fall of 1915 and celebrated his twenty-seventh birthday. As the drought continued in South Texas, he moved his cattle to greener pastures outside of Austin so he could fatten them up for the market. As he juggled his teaching and ranching duties,

Dobie cowboying in South Texas, ca. late 1910s. Southwestern Writers Collection/The Wittliff Collections, Texas State University–San Marcos.

Dobie began appearing on campus in khaki pants and boots. Before long he began to gain a reputation as something of an oddity—a cowboy professor.

Dobie was also becoming known as the young man who refused to earn his Ph.D. The doctoral degree was an absolute requirement to win tenure and promotion to full professor. Friends, colleagues, and even Bertha pleaded with him to finish his graduate work, but Dobie remained steadfast. He maintained faith in his originality—even though he hadn't yet figured out how to use it—and he feared that more formal scholarship would sap his vitality.

Such a position represented an obvious sacrifice to his academic career, and Dobie became increasingly bitter about his low prospects. He remained in debt to his parents, who had financed much of his graduate study, and he wrote his mother that he was having trouble repaying his loan because "a college instructor simply can't live with as little expense as can a grocery clerk."[18]

He had never been able to hide his disgust at the expected sycophancy within the English department, and he watched in dismay as more pliant instructors were promoted ahead of him. He told his mother that he preferred the company of ranchers to professors. She responded sharply, noting that some of the ranchers she knew "don't have brains enough to fry an egg in."[19]

In letter after letter to Bertha he poured out his complaints about departmental politics. "I have more originality than any man I know," he told her, yet "I publish nothing; I have no Ph.D.; therefore I am fit only for freshman rhetoric. Curse business, curse politics, curse the materialist world . . . there is in it nothing so ludicrously pedantic, unfair and puerilely narrow as the petty jealousies and spelling-bee standards of judgment to be found in academic circles."[20]

This time, however, Bertha's response was not as sympathetic as he might have hoped. She had lost her position at the private college and was relegated to teaching at a high school in Galveston. She missed the more prestigious academic environment. She wrote to him, "I think this bitterness does you no good. It wastes your energies." Then, giving him a little tweak, she suggested that if he wanted to become a serious writer, then "perhaps he should not marry her but go off to New York to write."[21]

He became contrite, telling her, "Although I am selfish and hard enough, God knows, I love you and want you more than I want any other one thing or all other things put together. . . . I may be unable to succeed, but, nevertheless, I want you, and I am not afraid to try with you."[22]

A few weeks later, with their mutual understanding complete, J. Frank Dobie and Bertha McKee consummated their six-year courtship by marrying on September 20, 1916. There was no honeymoon for the financially struggling couple. Instead, they caught a quick train to Austin so Dobie could return to his teaching duties. After years of being physically apart, the two lovers could count at last on sharing the same household. The arrangement would last six months.

# The Great War
## 1915–1919

**D**URING THE DOBIES' two-year engagement, the Great War consumed Europe, pitting the colonial powers against each other. Most Americans opposed any involvement, and isolationism became the safest political position. The pacifist movement also gained attention, thanks to its advocacy by prominent writers and intellectuals. Woodrow Wilson won reelection in 1916 by campaigning as the peace candidate.

Dobie, however, remained out of step. His passion for British literature made him into something of an Anglophile, and students in his classes heard him condemn Germany's attempts to "destroy British civilization." He also had more personal reasons for resenting Germany. "Through the Teutonic Ph.D. system," he opined, German intellectuals "long ago dehumanized the humanities in American colleges and universities."[1]

Dobie openly favored U.S. intervention and he made no secret of his desire to rally others to war. He again came to the attention of the *Austin American*, whose editorial policy favored neutrality. In a dig at Dobie, the paper wrote, "The amiable alien harbored in the University is at it again. In addition to preaching the British propaganda to his class, he has taken occasion to advise it that *The American* is a 'diabolical' newspaper. Of course Old Sweetie prefers to fight Great Britain's battles in the University rather than on the firing line . . . . "[2]

As the war continued to spread, concern grew in America about attacks from south of the border. Mexico had grievances, after all, having lost much of her territory to the United States in 1848. Mexico was also embroiled in its ongoing revolution, which destabilized the border. As early as 1914, when Dobie was still in New York, people were calling for the United States to invade Mexico and instill order. At that time Dobie wrote to Bertha that such a war would be "a farce" and "there would not be much action in it." He even suggested—perhaps to provoke a reaction—that if such a conflict erupted, "I should prefer fighting on the Mexican side." But then he assured Bertha, "as the South is still attached to the United States . . . I would not fight against the nation."[3]

The border situation intensified in 1915, when Anglos discovered that Mexicanos in San Diego, Texas—some forty miles from the Dobie Ranch—were plotting a revolution. The Plan of San Diego, as the manifesto became known, called for the liberation of the territory lost by Mexico in 1848—Texas, New Mexico, Arizona, Colorado, and California. All people of color—Mexicanos, African Americans, Native Americans, and Asian Americans—were encouraged to join the fight to form a new independent republic. Chillingly, the document also called for exterminating all white males over the age of sixteen. Dobie, who had grown up casually bossing Mexicanos, was now one of their targets.

Stories of the plot appeared in Texas newspapers and tensions ran high as people braced for a possible race war. In the summer of 1915, guerrilla raids began in South Texas. Groups of armed Mexicanos, ranging in size from a dozen men to fifty, burned railroad bridges, cut telegraph and telephone wires, and attacked army outposts, supply stations, and trains. On August 8, they raided the southernmost section of the King Ranch, near the Mexican border. Workers held them off until reinforcements arrived and the raiders were forced to retreat.

As this attack took place, Dobie was back in the Brush Country, trading for cattle and herding them back to his family's ranch with some vaqueros. Unconcerned about the raid on the King Ranch, he wrote to Bertha that they had driven the cattle "through a country of 'muchos amigos'—many friends—where the brood hospitality of one cow man to another showed itself."[4]

A handful of other raids occurred over the next few months. A total of seventeen Anglos died—eleven soldiers and six civilians. If the revolutionaries were counting on a massive uprising to support their aims, they badly miscalculated. Further, their habit of retreating across the border left the native Texas Mexican population exposed to reprisals that were far more violent than the original raids. Over the next few months, Texas Rangers and other Anglo law enforcement officials stormed through Texas Mexican settlements, lining up brown-skinned people and shooting them down. Others were lynched. Lands were confiscated. No one knows how many innocent people were killed during these attacks; estimates range from the hundreds to the thousands. Thousands more Texas Mexicans fled across the border, believing that life was safer in revolution-torn Mexico than in their home state.[5]

Just as the violence on the Texas-Mexico border was quieting down, Pancho Villa invaded Columbus, New Mexico in March 1916, killing sixteen Americans. U.S. General John Pershing launched a punitive expedition in return, going deep into Mexico on a futile search for Villa. Pershing was still in Mexico the following year when British intelligence intercepted the Zimmerman Telegram, which brought to light Germany's intent to form an alliance with Mexico against the United States. Americans were outraged, and all pretensions of neutrality were cast aside. Within a few weeks, the United States declared war against Germany.

The war gave Dobie a chance to engage in the adventure he had long craved. He immediately volunteered for the cavalry. In his application letter, Dobie disregarded the European war. Instead, he focused entirely on Mexico. "I know the Mexican genius," Dobie wrote, adding that he had "managed good-sized bodies of workmen, Mexicans especially. . . . I can and will raise a company of one hundred men out of the ranch countries of Southwest Texas. These men would be hard of physique, efficient as to riding and shooting, and knowing as to Mexican territory. . . . They would be well mounted."[6]

The Army, however, refused to accept him. He had varicose veins in his legs, making him ineligible. Undeterred, he underwent an operation to have them cut out. After recovering, he enlisted again. No cavalry assignments were available, so he was assigned to artillery instead. He sold off his cattle and Bertha was forced to move out of their home—which she had fallen in love with—in order to take a room at a boarding house. Dobie apologized to her, but explained that, given her delicate health, she needed to be around someone who could help look after her while he was at war.

Once in the Army, whatever relief Dobie felt from escaping the stuffy academic environment quickly evaporated. He was as much of a misfit in the military as he had been at the university. Pedantry and blind obedience were required, and, worse, he realized that a "certain refined sensibility kept me apart from my fellows. . . . I had too long soaked myself in poetry and novels." During his first two months in the service, Dobie recalled, "I suffered such a loss of self-confidence, such a void of personality as I hope to never realize again. I was dogged and cowed."[7]

His failures as a writer certainly didn't help. Mindful of how wartime had inspired great writing, Dobie asked the *Dallas Morning News* if he could become their war correspondent. They turned him down. He also continued to send out short stories, none of which were accepted. Though Dobie did not keep any of his early fictional efforts, one can gain a sense of the kind of material he was writing by considering Bertha's response to one of his manuscripts. "You know, Frank," she explained in a letter, "I don't believe you will sell stories until you leave out the supernatural. This is too sophisticated an age to appreciate things that aren't so."[8]

★ ★

Dobie gradually adapted to Army life. He came to understand the technical aspects of the artillery, and with "knowledge came power and self-confidence." Before long, "the natural robustness of my nature asserted itself," he reported. Soon, Dobie was in full rebel mode, describing his company's major as "common as pigtracks," the lieutenant colonel as one who "constantly licked the general's boots," and the general himself as walking "like a fat gander."[9]

Commissioned as a lieutenant, Dobie was not sent to France right away. Instead, much to his annoyance, he was kept stateside as a camp instructor in Georgia. He and Bertha continued to keep in close touch through their correspondence, writing almost daily. Among the issues they discussed was women's suffrage, which had recently lost a vote in the U.S. House of Representatives. Bertha complained about women's secondary status, and Dobie wrote back agreeing, although he added that women in Germany were treated far worse. He also pointed out that "women after this war will have a far larger part in affairs" and will soon gain full rights. He added, "I guess that you know my ideas coincide with yours, *entirely*, without reservation, in these matters."[10]

Given the shortage of manpower during the war, UT had allowed Bertha to take over her husband's teaching duties. Once at the university, she became much more sympathetic about his situation and wrote to him, "I

Lieutenant Dobie in uniform during World War I. Southwestern Writers Collection / The Wittliff Collections, Texas State University–San Marcos.

used to wish very earnestly that you would study for a Ph.D., even if it meant your being away from me for three years. . . . But, my dear husband, I would not have you, with your temperament, peg at this stuff. . . . To do so would kill everything that is you—things much more desirable and much rarer than Ph.D. degrees."[11]

Once Bertha finished the term, UT expressed little interest in keeping her on. She wrote to him that Dr. Callaway, the department head Dobie had clashed with, "isn't favorable enough toward women to give them a decent salary." However, Southern Methodist University in Dallas offered her a job, and the pay was also better, so Bertha began making arrangements to move to Dallas.[12]

Meanwhile, the Army finally shipped Dobie to France in October 1918. Two weeks later the Armistice was signed. He wrote to Bertha, "God knows, Burbie, I want to go home to you, but it is bitter to have trained so much and to have come so far . . . and then to be failed of one single battery volley into the Hun ranks. . . . I think I should be ashamed when I get back, never having endured one hardship or fought one fight."[13]

But Dobie received a major consolation—he fell in love with France. He visited the Louvre, took in plays in Paris, and drove around the countryside, admiring its beauty. The Army allowed him to enroll in the Sorbonne "as a special student in French history and literature."[14] There Dobie became introduced to the great sixteenth-century essayist Michel de Montaigne. Unlike the smug and condescending scholars Dobie despised, Montaigne never bothered with amassing reams of objective facts and then exhaustively analyzing them. Instead, he believed that reality could be adequately captured through personal observation and good judgment. There was no need to "prove" everything with facts. In his writing, Montaigne developed a charmingly unique style—he blended high-concept scholarly ruminations with anecdotes taken from everyday life. He bridged intellectualism with relevance, and he became the model for Dobie's own writing.

Earlier in Dobie's education, the English Romantics had provided him with a poetic tradition that aligned with his naturalistic impulses. Now, he was exposed for the first time to an intellectual framework that meshed with his own personal philosophy. He became rapturous. He told Bertha in a letter, "When I feel myself so happy here, so congenial, and then I think of the ashen and fruitless days I spent at American colleges and universities, I could cry." He promised her that, upon his return, he would "set about making money so that you and I will not have to live amid the banalities of the 'Lone Star State.'"[15]

During this idyllic time, however, tragedy struck. A flu pandemic was sweeping the globe, killing an estimated twenty million people—more than had died in the war itself. Dobie caught the bug in France but quickly recovered. Bertha, however, was not so lucky.

On New Year's Day, 1919, Dobie received news that Bertha had become ill. A few weeks later, his brother-in-law, Edgar Kincaid, sent a cable explaining that she had nearly died, but was now recovering. She was being cared for at the Kincaid family's ranch outside of San Antonio.

Dobie could have applied for a transfer to return home immediately, but instead he decided to remain in France. His rationale, as he explained it in a letter to Bertha, was primarily financial. If he returned early he would have no guaranteed job, whereas if he stayed in France the Army's salary would help pay for her care. He wrote to her, very carefully explaining, "do not be hurt at me or think I do not want to come now."[16]

Bertha sent a note informing him that she was recuperating but would likely be an invalid for some time. Dobie wrote in his defense that his time in France "has meant a great deal to me, and you will see, in the future, that it has made me abler. I was *destined*, in a way, to learn something of the foreign. There was in me a vacancy that, for my work, must be filled with life abroad. It was not a whim, not a child's love of romance, not a fool's paradise of traveling, not a mere gratification of desire for experiences that kept me in France. You will understand this."[17]

Then Dobie received an ominous telegram. This one read, simply, "Bertha critically ill." Dobie immediately put in for a transfer home. The Army granted his request, although it was several more weeks before he could ship out. He finally returned to Texas in May 1919. He had been in France for six months—five of them after learning of Bertha's illness. Bertha was alive, but there was no assurance that she would last longer than a few more months. While convalescing, she had written a letter to her husband that she decided not to send. In it, she poured out her bitterness, noting that, "only the direst extremity could have won my consent to sending for you. . . . [Had others] not assumed a responsibility that is yours, I should not be alive at this hour." In a letter infused with harsh truths about her husband's nature, one line stands out. J. Frank Dobie, Bertha wrote, "cares a thousand times more for experience than for me."[18]

*The Rising Star*

# A Rangeland Epiphany
## 1920–1921

**A**FTER HIS DISCHARGE from the Army, Dobie rejoined the University of Texas, although there was little cause for celebration. He was thirty-one years old, entering middle age, and his salary was little improved from his teaching days at Alpine nearly a decade before.

While Dobie seemed to be standing still, America was entering the Jazz Age. Women were finally granted the right to vote in 1920, and prohibition went into effect that same year. The automobile had fully supplanted the horse and the economy was booming. The country's traditional agrarian society crumbled before the onslaught of industrialization, and millions of people left farms for factory jobs in the cities. By 1920, for the first time, a majority of Americans lived in urban, rather than rural, environments. As the historian Nathan Miller observed, the nation "was being homogenized by national advertising, chain stores, standardized products, radio networks, newspaper chains, and mass circulation magazines—foreshadowing the rise of mass culture and the decline of regional variety."[1]

Yet there was a countermovement afoot—a desire to preserve, or at least document, America's rapidly vanishing rural heritage. The leaders in this movement were folklorists, and at the University of Texas, John A. Lomax was chief among them. Lomax made a national reputation by collecting and disseminating traditional cowboy songs. Like Dobie, Lomax detested Morgan Callaway, the head of UT's English department. Back in the 1890s when Lomax was a student at the university, Callaway had told him that his interest in cowboy songs was "tawdry, cheap, and unworthy."[2]

In 1906, Lomax went to Harvard for graduate study, and the Eastern establishment embraced his interest in cowboy songs. He published his first collection, *Cowboy Songs and Other Frontier Ballads*, in 1910. Interest in Lomax's material was so high that the introduction for his book was written by none other than President Theodore Roosevelt.

Dobie found Lomax inspiring in many ways. Not only had he managed to prove the arrogant Callaway wrong about the value of Texas's indigenous culture, he was also something of a late bloomer, and had not published his first book until he was forty-three. For Dobie, who was still searching for his first success, Lomax proved it was not too late for him.

Like Dobie, Lomax had a prickly relationship with academia. He was fired from UT in a political purge under Governor Jim "Pa" Ferguson, but later returned after Ferguson was impeached. Lomax often took long leaves of absence, traveling thousands of miles in search of the folk songs that were his passion.

Lomax took Dobie under his wing, hiring him to write articles for the *Alcalde*, the university's alumni magazine, which provided the Dobies with a bit of extra income. Dobie gained even greater confidence in his writing when, at last, he had articles accepted by an academic journal. In 1919 and 1920 he placed three essays in the *Texas Review*. Two were meditations on the pleasure of reading, written while he was still serving with the Army in France.

The third article was a review essay of Lomax's new book, *Songs of the Cattle Trail and Cow Camp*. Dobie offered generous praise, concluding that Lomax's ability to capture "the spirit of these cow folks" will have resonance "long after the fatuous thesis of many another son of Harvard shall have turned to dust on its undisturbed shelf."[3]

Despite this modest publishing success, Dobie's life at the university continued much as before. "My wife and I were doing worse than starving to death on a government claim," Dobie observed. "I was at the bottom of the ladder with very little prospect of getting higher up until I got a Ph.D. degree, and I did not intend to get one."[4]

In the spring of 1920 Dobie received a visit from his Uncle Jim, a successful rancher who had considerably expanded his holdings. The cattle industry was still booming and Jim didn't understand how his nephew could

John Lomax. Southwestern Writers Collection/ The Wittliff Collections, Texas State University– San Marcos.

prefer teaching to ranching. He offered Frank one hundred and fifty dollars a month to manage his Los Olmos Ranch in South Texas. Dobie considered the pay low, yet it did represent a substantial increase over his university salary.

Dobie accepted the job even though Bertha argued against it. She was still convalescing, confined mostly to bed, and there was fear that she "would always be an invalid." They both knew that it would be impossible for her to live with him at the remote ranch headquarters. Dobie was "immensely apologetic for this new separation," and he arranged for Bertha to live in a small house in San Antonio, eighty miles north of the ranch. He promised to come visit every weekend.[5]

Dobie's area of responsibility covered nearly five hundred thousand acres, and included a large spread in northern Mexico that was subject to a land dispute. He negotiated business deals, rode with the vaqueros, roped wild hogs, stared down poachers, and bossed a bunch of Mexicano laborers as they built stock tanks and repaired fences. He was often the only Anglo around. "I had never been entirely weaned from ranch life," Dobie wrote. He later added, "I knew that I had just about reached paradise."[6]

To Bertha, however, he was more tactful. He wrote to her that this was "about the first time I ever went to a new place without enjoying it. I am too homesick for you to enjoy anything."[7] He had plenty of meat sent to her from the ranch, overloading her with more venison and quail than she could ever eat. He wrote often, but weekly visits proved impossible.

Dobie's adventures were not limited to simple ranching. Prohibition had sparked a wave of cross-border smuggling, and the ranch was on a main route between Mexico and San Antonio. "I didn't care how much tequila was passed," Dobie wrote later, "but the Rangers and the river guards and customs men were strong against the traffic."[8] On one occasion, Dobie came to the aid of a Mexicano bootlegger whose truck had gotten bogged down in the mud. Dobie ordered ranch hands to help free the truck, and he in turn was rewarded with a half dozen bottles of tequila.

Continuing problems with poachers led the sheriff to deputize Dobie, and he was proud of his warrant. He wrote to Bertha, "I carry it with me and am itching to use it."[9]

He didn't have to wait long. A group of Texas Rangers set out to raid a nearby bootleggers' camp and invited Dobie to join them. Shots were fired, and one of the Mexicanos was killed. Six others were captured, and Dobie and the Rangers confiscated the tequila. Dobie wrote to Bertha that news of the violence had spread throughout the area. "Mexicans in the county are literally afraid of sticking their heads out of their houses," he told her, adding, "I've never enjoyed two days so much in my life."[10]

Though Dobie's new occupation seemed infused with vigor, intellectual pursuits were never far from his mind. He read constantly and continued to work on scholarly articles. He wrote to Bertha, "While I am in one world it is forever my fate to hear the music of the other: in the university I am a wild man; in the wilds I am a scholar and a poet. It is terrible for you to be married to such a man, for I am plainly not a success."[11]

Dobie's ambivalence carried over into his feelings about the Mexicanos. On the one hand, he bragged of having terrorized them. On the other, he felt a deep kinship with people who were as attached to the land as he was. To Dobie, the rural Mexicanos symbolized the frontier past—a way of life he revered all the more because it was clearly slipping away. Though Dobie knew little Spanish, he liked the way his name "Frank" sounded when the vaqueros spoke it. He let it be known among his Anglo friends that he didn't mind being called "Pancho."

Among the Mexicanos working on the ranch was Santos Cortez, who

Dobie considered "an indifferent vaquero" but a sublime companion, a man who "craved conversation on higher things."[12] In the evenings, as the men sat around the campfire, storytelling served as their chief form of entertainment, just as it had for generations of range folk before them. Cortez was a terrific storyteller, and he shared with Dobie many Brush Country tales of ghosts and buried treasure. Such accounts were a common part of the Southwest's oral tradition, and Dobie had always taken them for granted.

Stories of lost riches were among the most popular tales. Back in the old days, banks were unheard of and so people buried their wealth in order to protect it. As a child, Dobie had grown up hearing legends about buried gold on his family's ranch. The original owners, the Ramirezes, were said to have been very rich, so "when they were massacred by Indians, they left their wealth for some stranger to find," Dobie recalled.[13] A half uncle of his spent thirty years digging around the Ramirez ruins. Though he never found anything, he remained convinced that lost treasure existed throughout Spain's former territory, and he loved to tell such stories to the Dobie children.

Occasionally small treasures were found. Eight hundred Mexican dollars were recovered from "under a mesquite tree in Atascosa County." In nearby Frio County, hogs rooted up four hundred dollars in Mexican coins. Cortez was among those who believed that buried treasure existed on Los Olmos Ranch. One account suggested that Spaniards had lost thirty-one mule loads of silver near the Nueces River. After hearing this story one evening, the men decided to look for it. Dobie accompanied the Mexicano laborers, who "set to work, constructed a small derrick of mesquite limbs, and sent down a drill." Thirty-five feet into the earth, the seekers gave up. On another foray, the men "excavated a hole so large a wagon and a team might easily have been buried in it, but they found no treasure."[14]

Such a find would have been a boon to Dobie. He had few financial prospects, and the cattle industry went into a slump soon after he arrived at the ranch. His Uncle Jim was encountering hard times and Dobie knew that a change was coming. He could no longer put off choosing his life's course.

For years the idea of folklore had been percolating in his subconscious. His friendship with a successful folklorist like Lomax helped him realize that such work could become valued, despite lingering opposition from tradition-bound academics. Yet Dobie had not yet realized that his Brush Country heritage could provide the basis for his own folklore collecting.

In the evenings at Los Olmos Ranch, as Cortez told his stories, a new idea kindled inside of Dobie. While "Santos talked, while Uncle Jim Dobie and other cowmen talked or stayed silent, while the coyotes sang their songs, and the sandhill cranes honked their lonely music, I seemed to be seeing a great painting of something I'd known all my life," Dobie recalled. "I seemed to be listening to a great epic of something that had been commonplace in my youth but now took on meanings."[15]

Dobie had a revelation. "I would collect and tell the legendary tales of Texas as Lomax had collected the old-time songs and ballads of Texas and the frontier."[16] He could now unite his opposing halves—the love he felt for the Brush Country in his bones with the love for literature he felt in his soul.

# The Making of a Folklorist
## 1921–1923

OBIE DIDN'T HAVE to wait long to engage his newfound passion. Less than a year into his tenure at Los Olmos Ranch, the cattle market collapsed and his Uncle Jim went broke. Ranching was now out of the question, and Dobie decided, "I should go back to my old job at the University of Texas." Convincing the English department to take him back wasn't easy, but his advocates within the university managed to prevail. Dobie was grateful for their help, but he remained adamant in his feeling that, "It was certainly lucky for me that I left the university in 1920 and learned something."[1]

Bertha was thrilled at the opportunity to return to Austin, but by now she was wise to her husband's ways. She had supported his moves for the last several years, even when she didn't agree with them. This time, however, she consented to accompany him only after he promised to stop his "endless belly-aching" and "thousands of fits of anger" over English department politics.[2]

When Dobie rejoined UT, he found the climate more hospitable than before, as he realized he could nourish his intellectual interests through the Texas Folklore Society. The organization, which had been founded by John Lomax and Leonidas Payne in 1909, had become moribund during the Great War. When Dobie returned to campus in 1921, he teamed up with

Payne to resurrect the Texas Folklore Society. Payne became the president; Dobie was elected secretary-treasurer. He also took over as editor of publications and began soliciting contributions for a compendium of folklore articles.

At every opportunity Dobie left Austin and headed out into the backcountry, hunting for tales of old-time Texas. He traveled by automobile when absolutely necessary, but he much preferred to make his way by horseback, burro, wagon, or carriage. He met with old-timers and sat around their campfires. "I belong to the soil myself," Dobie observed, "and the people of it are my people. I have certainly met many interesting talkers among them. . . . We hear each other gladly."[3] He was more than just a good talker; he was a great listener, and he had a way of projecting thoughtful attention as others spoke.

A friend recalled encountering Dobie on one of his expeditions: "He was wearing some scuffed old high-heeled boots, about a dollar and a half's worth of clothes, and a Stetson hat that would keep the sun off his face. He was starved and eating stew with both knife and fork as he listened to an old rancher tell an old tale. I never saw a happier man."[4]

Dobie was the first academician to make a systematic effort to collect Texas's folk heritage, and a whole new world opened up, just for him. His informants shared stories of old-time cowmen and trail drivers, Brush Country ghosts, and tales of the Southwest's horses, cattle, coyotes, roadrunners, and rattlesnakes.

Dobie's favorite stories, however, were those of buried treasure. He believed that "the men who told the tales and participated in them, together with the ground on which they acted and to which they belonged . . . [were] the most vital part of the narratives." More than once, Dobie's interest reinvigorated a dormant quest, and he joined the dreamers on a new search, "helping spade about in the earth for buried silver and gold."[5]

Dobie also became "an unflagging letter writer," sending inquiries to anyone who could help in his quest—cowboys, hunters, prospectors, and newspaper editors. He became obsessed with finding tales, writing, "I look for them, lay for them, listen for them, hunt them, trail them down, swap for them, beg, borrow, and steal them, and value above rubies the person who gives me a good one."[6]

Dobie's new pathway led quickly to academic success. Within months, he became the dominant figure in the Texas Folklore Society and he also placed two articles in the *Journal of American Folklore*, which was still being edited by Franz Boas at Columbia University. Both of Dobie's articles focused on the Texas-Mexico border. In one, he presented a corrido sung on his Uncle Jim's ranch by the vaqueros. In referencing how he had come to collect the ballad, Dobie noted that, "Originally, the song was written down for me by a Mexican named Santos."[7] Dobie, in true patrón fashion, did not bother to provide a last name, but this was Santos Cortez, the man whose stories had helped him discover his calling.

In December 1922, Dobie traveled to Cambridge, Massachusetts, to attend his first national meeting of the American Folklore Society—the national organization the Texas Folklore Society reported to. There he presented a paper and got himself elected to the national council. By now Dobie was glowing with confidence. He met with the prominent leaders in the field, including Franz Boas. When the two men spoke, Dobie took pains to point out that Boas's *Journal of American Folklore* had never updated its listing of Texas Folklore Society officers. Essentially, Dobie's complaint amounted to the fact that his own name did not appear in the journal as it should. Correcting such a matter was apparently not at the top of Boas's agenda, as Dobie sent two subsequent letters following up on this same issue.

Dobie also sent Boas a letter complaining that the journal published Spanish-language materials without translations. He argued that, "a number of people who are humanly interested in folk-lore are estranged because of the Spanish." Boas rejected Dobie's request to provide translations, but he did take time to point out that a Spanish usage in Dobie's recent article had been incorrect.[8]

The divide between Boas and Dobie widened when Dobie casually informed Boas that he was opening the Texas Folklore Society to amateur folklorists as well as professional scholars. Such amateurs included his wife, Bertha, whom Dobie had asked to contribute articles for an upcoming publication. Boas was not amused, as he had been discouraging participation by nonprofessionals for decades. Back in the early years of the American Folklore Society, Boas had "even raised questions about the appropriateness of Mark Twain's membership in the society."[9]

The American Folklore Society viewed folk tales as raw data, which professional folklorists cataloged in order to analyze the cultural transmission of such stories. The need for careful, strictly literal collecting was of utmost importance to Boas and his colleagues, because corrupting the data could result in flawed conclusions. In Dobie's first few months with the Texas Folklore Society, he understood and accepted these mandates. His instructions to collectors were in keeping with established practice: "no legend should be adorned, 'doctored,' or changed from its usual form. It should be written as it is usually told."[10]

Yet during his time out in the field, Dobie discovered a problem. As much as he liked the stories, he realized that they didn't always stand up to literary scrutiny. He would find instances in which the informants left out a necessary detail, or got the chronology wrong, or gave away the ending too early, thus forfeiting all its suspense. Reprinting such tales literally, as the folklore profession required, meant diminishing their literary value. Dobie, as a natural storyteller and a keen student of literature, realized that some sifting could produce literary gold.

Dobie was not the first to recognize the conflict between scientific and literary uses of folklore. Previous generations of American writers, such as Washington Irving, had freely adapted folktales from their native region into literature. In the 1920s, Zora Neale Hurston became a leading writer of the Harlem Renaissance by rewriting folk tales from the rural South. Now it was Dobie's turn to recognize that, as far as literature is concerned, "the story belongs to who tells it best." He believed that he had discerned "the underlying relationship between simple storytelling and great literature."[11]

In Dobie's view, folktales were about "life's romance, vitality, flavor, humanity, humor, gusto," and more. Whereas most of the cognoscenti considered the Southwest a literary backwater, Dobie believed that his native region offered a wealth of folkloric stories. "We are inheritors of a vast body of tales about cunning coyotes, matchless mustangs, fabulous mines, gigantic bears, phantom stampedes, daring riders and scores of other phenomena characteristic of our land," he wrote. "We do not have to go . . . to Grimm for folk tales any more than the Grimm brothers themselves had to go outside Germany for theirs." Dobie saw folklore as "the essence of a cultural inheritance"—not to be dissected by academics, but rather belonging to the people—and also to himself as his people's chief literary interpreter.[12]

# The Rising Star
## 1923–1926

**I**N THE SUMMER OF 1923, thirty-five-year-old J. Frank Dobie left Austin to continue his tale gathering. His reputation was growing, and his spirits were high. "I can smell a legend as far as a buzzard can smell a dead cow," he later wrote to a friend. Bertha, meanwhile, traveled to Fredericksburg, an old German town seventy miles west of Austin, for her "summer rest cure." As was usual during their separations, the two kept in constant touch through letters.[1]

Despite Dobie's successes, he was troubled by the continuing resistance to his work at UT. Many of his colleagues criticized him for not performing "true academic research," and administrators still refused to promote him above the rank of instructor. But other colleges were beginning to take notice of him and his work. That summer, the president of Oklahoma A&M College (now Oklahoma State University) in Stillwater offered him a job as the chair of their English department. The salary was significantly higher than the pay offered by UT and the position carried more prestige.

He sent Bertha a letter explaining that he "hastily accepted an offer hastily made." She was devastated. Stillwater possessed few of Austin's charms and it was far away from friends and family. She did not want to leave Austin, "and she was to be miserable . . . from the start."[2] Despite Bertha's anger at her husband's rash decision, his instincts proved to be correct, and the move to Oklahoma turned out to be advantageous for them.

In Oklahoma, Dobie continued his frenetic pace. He cofounded and became the first president of the Oklahoma Folklore Society. He also maintained his position within the Texas Folklore Society. "I have worked, eaten, and slept with the Texas Folk-Lore Society for three years now," he wrote in a letter. "I am more interested in it than anything in the world."[3] He was almost finished with *The Legends of Texas*, a book of collected folk tales that he was editing, and he was confident of its success.

As a college town, Stillwater received its share of visits from traveling writers. Dobie, as the department head, was well positioned to make the most of these opportunities. He met Carl Sandburg, and the two immediately hit it off, forming a lifelong friendship. Even more profitable for Dobie was a visit from E. H. Taylor, who edited a large-circulation, Philadelphia-based magazine called the *Country Gentleman*. During his visit to the Dobies' home, Taylor listened to stories of the open range while the two men sipped on the bootleg tequila Dobie had acquired on his Uncle Jim's ranch. By the end of the convivial evening, Taylor was asking Dobie to write an article for his magazine. Taylor wanted a story on the ever-popular topic of cowboy songs—Lomax's terrain. Dobie suggested an article on cattle trail drivers instead. "Well," Taylor told him, "try us out first on cowboy songs."[4]

The *Country Gentleman* not only paid very well, it also promised to introduce Dobie to a national audience. He quickly arranged for a leave of absence from Oklahoma A&M to work on the story. The university allowed Bertha to take over his teaching duties.

Anxious that he might enlarge his own reputation at the expense of his mentor's, Dobie wrote Lomax to explain his position, and to ask for permission to do the article. Lomax wrote back, telling Dobie not to worry, adding, "You have about supplanted me in everything pertaining to the Southwest."[5]

After submitting his article to the *Country Gentleman*, Dobie got a telegram telling him that it was "received with much enthusiasm. Please go to San Antonio and write two pieces on trail drivers." When he saw the published article, Dobie became angry about how his writing had been edited, noting in a letter to a friend that the magazine "cut out some of the most meaty paragraphs and then sliced the others up into something that resembles bat-droppings." Still, the two hundred dollar check proved a nice salve. So did Taylor's subsequent note inviting him to Philadelphia to discuss a whole series of articles. Dobie would publish a dozen more articles in the high-profile magazine over the next three years.[6]

Dobie in Stillwater, 1924.
Southwestern Writers
Collection / The Wittliff
Collections, Texas State
University–San Marcos.

Dobie's first *Country Gentleman* article appeared just as his long-awaited book for the Texas Folklore Society, *The Legends of Texas*, came out in 1924. The volume contained seventy items from thirty-five writers, and Dobie was the clear star, writing the introduction and penning far more articles than any other contributor. Many of the accounts reflected Dobie's own interests, consisting of stories about buried treasures and lost mines in addition to tales of the supernatural.

Many selections, including Dobie's, were avowedly literary, rather than scientific, treatments of the source material, and the reading public in Texas loved it. *The Legends of Texas* shot to the top of the state's bestseller lists and was praised as "a work of permanent value." Dobie in particular received accolades for his "style and substance, at once sparkling and scholarly . . . [that gives] the entire collection a literary flavor and quality which greatly enhances its appeal and value."[7]

*The Legends of Texas* also enjoyed good publicity nationwide, winning positive reviews in the *Nation* and the *Saturday Review of Literature*. Yet the *Journal of American Folklore* remained silent. Dobie sent letters asking them to acknowledge it. Finally, over two years later, the journal ran a short,

66

unsigned review that offered lukewarm praise, noting that, "The collection is of more interest to the local historian than to the student of folklore in general."[8]

As Francis Edward Abernethy, former president of the Texas Folklore Society, notes in his history of the organization, Dobie must have been particularly embittered by this put-down, because he had "tried to be an active and accepted part" of the American Folklore Society.[9] Dobie had experienced a slow burn over the years while the national journal delayed in carrying news of Texas Folklore Society meetings, failed to update its list of Texas Folklore Society officers, and, worst of all, tepidly reviewed *The Legends of Texas*. Dobie realized that his literary treatments of folklore would never mesh with the American Folklore Society's scientific focus. So he decided it was time to rebel.

Under Dobie's leadership, the Texas Folklore Society had thrived, making it the largest state chapter in the American Folklore Society. Dobie decided that the Texans no longer needed the national organization, and under the force of his personality, the Texas Folklore Society broke away, becoming an independent entity. Dobie explained his rationale by pointedly criticizing the American Folklore Society's approach to folklore: "I care next to nothing for the science of folklore which some scholars reverence," Dobie wrote. "The dullest of wits can add up footnotes as endlessly as an adding machine can add up figures."[10]

The schism between the two organizations has remained in place ever since. The Texas Folklore Society is a haven for grass-roots folklore, and its meetings showcase folk performances, such as songs and storytelling, conducted by the members themselves. The American Folklore Society, in contrast, remains scrupulously scholarly. Its meetings are much more formal, consisting of academics presenting reports of their research.

As former Texas Folklore Society President Rollo K. Newsom reported, many of the scholarly folklorists "hold Texas folklorists in disdain because of what Dobie did with our meetings and publications." Yet there seem to be few regrets among the Texans. As Abernethy, another president of the Texas Folklore Society, pointed out, the organization has published "more folklore and folklore studies than any other state folklore society. And its meetings are more interesting than many AFS [American Folklore Society] meetings I attended."[11]

Dobie's commanding stature as the guiding force behind the Texas Folklore Society, along with the success of *The Legends of Texas* and his publications in a national magazine made Dobie a much sought-after figure. He received a flurry of new job offers. The most intriguing came from the president of Texas Technological College (now Texas Tech University), which had just opened in Lubbock, who offered him an astounding thirty-six hundred dollars a year to join its faculty. This was far more money than Dobie had ever made before. Yet accepting the offer meant that he would be consigned to "libraryless Lubbock," and he much preferred "to be back in libraried Austin."[12]

Meanwhile, Dobie heard stirrings from the University of Texas at Austin. His friend Leonidas Payne, one of the original founders of the Texas Folklore Society, led an effort to get Dobie rehired at UT. Although the majority of the English department remained opposed to Dobie, Payne took his case to the university's president, who overruled them and agreed to extend an offer.[13]

The proposed salary was less than Texas Tech's, but it came with assurances that he would receive "time to pursue independent research and writing, moral support and intellectual independence."[14] Bertha began packing their bags.

Perhaps most significantly, Dobie's return to UT carried a promotion to the rank of Adjunct Professor. This made him the first person in the history of the university to rise above the status of a simple "instructor" without the benefit of a Ph.D.[15] Dobie, who had adamantly followed his own instincts, rather than the usual paths, seemed at last to be finding success. He was fighting the entrenched academic interests and winning.

9

# Voices of the Southwest
## 1926–1930

ON THANKSGIVING DAY, 1926, Frank and Bertha Dobie moved into a pleasant two-story frame house in Austin, nestled along the banks of Waller Creek just north of the UT campus. A room upstairs served as Dobie's study. With Dobie's hard-won prestige and decent salary, he and Bertha could at last settle down. The couple would live in this home for the rest of their lives. Dobie recalled years later, "We had to buy it mostly on credit, but it was the *Country Gentleman* that paid for it. I guess if I'd been dependent on the salary that I was at that time getting from the University of Texas I'd still be paying for it on the installment plan."[1]

Dobie's growing acclaim was not merely regional. His work in the *Country Gentleman* brought him to the attention of other editors, and before long he was publishing stories about buried treasure, Southwestern characters, and animal life in *Holland's*, the *American Mercury*, and the *New York Herald-Tribune*. He also placed numerous articles in academic journals. He was becoming one of UT's best-known faculty members.

Bertha's own writing career was still developing in fits and starts. She wrote nearly as much as Frank did, but with much less success. Her husband tirelessly promoted her work, and thanks to him, she had published in *The Legends of Texas*. He also named her the assistant editor for Texas Folklore Society publications, and Bertha proved to have a very capable talent for editing. Yet Bertha enjoyed only a few modest achievements outside of her husband's immediate orbit, such as a book review on Edna St. Vincent Millay for the *Dallas Morning News*. Most of her writing during this period consisted of literary criticism and short stories, none of which found a willing publisher.

While many Texans were praising Dobie for leading the Southwest's literary culture out of darkness, several other Texas writers were making their voices heard, and most of them were women. One was Dorothy Scarborough, who like Dobie attended graduate school at Columbia University in the 1910s. Unlike Dobie, Scarborough went on to earn her Ph.D. at the university. She published several books during the 1920s, including *The Wind*, a controversial novel that described a woman "driven insane by the incessant wind and drought-plagued frontier environment."[2] Many Texans condemned the book for fostering a negative image of the state, but nonetheless in 1927 it was made into one of the last great silent films and starred Lillian Gish.

Another successful writer was Winifred Sanford, a Wichita Falls resident who chronicled the effects of the Texas oil boom in a series of finely observed, well-written short stories that remain very readable today. Most of her work was published in the *American Mercury*, a magazine edited by one of America's foremost journalists, H. L. Mencken. Three of her stories also appeared in the 1926 edition of *Best American Short Stories*. A collection of Sanford's work remains in print and is available for contemporary readers.

Most impressive of all was Katherine Anne Porter, two years younger than Dobie, who had fled Texas and embraced literary modernism as she lived a bohemian lifestyle. Porter wanted to join the American expatriate community in Paris during the 1920s, but she didn't have enough money to make the trip, so she went to Mexico instead. There she fell in with revolutionary artists such as Diego Rivera, Frida Kahlo, and Manual Alvarez Bravo. She learned Spanish and published essays and book reviews in Mexican newspapers. She also began writing acclaimed short stories that would win her an international reputation.

Like many young writers of the era, Porter was politically very liberal, and in New York City in 1927 she was arrested, along with other writers and intellectuals, for protesting the execution of Italian anarchists Sacco and Vanzetti. Porter rarely returned to Texas because she resented the state's cultural conservatism. However, her Texas roots were often an important element in her fiction.[3]

Meanwhile, a new literary movement was springing up in the Southwest as a direct response to the Great War. Mabel Dodge, the wealthy socialite who had sponsored the literary salon in New York City during the 1910s, was among those who became disenchanted by the "machine age" after the mass carnage inflicted during the war. Like many artists, she began to view Western civilization as irredeemably corrupt, and she sought refuge away from its nerve centers.

Dodge believed that she had found such a place in Taos, New Mexico, where painters had been settling since the beginning of the century. The air was clear, the light was dazzling, and the local Native Americans retained many of their traditional ways. The cost of living was cheap. For those seeking an escape, northern New Mexico seemed ideal, particularly once marketing connections to New York were established.

Soon after her arrival, Dodge married a Taos Pueblo chief, Tony Luhan, and she began inviting artists and writers to visit. Among those who came was Georgia O'Keeffe, who later decided to relocate there permanently. Eminences such as Carl Jung and Aldous Huxley visited, and Dodge also lured British writer D. H. Lawrence, who stayed intermittently during the mid-1920s. Numerous other writers became identified with the New Mexico literary scene, including Mary Austin, author of the classic Southwestern work *The Land of Little Rain*, and Oliver La Farge, who would win a Pulitzer Prize in 1930 for his Navajo-themed *Laughing Boy*. Also present was Willa Cather, who won a Pulitzer in 1923 and subsequently wrote her own New Mexico novel, *Death Comes to the Archbishop*, in 1927.[4]

Many of the New Mexico writers incorporated Modernist techniques and experimented with style, but, like Dobie, they were primarily interested in adapting local history and folklore into their work. They celebrated indigenous peoples as a countermeasure to Anglo culture, which they saw as materialistic and deadening. This resistance was not just artistic and political, it also became spiritual, and many of them explored eastern philosophies and Native American religious traditions.

The New Mexicans' emphasis on spirituality, indigenous culture, and the transformative power of landscape nurtured a literary approach that has paid dividends for generations, continuing into the present, with the success of such writers as Rudolfo Anaya, John Nichols, Tony Hillerman, and Leslie Marmon Silko.

Dobie made a few trips out to northern New Mexico in the course of his folklore research. He struck up a mild friendship with the writer Mary

Katherine Anne Porter, ca. 1930s. Papers of Katherine Anne Porter, Special Collections, University of Maryland Libraries.

Jovita González, ca. 1930s. E. E. Mireles & Jovita G. Mireles, Special Collections & Archives, Texas A&M University–Corpus Christi, Bell Library.

Austin, but he never connected with the group. Like them, he denounced the machine age, and he appreciated his own "indigenous" people—Texas Mexicans—for being "a holding line against the intrusions of modernity."⁵ But Dobie could never make the leap across the cultural divide and view the Mexicano culture as an antidote to modern society's ills.

Dobie's remedy, instead, was to look back to the pioneer Anglo settlers—his own ethnic stock. If people only emulated their values, his work often suggested, the world would be a better place. In making this choice, Dobie never acknowledged what was obvious to the writers in New Mexico: it was the Anglo American culture that had created the machine age, and it was the Anglo American ranchers who had fenced off the open range.

Dobie made a sharp distinction between "good" Mexicans—those who accepted Anglo hegemony and worked well within Anglo society—and the "bandits" who resisted Anglo domination. Dobie had a colonialist's contempt for the rebels, writing in an early folklore article that it "is characteristic of any lowly people . . . that they should heroize a rebel against law and property. Hence, whenever a bandido or revolutionist dies in Mexico, he is almost sure to be 'put into a ballad.'"⁶

However, when Dobie determined that a Mexicano was a "good" one, his heart would open up and he would do all he could to assist the person. He found such a friend in the mid-1920s at the University of Texas.

Jovita González was a pretty young woman who grew up on a ranch near Roma, along the Texas-Mexico border. She was said to come from a landowning family, and she enrolled at UT in pursuit of a master's degree in 1925. There she was introduced to Dobie and noticed immediately, "He walks just like a cowboy."⁷

González was interested in folklore and in writing, and soon Dobie became her mentor. He solicited articles from her, helped edit her manuscripts, and promoted her membership within the Texas Folklore Society. He and Bertha underwrote bank loans to help her to continue her education, and she became a frequent visitor to the Dobie home, where she joined Dobie, Bertha, and other guests for dinners and conversation.

González was twenty-three years old when Dobie suggested to Texas Folklore Society members that she should be chosen to give the featured presentation at its 1927 meeting. No one dared oppose him, and González gave a talk on "Lore of the Texas Vaquero" that drew statewide press attention. She began publishing articles in the annual folklore journal that Dobie edited, and thanks to his influence she became the organization's vice president in 1928. Then, beginning in 1930, she was elected to two terms as president of the Texas Folklore Society. This was an unprecedented accomplishment at the time for a woman and a Mexican American.

Yet there was a hitch. As later scholars have pointed out, González's folklore largely consists of paternalistic accounts that reinforced prevailing Anglo views of Texas Mexicans as simple, ignorant folk who had more or less accommodated themselves to Anglo dominance. Little of her work acknowledged the active spirit of resistance, which in reality formed a large part of the Texas Mexican folkloric tradition.

Many later critics have blamed Dobie for imposing his views on González, although no evidence exists that he ever did such a thing. In fact, Dobie gave every indication throughout his tenure that he favored complete intellectual freedom for all contributors to the Texas Folklore Society. Still, it would have been very difficult for González, as a young woman and an ethnic minority, to challenge the dominant views. It is also the case that many folklorists of the time sought to promote harmony between the races, and so they often downplayed intercultural conflict. In this way, González's folklore simply conformed to accepted standards of her era, and likely would have been mild with or without Dobie's presence.

González referred to her mentor as "Amigo mio don Pancho," but she was certainly aware of ethnic enmity. She considered South Texas history to be "a racial struggle" and believed that "some of those things that happened on both sides were very bitter." In an interview near the end of her life, she said that she made it a point to never go into one of Dobie's classes "because I would be mad at many things. He would take the Anglo-Saxon side, naturally. I would take the Spanish and Mexican side."[8]

Despite these differences, Dobie and González remained very close. They critiqued each other's manuscripts and Dobie helped her secure a Rockefeller Grant, which allowed her time to work on a novel. González was well on her way to becoming a major Texas writer in the 1930s. Then she married Edmund Mireles and suddenly quit writing for publication. She settled down into a career teaching school and subordinated her independent career to assist her husband's. Although she had completed two novels, they remained unpublished during her lifetime.

Her husband apparently stifled her creative output. During the 1970s, an interviewer asked González about her unpublished novels. Before she could answer, her husband spoke up, assuring the interviewer that the manuscripts had been destroyed. González, in a quietly subversive manner, made a small wagging motion with her hand to indicate that her husband was wrong and that the manuscripts still existed.[9]

In the 1990s, after González and her husband were both dead, her manuscripts were rediscovered, and her novel *Caballero* was published in 1996. Ironically, the book offers a harsh condemnation of its protagonist, a Mexicano patriarch, for his autocratic treatment of women. A much more sympathetic character is found in an Anglo man, who, like Dobie, maintains a far more progressive view of gender relations.

Two additional books by González have also been posthumously published, and now she receives much attention from new generations of scholars. Despite lingering ambivalence about her folkloric approach, she is regarded as a groundbreaking figure in Texas literary history. Under Dobie's "guidance she became, in effect, one of the first professional native scholars of Mexican-American culture and very probably the first woman."[10]

# Regionalism Goes National
## 1929–1930

OBIE'S OFFICE AT UT reflected his love for the Southwest. On his door hung a cow's thighbone, onto which he had inscribed "Office hours: irregular. If your messenger finds him not within, seek him in the other place yourself. Cursed be he that disturbs my bones."[1] Once entering his lair, students couldn't be blamed for feeling as though they had stepped into a ranch headquarters. Western art filled the walls, and coyote and deerskin rugs blanketed the floor. Visitors sat in rawhide chairs, where they had a good view of Dobie's old mesquite desk. Above everything, dominating the entire room, was an impressively huge skull from a Texas longhorn.

Dobie's devotion to regionalism encountered hearty opposition among many of his colleagues and superiors, and he hardly helped matters by publicly criticizing the university's lack of interest in its native soil. "I do not think the University of Texas will ever be dear to the vast territory of Texas and its millions of citizens," he said, "until it becomes more *of* Texas."[2]

By this time, Dobie was no longer a lone wolf in fighting the entrenched interests. The concept of regionalism was taking root in different corners of the country, providing him with models of how his own university might develop. At the University of North Carolina in 1924, Professor Howard Odum founded an institute to study the South's social and economic problems. Odum's center became a fulcrum for Southern studies, establishing a rich regionalist legacy. In Dobie's old stomping grounds north of the Red River, the University of Oklahoma Press was launched in 1928 on a "strictly regional program," signaling a conscious departure from "purely academic" books. Other regionalist enterprises were cropping up in Montana, Iowa, Nebraska, and Louisiana.[3]

In 1929, Dobie suggested establishing a course on Southwestern Literature at the University of Texas. The chairman of the English department questioned whether the Southwest had enough literature to merit such an offering. Dobie responded, "Well, there's plenty of life in it, so I'll just teach that."[4] Thus UT, however reluctantly, became part of the regionalist movement.

Dobie had enjoyed significant successes as a writer and an editor, but he had not yet published a book as an author. All that was set to change, as he had two new books forthcoming, positioning him to attain greater heights.

*A Vaquero of the Brush Country* was published in 1929 as Dobie turned forty-one and the stock market crashed. The book is "partly from the reminiscences of John Young," the old cattleman Dobie had met as a schoolteacher in Alpine nineteen years earlier. Young—the "vaquero" referred to in the title—believed that his memoirs would bring in a trainload of money, and he planned to use the proceeds to build a ten-story marble hotel in downtown San Antonio. Because he was not a writer himself, Young enlisted Dobie's aid in telling his story. Dobie agreed and took over as author.[5]

By the time the book appeared, the heroic image of the American cowboy had already imprinted itself in the popular imagination, thanks to scores of dime novels, Wild West shows, and western movies. For all the talk of literary modernism during the 1920s, the fact remained that Zane Grey's western pulp fiction far outsold the works of Fitzgerald, Joyce, Hemingway, and Faulkner combined. Americans loved to see lone cowboys gunning down bad men.

Dobie despised such treatments, and his aim was to provide an authentic picture of the Texas cowboy, in contrast to the "sensation mongers and sentimentalists." Nevertheless, Young comes across as a rousing figure, and Dobie provides plenty of detail about his various scrapes. Young's spiritedness is summed up by an episode in which he and some companions planned to invade Mexico in order to rescue a jailed friend. The man was released before they could carry out the attack. Young conceded that, had they gone through with the plan, they probably would have been killed. But then, "we loved living more than we loved life."[6]

Despite the heroism with which Dobie portrayed Young, the book was not what the old cattleman expected. As Dobie observed, "I made him more a figure of the earth than the hero of his own imagination." Instead of simply chronicling Young's life story, as Young had hoped, Dobie instead saw him as largely symbolic, "representative of the unfenced world." Dobie used Young's life as a point of departure to tell the story *he* wanted to communicate: "the brush and the brush land [which] has never been written." Dobie wanted to "help the reader to imagine what those old days in the brush were like."[7]

While Dobie deflated Young's self-importance by refusing to make him the hero of his own memoir, his instincts proved to be prescient. He consciously rejected the "Great Man" approach to history, choosing instead to work with a broader canvas, one that more fully considered the lives of common people.

Dobie's social history of the Brush Country reaches its apex in the book's critical chapter—"The Bloody Border"—in which he tells "a part of the dark and unknown story of that border land between the Nueces and the Rio Grande, where Texans and Mexicans for generations killed and raided in a way to make all Indian troubles of the region seem insignificant . . . ."[8]

Dobie's perspective on the region's history left something to be desired. He relied heavily on slanted newspaper stories and official reports that gave a one-sided view of South Texas's ethnic clashes. As the scholar James McNutt observed, Dobie's book is "an apology for Anglo oppression."[9] On the critical issue of how Mexicanos lost so many of their South Texas ranches, Dobie writes only that "shrewd" Anglos gained control of the lands, ignoring the obvious fact that many Texas Mexicans were victims of unscrupulous and even illegal behavior.

In Dobie's view, any Mexican American who challenged the status quo was wrong. Such was the case of Juan Cortina, who led the uprising in 1859 that bested the Texas Rangers. Dobie downplayed Cortina's popular appeal and military successes, and instead portrayed him as "a supreme chieftain over some hundreds of bandidos." Dobie described Cortina as a man "so ignorant that he could hardly sign his name, 'the expression of his face sinister, sensual, and cruel.'"[10]

Yet Dobie's book was progressive by the standards of the day. He was far more sympathetic to Mexican Americans than other Anglo Texas writers of the time. For one thing, he made it clear that the Texas cattle industry was started by Spanish Mexicans—a view that many Anglos had trouble accepting. He also pointed out that there were times when Anglo cowboys "crossed the Rio Grande and got more cattle" by stealing them from Mexicans.[11] This was not something that most Anglo Americans expected to read, being conditioned to regard Mexicans as the source of all border provocation and thievery.

Perhaps most significant was Dobie's description of the infamous "Cart Wars" of the 1850s, during which Anglos murdered Mexicanos who were charging lower prices for transporting goods across the state. Dobie called such events disgraceful, "nothing less than an effort on the part of certain Texas ruffians to run Mexican freighters out of business."[12] This was one of the very few times any Anglo writer had voiced support for the Mexicano side.

Dobie also took pains to point out that, despite the image of a "bloody border," in truth "strong ties of friendship existed between many Anglo Texans and Mexican Texans" in South Texas.[13] In this view, too, Dobie was far ahead of his time, even leapfrogging later generations of revisionist scholars. Prior to the 1980s, most Anglo historians wrote accounts that emphasized Mexican cruelty. Revisionist Chicano scholars reacted by writing accounts that emphasize Anglo cruelty. Both sides have contributed to a historical portrait that stresses ethnic enmity and violence.

In recent years, a new picture has developed. This view is far less colorful, but it does have the advantage of perhaps being more accurate. Scholars such as Armando Alonzo have done careful studies indicating that, despite occasional flare-ups of intense violence, the overwhelming reality for most people in South Texas—Anglos and Mexicanos alike—was a spirit of accommodation, at least during the era Dobie was writing about.[14] As future generations of scholars find ways to more carefully examine the complexity of intercultural relations, many of Dobie's writings will appreciate in value because, despite his lapses into cultural jingoism, much of his work also contains sharp glimpses of reality.

★ ★

*A Vaquero of the Brush Country*, alas, did not earn John Young enough money to build a marble hotel. It did become a minor success, at least in Texas, by selling nearly one thousand copies during its first year of publication. It was generally well received by both the public and reviewers, thereby helping to build name recognition for Dobie's next book, which became his breakout work.

For several years Dobie had collected stories of men who were "lured ever onward by the tantalizing tales of gold and silver and other romantic

Dobie in Dallas, 1931.
Southwestern Writers
Collection/The Wittliff
Collections, Texas State
University–San Marcos.

riches hidden away beneath the land." The treasure stories Dobie included in 1924's *The Legends of Texas* were the best-received part of that book, and he planned to produce a new compendium focusing exclusively on treasure stories, with contributions from many different writers. Yet as Dobie worked up his own material in anticipation of the volume, he grew to realize that "I can easily make this book without using any one else's contributions." He combined his new stories with those he had originally written for *The Legends of Texas*, and by 1930 the book was ready.[15]

He called it *Coronado's Children*, in honor of those who followed in the footsteps of the region's original treasure seeker, Francisco Vasquez de Coronado, who traveled across the Southwest in 1542 in a futile search for the Seven Cities of Gold.

The book was published by the Southwest Press, the same Dallas-based regional publisher Dobie had used for *Vaquero*. Dobie believed the Southwest was ripe for a literary boom, and publishing locally was his way of expressing support for regionalism. It also allowed him to avoid the more complicated issue of taking the book to New York, where editorial acceptance might not be so easy. By 1930, however, the Southwest Press was struggling against the Depression, and Dobie agreed to take deferred royalty payments to ensure smooth delivery of the book. He hoped to make some money, but "the honest truth is that I'd give my life to make the heritage of my soil a living part of the people existing on it."[16]

In *Coronado's Children*, Dobie's warm, open voice is at its best as he guides readers on journeys to remote corners of the Southwest. The author's vigorous presence is clear throughout as he describes going out into the wild, camping out under the stars, and meeting up with prospectors and dreamers. The sense of adventure is palpable, and Dobie's storytelling is imbued with a folksy, almost oral quality. With some imagination it is possible for readers to feel that they, too, are sitting around Dobie's campfire as the tales unfold.

While gold and silver are the lures, the stories are really about the people and the land. Caches of riches are briefly discovered during times of distress, as in the case of a man who survives an Indian attack by burrowing into a small earthen cave, only to discover that he is hiding among gold. Another time a young girl gets lost in a dust storm and, when the air clears she finds herself standing on a mountain of gold. The lost travelers always return to civilization with just enough gold to send people into a fever. But the riches are never found again.

Many times, extraordinarily detailed maps lead travelers to the precipice of a great discovery, only to have fate intervene. Occasionally the fortune seekers manage to grasp the treasure, only to see it slip away. In one instance, boxes of money said to be buried by Mexican President Santa Anna are actually recovered, but before they can be secured they fall into bottomless quicksand, lost forever.

Despite Dobie's contempt for "scientific" folklore, his scholarship is superb in *Coronado's Children*, as he traces the tales back to their beginnings, showing how they became increasingly exaggerated over the years. His endnotes, too, showcase the mind of a man with an extraordinary command of printed material relevant to the subject. In addition to being a teller of folktales, Dobie was also clearly establishing himself as the leading literary authority on the Southwest.

The timing for *Coronado's Children* couldn't have been better. Treasure stories were of supreme interest during the Great Depression, and the collapse of industrialism created a wave of nostalgia for the country's vanishing rural heritage. *Coronado's Children* took readers back to a simpler time while exploring the tantalizing possibility, however distant, of getting rich quick.

Dobie fully expected *Coronado's Children* to do well in Texas, but no one anticipated the national reception. Prominent reviews ran in eastern newspapers, and the *New York Times* hailed the book as "a fascinating record of adventurous search for hidden riches . . . as entrancing a volume as one is likely to pick up in a month of Sundays."[17]

In February 1931, one of the country's major book clubs, the New York Literary Guild, announced that *Coronado's Children* was its featured selection. This was the first time any title from America's interior had been so honored. Waves of publicity washed over Dobie and his book became a national bestseller. People in Texas hailed his achievement, and he was invited to New York for a media tour. The triumphant author returned to the scene of his earlier failure, feeling that justice had been served at last. New York reporters gathered around him, eagerly scribbling notes as he lectured them on the importance of his native Southwestern culture. He had, in a word, arrived.

*Mr. Texas*

# Dobie in Bloom
## 1930–1934

OBIE'S NATIONAL SUCCESS proved to be a transformative event for Texans. Previously, writers such as Katherine
Anne Porter and O. Henry had left the state in order to carve
out their careers. As Dobie's triumph indicated, it was now "possible for a
Texas writer to stay home and make a living."[1] He also showed that Texas
pride could now extend to its literature, and the state was capable of making real contributions to America's national culture.

When editors in New York wanted someone to explain Texas or the
Southwest, Dobie was often the person they called upon. Following the
publication of *Coronado's Children*, he was besieged with offers. He read-
ily complied, publishing dozens of stories within the next year, including
an astounding eighteen articles in the *New York Herald-Tribune*, one of the
nation's leading newspapers at the time. Even with this national exposure,
Dobie took care to ensure that his byline also appeared regularly in regional publications.

For reporters, Dobie was irresistible copy. Charismatic, highly quotable,
and sharply opinionated, he never shied away from publicity. He projected
a comforting rusticity, dressed in rancher's clothing, and puffed on his ever-
present pipe. When he wanted to appear more formal he favored white
suits, just like Mark Twain. Dobie punctuated these with a brightly colored
rose plucked from Bertha's garden.

People remarked how much he resembled Will Rogers, Carl Sandburg, or Robert Frost. Indeed, he came across as a Texas version of those more famous personalities. Articles by Dobie, about Dobie, and quoting Dobie cropped up regularly in Texas newspapers, along with photographs of "the picturesque author."[2] Before long he became famous even among those who had never picked up a book. For many Texans, J. Frank Dobie was the only writer from the state they had ever heard of.

Dobie found himself in demand as a public speaker, and he earned extra income giving readings and lectures, which had the nice benefit of getting his name yet again into local papers. By 1934 he became popular enough to take his act on the road, making stage appearances as an oral storyteller in Texas, New Mexico, and Colorado. Bertha, as usual, took over his classes during these absences.[3]

Dobie's role as spokesman for Texas and the Southwest made him a magnet for people who wanted to share their own stories. He began receiving hundreds of letters each year about everything from swimming rattlesnakes to secret gold mines. The letters often contained offerings—Bowie knives, spurs, coyote heads, pottery, and arrowheads. Dobie kept many of the mementos, which he added to his growing collection of Southwestern artifacts. But more importantly, he recognized that these contributed tales and anecdotes could make him even more prolific, and he gratefully incorporated this shared material into his writing.

★ ★

America's literary landscape had changed a great deal since the Roaring Twenties, and the emerging trends played right into Dobie's hands. The Great Depression caused a loss of faith in mass production, and people turned against standardized, homogenous environments. For the first time in America's history, rural areas gained population at the expense of the cities.[4]

This movement, naturally, influenced the arts. In the 1920s, Modernists experimented so much with style that they often cared little for setting. The rise of regionalism, in contrast, celebrated the authenticity of local cultures. Painters such as Thomas Hart Benton and Grant Wood rejected Abstract Expressionism in favor of agrarian stolidity by creating realistic portraits of Midwestern farmers. In literature, America's best-selling novels during the 1930s also had a strong regionalist bent, including Margaret Mitchell's *Gone with the Wind* and John Steinbeck's *The Grapes of Wrath*.

A triumphant Dobie, ca. 1930s. Southwestern Writers Collection / The Wittliff Collections, Texas State University– San Marcos.

Franklin Roosevelt's New Deal deployed federal funding in support of regional arts. The Works Progress Administration (WPA) employed writers to put together a series of travel guides to each state. The WPA also sponsored the post office mural project, which commissioned artists to highlight local culture. The federal government also undertook a massive effort to collect oral histories of rural folk, including the first-ever program to interview former slaves. John Lomax, traveling with his son Alan under the auspices of the Library of Congress, recorded folk music in the rural south, discovering performers such as Leadbelly. Perhaps most significantly, the Farm Security Administration sent out photographers such as Dorothea Lange, Walker Evans, and Russell Lee to document people in their native environments. Their work created an indelible visual record of the Great Depression.

As one geographer noted, this buzz of activity during the 1930s represented "a search for what might be called the indigenous or the primal basic America, a desire for a stable communal identity, and a reverence for the past—especially the memories that could bring a sense of order and certainty to a tumultuous present."[5]

Dobie, of course, had always looked to the past. Now the rest of America was finally catching up with him. Many people, especially in Texas, saw him as their leader and he became a living legend among his many admirers. One man, J. Forrest McCutcheon, went to the trouble of privately printing and distributing a Christmas pamphlet in 1932 titled "J. Frank Dobie—Texan: An Appreciation." The pamphlet described Dobie in heroic terms: "He is preserving for the Southwest a heritage and an heirloom far more golden and entrancingly beautiful than any of her other legacies . . . it is by the very simplicity and preciseness of his style that he obtains the mellowness, charm, vividness and gusto that is so patently present in every paragraph he has written."[6]

Part of Dobie's success was due to his wife, Bertha, who served as his chief critic and editor. As Bertha recalled, "When he finished a first-draft of a chapter, he'd give it to me to read. I'd put check marks in the margins and later we'd talk about them. Sometimes he would come to my point of view, and sometimes not."[7]

Bertha's main aim was to offset her husband's disregard for structure. Dobie enjoyed the random, digressive character of oral storytelling, and he wanted to preserve some aspect of that quality in his prose. While such idiosyncrasies might be charming in conversation, Bertha didn't believe they translated well to literature, and she attempted to organize his writing by "changing paragraph sequence, and making the story tighter, more of a unit."[8]

Dobie didn't always take well to such suggestions, and in these early years, Bertha said, "I'd hold my views rather strongly, and we'd often get into a furious argument. Anyone listening might think we were angry. But later on I became more philosophical, and if he didn't agree with me, I'd say no more."[9]

Despite his resistance to such word herding, Dobie recognized his wife's contributions, and he gratefully acknowledged her help in all of his books. In one of his dedications he wrote, "Through the years I have derived as much from her habit of clear thinking as from her particular criticisms. She is the most incisive and the most concretely constructive critic I have ever known. Her sense of form and fitness and her precision in details have gone into every book I have written."[10]

In addition to being her husband's helpmate, Bertha was at last enjoying some literary success of her own. Since moving into their Austin home, Bertha had turned the curving bank of Waller Creek behind their house into

Bertha McKee Dobie in her garden, ca. 1930s. Southwestern Writers
Collection/The Wittliff Collections, Texas State University–San Marcos.

a dazzling garden. She focused on native vegetation and kept the arrangement informal, planting dogwood, wild peach, Texas holly, lantana, Cherokee plum, mountain laurel, wisteria, honeysuckle, and the chilipiquines her husband favored. Rose bushes were everywhere, and flowers bloomed ten months of the year. She avoided cactus, as she wrote, because her yard's "great elm and the creek bank say so. Spines and stiff forms would be out of place where the natural tone is soft, lush, and extravagant."[11] In Austin, many people came to recognize the Dobie home as much for Bertha's garden as for the fact that a famous writer lived there.

Bertha's passion for gardening found its way into her writing, and for the first time, she found a ready market for her work. She was undoubtedly helped by her husband's stature and the fact that he talked her up to editors wherever he went. In December 1930 she published an article on Texas gardens in *Nature* magazine. Her husband also appeared in that issue, and so she used her maiden name, Bertha McKee, "to avoid having two Dobies in the same issue."[12]

In 1931 Bertha enjoyed her biggest success to date, developing a column on gardening that was published in Austin and Dallas newspapers. The column appeared every week for the entire year, bringing her significant attention as a leading authority on Texas gardens. She received letters from appreciative readers, and her husband's publisher, Southwest Press, agreed to publish her book on the topic as soon as she completed the manuscript. Just as her husband had spun his love for folktales into literary gold, so too did Bertha hope to make her passion for gardening the foundation for her own writing.

★ ★

Dobie began offering his new course, "Life and Literature of the Southwest," in the spring of 1930. Students received an education unlike anything before. They had grown up believing that American history began with the arrival of the Pilgrims and the founding of the thirteen colonies. Dobie aimed to set them straight. He pointed out that the city of San Antonio was established years before George Washington was born, and that Santa Fe, New Mexico, had been a territorial capital before the first Pilgrim ever landed at Plymouth Rock. Though the Southwest had long been overlooked, Dobie argued, it offered just as much relevant history as New England.

Dobie showed up in class with "a battered briefcase stuffed with books." He would tell students to forget "sermons of dreary New England preachers."[13] Instead, he told them the story of Cabeza de Vaca, the Spanish explorer who lived among Texas Indians in the 1500s. No other English professor in the country paid the slightest attention to Cabeza de Vaca at the time. In the years since, however, the Spanish explorer's story has become an important part of the American canon, and many schoolchildren across the country are made aware of his significance.

Dobie's lectures were wide ranging. He taught his students how to survive in the desert on prickly pear cactus, and he explained how to calm a nervous herd of longhorns during a lightning storm. Dobie also pointed out the beneficial qualities of the mesquite tree: "How you could stuff your hat with the leaves to keep cool, or chew them for a headache." He brought samples of rawhide to show the class and he told "wondrous tales" about it, how it could be made either elastic or hard, and "how Indians used it to bind and rack a spread-eagled victim, or how Charlie Goodnight threw a hide on the floor [for an overnight visitor] and told his guest, 'Here, you take this. I'll rough it.'"[14]

Dobie also encouraged his students to live their lives to the fullest. On one of his end-of-the-semester tests he added a note: "I hope you'll always be able to eat when you are hungry—and that you will be very hungry; that you'll always be able to drink when you are thirsty—and that you will often raise a powerful thirst; and that you'll really live until you die."[15]

Dobie's class was not easy, and students were expected to do a lot of writing. He helped corral the best of their work into privately printed keepsake publications, which he helped pay for and promote. Whenever he had an exceptional student, Dobie was a generous mentor. He would give the student personally inscribed copies of his own books, and he would also loan or give important books by others that he thought the pupil should read. Dobie would also go to great lengths to help young writers get published, and many of his students went on to produce work for the *Southwest Review* and the Texas Folklore Society. Several went on to successful careers of their own, such as humorist and storyteller John Henry Faulk and novelist Fred Gipson, author of *Old Yeller*.

Although Dobie's course was ostensibly about the Greater Southwest, he did not teach the works of the contemporary New Mexico writers who were making a national impact, such as Mary Austin, Willa Cather, and Oliver La Farge. Instead, Dobie's focus was on old-time Texas, and therefore his students read Davy Crockett's autobiography, the life story of Texas Ranger Big Foot Wallace, and Andy Adams' *Log of a Cowboy*. Precious little information was shared about Native Americans, other than accounts of warfare written from the Anglo point of view.

Many of his students, captivated by the wonders they discovered in Dobie's course, wanted to continue the journey. For them, Dobie developed a reading guide containing an extensive list of books, organized by topic. He also added erudite, often charming observations on each title. He made mimeographed copies of the guide available to his class, and in 1931 the Southwest Press published a book, *Finding Literature on the Texas Plains*, which included Dobie's bibliography. He continued to expand his list, and a few years later his *Guide to Life and Literature of the Southwest* was published as a stand-alone book. It remains one of his enduring works and is an essential volume for any Southwestern bookshelf. Dobie's generosity of spirit is evidenced by his refusal to copyright the publication. On the title page, where the legal disclaimers normally appear, Dobie wrote, "Not copyright. . . . Anybody is welcome to help himself to any of it in any way."[16]

Dobie's course "Life and Literature of the Southwest" quickly gained a reputation as UT's most popular elective, and several other universities have adopted the idea over the years. Not every student, however, appreciated Dobie's teaching. In 1933, one pupil wrote a final exam essay that directly challenged his professor. The student noted that he had begun the course "with eager anticipation," but that his "enjoyment of it decreased" as he read the books Dobie assigned. The student complained that the "dull, mediocre books" did not compare well to the novels of luminaries such as Willa Cather. Dobie's choices, the student wrote, "are exceedingly uninteresting from the standpoint of both style and content." In summing up, the student posed a question: "So I ask again, why read them? And the only answer I can think of is, you have to do so to pass a course and get three more hours of credit."[17]

Dobie saved the student's essay, retaining it among his personal papers. Obviously approving of the young man's bravado, he marked the essay with an "A," not an easy grade to get in his class.[18]

Over the next few years, Dobie did begin updating his reading list, expanding his notion of the Southwest to include more works about Native Americans and Spanish Mexicans. By 1938 he was advising students, "The main aim of this course has been to come to a realization of the elements that have blended together to form the *culture* of the Southwest."[19]

★ ★

Walter Prescott Webb in Alpine, Texas, 1924. Southwestern Writers Collection / The Wittliff Collections, Texas State University–San Marcos.

J. Mason Brewer, photograph by Walter Barnes Studio. Southwestern Writers Collection / The Wittliff Collections, Texas State University–San Marcos.

94 Dobie was not the only regionalist at the University of Texas. Hot on the heels of *Coronado's Children* came the publication of *The Great Plains*, the first book by his colleague, historian Walter Prescott Webb. Like Dobie, Webb was something of a late bloomer. He was forty-three when his first book appeared.

Webb had not earned a doctorate either, and he sought to write for a popular audience rather than academic specialists. *The Great Plains* didn't achieve the commercial success of *Coronado's Children*, but it became hugely influential among historians. In his book, Webb practically invented the field of environmental history by pointing out that the plains' arid climate had strongly influenced human settlement patterns. Webb's revelation overturned previous approaches to history, which often considered factors such as divine intervention to explain human behavior. Webb's new regionalist approach became a turning point in American historical writing, and in 1950 a panel of American historians chose *The Great Plains* as the most significant book written by a living historian.[20] The book is still taught today in college courses.

Webb had a coolly analytical mind, and his somewhat morose personality was leavened by a sharp, biting wit. However, he proved a bit unhinged when it came to matters of race. He did not grow up among Mexican Americans, as did Dobie. Raised on a hardscrabble farm in North Texas, Webb understood Mexicanos only as a historical enemy. In *The Great Plains*, he infamously observed that the Mexicano's blood, "when compared to that of the Plains Indian, was as ditch water."[21]

In his subsequent work, *The Texas Rangers*, published in 1935, Webb carried his race-baiting to another level entirely. His aim was to justify the Anglo domination of Texas, and to that end he was contemptuous of prior Indian and Mexican claims to the land. The Indians, he wrote, were "fickle, irresponsible and primitive people" who "knew just enough history to confuse them." The Indians, however, looked pretty good when compared to the Mexicanos, whom Webb described as having "a cruel streak in [their] nature, or so the history of Texas would lead one to believe." Webb described Mexicanos as "wholly unequal" to Texans and he suggested that they were cowards besides. The Mexicano, Webb wrote, "won more victories over the Texans by parley than by force of arms. For making promises—and for breaking them—he had no peer."[22]

Webb and Dobie had known each other casually since the early 1920s, but they were never particularly close friends. In some ways, Dobie related better to John Mason Brewer, a professor in Austin who had a very similar background to Dobie's. Brewer was born and raised in South Texas; his mother was a teacher and his father had driven cattle up the trail to Kansas. He was well educated and served in the Army during the Great War. Yet unlike Dobie, Brewer was fluent in French, Spanish, and Italian, and he worked as a translator during the war. Brewer was quite interested in poetry, as Dobie had been; however, he'd had much better luck publishing his poetry than Dobie had. Like Dobie, he had been a high school teacher and principal, but then he left to go into private industry in order to make more money. Finally, like Dobie, Brewer used only the first initial of his given name. He went by J. Mason Brewer. Yet there was one significant difference between the two men—Brewer was African American.

Brewer lived in Austin, where he taught at the city's black college, Samuel Huston (now Huston-Tillotson University). One Sunday afternoon in 1932 he called Dobie to tell him that he had been collecting Negro folk tales. Dobie arranged to meet with him that same day.

Dobie read over a couple of Brewer's tales and quickly realized "the Texas Folk-Lore Society's next book would have a treasure." Dobie agreed to edit Brewer's manuscript, and the lead article in the next Texas Folklore Society publication was Brewer's "Juneteenth." Dobie himself introduced the piece, noting, "as folk-tales and as a revelation of the race that has engendered and fostered them, they are, all in all, a distinct contribution."[23]

As he had earlier with Jovita González, Dobie again broke a color barrier within the Texas Folklore Society. In 1934, he asked for and received approval to make J. Mason Brewer the Society's first African American member.

Despite his friendly relations with Brewer, Dobie's views on African Americans were hardly progressive. Dobie did believe, along with most Anglo folklorists, that collecting Negro folklore was a worthy effort, but he did not consider African Americans to be equals. Though he aided Brewer and praised his published article, Dobie also made a point of telling others that Brewer's original manuscript was very ragged, and that it only became publishable as a result of Dobie's own editing efforts. "I have spent less time composing forty-five pages of my own writing," Dobie later observed, "than in editing J. Mason Brewer's 'Juneteenth.'"[24]

In his own writings, Dobie expressed little regard for African Americans. One of his stories in *Coronado's Children* was the tale of "The Lost Nigger Mine." Modern readers may cringe at the use of the word "nigger," but

Dobie had every right to identify the mine by its common name. What was bothersome about Dobie's account, however, was that he continued to use the word "nigger" long past the point it was necessary. At times, he even invoked the word gleefully, as when he wrote: "At any rate, the nigger left suddenly on a 'borrowed' horse . . . . "[25] The word "nigger" was viewed pejoratively among enlightened people of the 1920s and 1930s. Dobie, clearly, was not among them.

Despite Dobie's ingrained prejudices, he had a strong belief in personal freedom, and he encouraged its practice in others. As editor of the Texas Folklore Society annual publications, Dobie was well known for refusing to set limits on the other members. In 1926, when a Texas Folklore Society volume he edited contained several Negro folksongs, all of which were collected by whites, Dobie issued the book with a rather startling editorial note. Dobie's introduction spoke to both his own prejudices as well as his tolerance for all other views. Dobie, who chose to spell the word "Negro" with a small "n," wrote: "The editor disclaims any responsibility for the opinions and information set forth by the varying contributors on the subject of negro folk-songs printed in this publication. If one wants to spell negro with a capital N and another with a little n, the editor has nothing to say; if one considers a negro as a shining apostle of sweetness and light, another as a gentle old darkey, and still another as 'phallic kinky,' it is none of the editor's business."[26]

★ ★

Dobie's closest friend was J. Evetts Haley, who, like Dobie, was out of the old rock. Haley's ancestors fought in the Texas Revolution and the Civil War, and he grew up herding cattle on West Texas ranches.

Haley, who was born in 1901, came to UT as a graduate student in the mid-1920s, and Dobie saw in him a younger version of himself. When Haley was twenty-six years old, he sent Dobie a letter condemning "standardization, conformity, and conventionality." He added, "I have longed for the time when I could get back and hear the roar of the hoofs of the remuda."[27] Dobie had expressed the very same sentiment a dozen years earlier as a twenty-six-year-old graduate student in New York.

Before coming to the university, Haley worked for the newly established Panhandle-Plains Historical Society. He went out into the field to interview old pioneers and he collected artifacts and archives for a planned museum on range life. During these travels Haley met and befriended the

J. Evetts Haley, ca. 1930s.
Haley Memorial Library
& History Center, Mid-
land, Texas.

legendary Texas cattleman Charles Goodnight. He also scored an archival coup by securing the papers of the XIT ranch, one of the most famous
cattle empires in Texas history.

In Austin, Dobie got Haley involved with the Texas Folklore Society,
and the younger man published articles on cowboy songs and the "Lore
of the Llano Estacado" in the Texas Folklore Society's 1927 volume. After
graduation, Haley returned to his job in the Panhandle, and from West
Texas he helped Dobie track down stories for inclusion in *Coronado's Children*. Haley was also hard at work on his first book, a history of the XIT
ranch. He and Dobie kept in constant touch through letters, and in 1928
Haley sent Dobie a draft manuscript of his XIT book for comments.

Dobie's critique was withering. He wrote to Haley, "In the first place
you exaggerate and aggrandize and eulogize too much." Dobie also informed Haley that his writing style "is cursed with circumlocution, trite-
ness, verbosity, and nearly every other possible sin against strong, direct
diction. If there is anything at all characteristic about the language of men
of the soil it is directness and economy." Dobie rewrote several passages
to show Haley how his work could be improved, and told him "You will
never make a historian until you learn to write."[28]

At the end of his letter, Dobie softened a bit. "I have been severe on purpose. I could not blame you if you ceased to like me. Yet my whole purpose has been to make some criticism of value. . . . Let me repeat that you are doing something very much worth doing. And all in all you are doing it well."[29]

Such a stern criticism would have derailed a lesser man, but Haley was made of strong stuff. He wrote back to Dobie, "I want to thank you for being so frank. I admit that you gave me a hell of a jolt in several places, but I know that is what I need. . . . I guarantee that there will be less verbosity in the chapters that follow."[30]

Haley substantially revised his work, and it got published in 1929 as *The XIT Ranch and the Early Days of the Llano Estacado*. Dobie was among those who reviewed Haley's book favorably. Writing in the *Dallas Morning News*, Dobie praised Haley's "happy combination of accuracy and flavor" and predicted that his book had "set a standard for ranch histories that will probably never be reached by any other record."[31]

In the wake of his book publication, the University of Texas hired Haley to collect material towards a planned "Texas collection" at the university library. Haley's move to Austin solidified his friendship with Dobie, and the two men spent much time together. Like Dobie, Haley detested much of academia, and in a letter to his friend he condemned "the smugness, the pettiness, the superciliousness, the whole damned outlook so out-of-joint, so unnatural, as to be almost intolerable." Haley's devotion to Texas pride also mirrored that of Dobie's. In a letter to Dobie composed on Texas Independence Day, Haley noted, "My deep regret is that Texas ever joined the damned Union."[32]

Many of the faculty members at the university, including Walter Prescott Webb, were politically liberal. (In those days, progressive views on race were not a requirement for liberalism, especially in the South.) Many at UT were in step with the country's political trends, which moved to the left during the Great Depression. Even the state of Texas had a liberal governor, Jimmy Allred, during these years.

Haley, however, strongly opposed "the loose spending, and the loose morals of the Roosevelt Regime," and he published an article in the *Saturday Evening Post* denouncing Roosevelt. Haley much preferred things the way they were in the past: "How simple, natural, wholesome and right it all was," he wrote, before government programs came along "to bail out the lazy." Haley soon began a "vigorous fight" against Roosevelt and "the insidious invasion of socialistic federal power."[33]

Dobie was not as concerned with politics as Haley, but he was sympathetic to his friend's views. As a loyal grandson of the Confederacy and a rugged individualist, Dobie considered the federal government "almost a foreign menace to Texas rights and privileges."[34] In this regard, Dobie and Haley were closely aligned with other regionalists, particularly a group of twelve Southern writers who in 1930 published a manifesto, *I'll Take My Stand*, that called for safeguarding the South's traditional culture.

The emphasis on regional traditions could easily devolve into political reactionaryism, particularly in those places that enforced antiquated notions of class and race. Some of the contributors to *I'll Take My Stand* later became associated with right-wing politics as they endorsed pro-segregationist policies. Haley, too, would eventually gain a prominent reputation as a right-wing activist.

Dobie appeared to be set on a similar path. As a Texas traditionalist, he adhered to nineteenth century standards of personal freedom. The election of Franklin Roosevelt carried the promise of a more activist government, and Dobie was among those who opposed the New Deal. As the new president prepared to take office in 1933 Dobie wrote to Bertha, "I have no use for Roosevelt and no use for his plans."[35]

# Into Mexico
## 1933–1935

I N 1933, IN RECOGNITION of his achievements, the University of Texas promoted forty-five-year-old J. Frank Dobie to the rank of full professor—an unprecedented achievement for a man without a Ph.D. Dobie was pleased by the recognition, but by now he was making more money from writing than teaching, and he considered quitting his job, getting a literary agent, and becoming a full-time writer. He always enjoyed mentoring promising young people, but the vast majority of his students weren't serious about intellectual matters, and he didn't like wasting his energies on them. Worse, as his popularity grew, many students signed up simply to take "a course in J. Frank Dobie," rather than because of any interest in the material.[1]

Book publishers in New York were courting Dobie, and they were much better positioned to deliver him to a national audience, with attendant sales. His previous publisher, the Southwest Press, had not served him well. His books went quickly out of print as the press edged towards bankruptcy. "I should have started in with a good national publisher in the beginning," he wrote to a friend. "I thought that a publisher for the Southwest could be developed. That was a dream of impracticability."[2]

Dobie had several book projects in mind. New accounts of lost treasures were pouring in, and he could easily write a sequel to *Coronado's Children*.

He had also been busy collecting stories on a variety of subjects—in particular the animal folklore of the Southwest—coyotes, rattlesnakes, mustangs, and roadrunners, any one of which he could turn into a book. One animal of special interest was the Texas longhorn, which he saw as emblematic of "Old Texas."

The Southwest was wide open for him, and yet Dobie could not escape Mexico's gravitational pull. He saw it as the mother country, the source for much of what he loved about his native region. He had already made several journeys into Mexico, including a memorable 1927 trip into the rugged barranca country of Chihuahua. There he undertook a search for the famed Lost Tayopa Mine, which became the subject of one of his articles for the *Country Gentleman*.

Traveling across rural Mexico on horseback gave Dobie some sense of what the open range in Texas and the Southwest must have been like before he was born. Modern America seemed very far away. As he wrote to Bertha, "I discover within myself a very strong subconscious feeling of freedom, of personal liberty in Mexico, that I don't feel here." He noted that, in Mexico, "the *gente* (people) well say, 'whoever finds freedom finds his country.'"[3]

In 1932 he received a Guggenheim grant that paid him a year's salary to go looking for folktales in Mexico. He took an unpaid leave of absence from the university, which allowed him time to put off his decision whether or not to resign. His immersion in the Mexican backcountry meant that his media exposure—both as a celebrity and as an author—would likely diminish, but it was a price he was willing to pay. His newly signed New York publisher, Doubleday, Doran, and Company, was enthusiastic about the book he would write on Mexico, and everyone expected a tremendous success.

Dobie knew enough "Boss Spanish" to give rough orders to vaqueros and to sprinkle a few Spanish words into his conversation, but he never mastered the language and he relied on interpreters to converse with native speakers. Going into Mexico, however, did not bother him in the least. He would simply find a good *mozo* (guide), one who could speak English.

He experienced trouble at the beginning. At Villa Acuña, across the river from Del Rio, the Mexican customs officials demanded a duty of eighty pesos for the old saddle he insisted on bringing into the country. He refused. Finally, after negotiations broke down, he went downstream some fifty miles to Eagle Pass, where he was waved across for nothing. He had the entire country before him, and still no guide. In the Mexican border town of Piedras Negras, he asked around, and before long the famous American writer was introduced to a retired Mexican general.

Thanks to the general's efforts, Dobie was outfitted with a mozo and he set off with a team of pack mules. Dobie described the journey as "twisting around, through, and across the mountains of northern Mexico to the west—always to the west—just looking, listening, and living the most independent form of life I have known. Except for a few fences and ranchos, the country was all open and unrestricted by man—a country immense, immense. It seemed to belong to me as much as to anybody else."[4]

Traveling with him was Henry Nash Smith, his colleague from UT. Their contingent consisted of four burros carrying supplies, their mozo, and their mozo's son. Dobie and Smith rode horses. The two Mexicanos walked behind them, guiding the burros.

Dobie and Smith went looking for primitive Mexico, and they found it. The Mexicanos they encountered, however, weren't always pleased by the Anglos' perspective on their country. One morning, after emerging from their hotel, Dobie asked Smith to take a photo. The scene showed an elderly mozo attending to the burros as Dobie looked on, pipe in mouth, hands in pockets, clearly in command. In his diary, Dobie recorded that "an officious individual informed [Smith] it was against the law" to take such a picture. Undeterred, Dobie "told Henry to take the picture anyhow." Later on, a Mexicana woman who saw Dobie's photos accosted him, telling him, "You remember only the backwardness of Mexico."[5]

Dobie stayed at a succession of big ranches, where he was received as an important traveler. After four months in Mexico, Dobie wrote to his brother-in-law, "My Spanish is still a starved, limping, faltering thing, but I get along a great deal better than I did when I started into Mexico and I can understand about everything that is told to me."[6]

Bertha also joined her husband for a time, taking a pack trip into Chihuahua with him. There she met with C. B. Ruggles, an American prospector who had spent a decade searching for a lost mine. Dobie had gotten to know Ruggles several years earlier, and Bertha wanted to help write the man's memoir, similar to what her husband had done with John Young in *A Vaquero of the Brush Country.*

From Chihuahua, Bertha made her way to Mexico City, leaving her husband to continue on his own wanderings. In the capital, she settled down and completed work on the Ruggles manuscript. She also wrote a

Dobie hunting in Mexico, 1929. Southwestern Writers Collection/
The Wittliff Collections, Texas State University–San Marcos.

children's book on Mexico. She traveled to different parts of the country and put her observations into a long feature article, "Lifting the Curtain on Mexico," which was published by the *New York Herald-Tribune* in 1934.

Back in the States, Bertha went to New York to peddle her manuscripts, but publishers proved uninterested. Dobie wrote to advise her that, since she was having difficulty with the Mexican material, she should concentrate instead on trying to get her gardening writing published. Bertha had earlier secured a commitment from the Southwest Press to publish a book on that subject, but the project never came to fruition due to the Press's financial difficulties.

Bertha was acquiring a minor reputation for her writing on gardens. In addition to her yearlong series in the Austin and Dallas papers, she published articles in *Southern Home and Garden* and *Holland's*. In 1935 she was elected president of the Texas Federation of Garden Clubs, and in Austin she took courses in botany and collected specimens for UT's herbarium. Over the next few years she continued to publish occasional stories in Texas newspapers, and for a time it seemed that she would put together an entire book on gardening. She found a New York publisher, MacMillan, which expressed an interest. Yet as the years passed, no manuscript was ever completed. Though Bertha would remain her husband's chief editor for the rest of her life, she gradually drifted away from pursuing her own career in writing.

★ ★

Dobie found several folktales during his year in Mexico, including a story, "Juan Oso," about a half man half bear. He also came across a version of *la llorona* (the weeping woman), a tale that has since become well known in the United States. But he "was not finding the wealth of surefire 'stories' that he knew existed."[7]

Dobie had run into roadblocks before in trying to collect Mexican folklore. Back in the 1920s, after he had joined the Texas Rangers in their deadly raid against Mexicano bootleggers on his Uncle Jim's ranch, Dobie wrote, "I am told that a very long song was composed on the subject, in which certain gringos, including myself, are not very well spoken of." He asked around about the song, but to his disappointment, "I have been unable to hear the song or to secure a copy of it." As scholar James McNutt later pointed out, Dobie could hardly expect Mexicanos who had been "afraid of sticking their heads out of the houses" when the event happened to now "turn around and sing a song criticizing him to his face!"[8]

Bertha McKee Dobie (center) in Mexico, 1932. At left is a mozo identified as "Inocencio," at right is the landowner Don Mariano Saucedo. Southwestern Writers Collection/The Wittliff Collections, Texas State University–San Marcos.

South Texas was full of corridos and folktales that resisted Anglo hegemony, yet Dobie never encountered such politically charged material in his own collecting. When he learned of a corrido about the 1915 Mexicano raid on the King Ranch, the version he came across, improbably, praised the ranch's *defenders*, including the hated Texas Rangers. Dobie seems to have been wholly unaware that a much more popular corrido, "Los Sediciosos," contained lyrics celebrating the day that *"a esos rinches desgraciados, muchas balas les llovía* (a great many bullets rained down on those cursed Texas Rangers)."[9] Certainly, Dobie's unfamiliarity with Spanish and his position as a member of the Anglo ruling class made it difficult for him to discern what people were really thinking behind the mask of obsequiousness.

Despite social and political divides between Dobie and potential informants, he did often connect well with other people at a gut level. "When I like a man, my nature goes out to him and warms him," he observed.

When Bertha joined him on a journey into Chihuahua, she recalled how "we came upon a Tarahumara Indian running and kicking a wooden ball. The Indian spoke no English or Spanish and of course Frank spoke no Tarahumara. Yet they were soon communicating with each other in the friendliest way. Frank traded for that wooden ball. We had it up in the study for a long time . . . ."[10]

Although he made himself comfortable among the most affluent members of Mexican society, Dobie more often empathized with those at the bottom of the social ladder. He noted that, "it has been a constant observation of mine that goat-herders, commonly called ignorant, make much better company than scholarly Doctors of Philosophy."[11]

As much as Dobie enjoyed his adventures in Mexico, he had few stories to show for it. Nearing the end of his final stay, he wrote to Bertha, "I think I'll have to modify the book from a pure book of tales to something of a chronicle of observations."[12]

Yet he looked forward to this new challenge because he needed to prove something. In the past, he had presented himself simply as a compiler of folk legends, although he expected readers to recognize his gifted work in reshaping the tales into compelling literature. He received much praise for his efforts, but there remained an undercurrent of doubt—of which Dobie was acutely aware—that he was not a real writer, but rather a peddler of "retold lore."

Dobie had been writing steadily for nearly twenty years, and he had a lot more in him than simply folktales. His new book about Mexico, *Tongues of the Monte*, would be his chance to show everyone that he could write lyrical, soaring prose that ranked with the best American writers.

*Tongues of the Monte* was published in the fall of 1935 and "appeared at the crest of a wave of intellectual interest for Mexico in the United States."[13] The book is a semifictionalized account of Dobie's travels in Mexico. He created a persona for himself named "Don Federico." He collated the various mozos he employed into a single character, assigning a name with heavy-handed symbolism: "Inocencio." Dobie was mighty pleased with how the book turned out, and he told friends that he was thinking of writing a full-scale novel for his next work.

The book unfolds as a series of strung-together episodes as Don Federico and the faithful Inocencio travel throughout the country, encountering people who share folktales with them. As Don Federico observes, "It is my nature to draw out of men anything strange or novel they have within

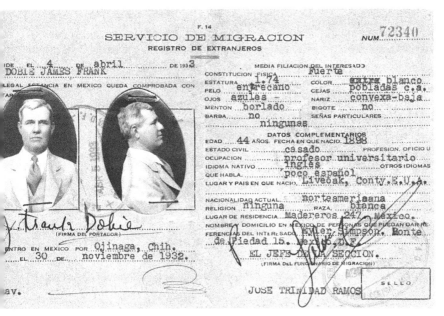

Dobie's immigration visa to Mexico, issued in 1932. Southwestern Writers Collection/The Wittliff Collections, Texas State University–San Marcos.

themselves, whether the matter be fact or not. In truth, I have no reverence for mere facts."[14]

Dobie reveals more of himself than in his earlier work, and in a passage that surely caused great concern to his mother Don Federico confesses to a "lack of [religious] faith." Dobie's own immigration visa to Mexico was also clear on this point. For the entry marked "religion" he answered "ninguna (none)."[15]

Many of the episodes related in *Tongues of the Monte* are compelling, and Dobie succeeds in capturing elements of what makes Mexico so romantic to gringo adventurers. Parts of the book, like all of Dobie's work, are brilliant. Yet his narrative runs into problems. He introduces melodramatic plot devices in order to string together the disconnected folktales. Most absurdly, he invents a florid love triangle, complete with a murderous villain named White Moustache who attempts to kill Don Federico, but is felled just in time by Inocencio's expertly thrown knife.

Worse for Dobie, he wrote with a lyrical romanticism that was completely out of step with contemporary American literature, and, indeed, with the entire twentieth century. In contrast to the increasingly direct language employed by American writers, Dobie's book possesses a nearly Victorian reticence. In one scene, set around a campfire, the men begin discussing women. The narrator then informs the reader that, "the talk took a direction I do not wish to record." This willful vagueness "is as precise as a nineteenth century novelist's," the *New York Times* noted in its review.[16]

Closer to home, the *Dallas Morning News* was more supportive, judging *Tongues of the Monte* to be the best literature ever produced by a Texan and "a landmark in the history of Southwestern literature." Of course, that review had the benefit of being written by Dobie's friend and fellow traveler, Henry Nash Smith.[17]

*Tongues of the Monte* "failed to arouse much interest in either the critics or the public," and its failure broke Dobie's heart.[18] Not only was he rejected at the national level, he learned that his core readers, Texans, didn't really care about Mexican folklore. Nor did his Texas readers want a sensitive, literary Dobie. They wanted the whooping and hollering tale-telling Dobie.

# The Flavor of Texas
## 1936

1936 MARKED THE one hundredth anniversary of Texas's independence from Mexico, and the state had long been eager to celebrate. It was back in 1900 that Governor Jim Hogg first proposed the idea of a grand centennial celebration, thus giving organizers a thirty-six-year head start on the project.[1]

All 254 Texas counties signed up to participate in parades and historic pageants. The state's normally tight-fisted budget makers threw open the coffers, and the federal government also chipped in, pledging millions of dollars for public works projects. Money poured out for parks, history museums, public sculptures, murals, and the restoration of old forts. To this day, many of Texas's most notable cultural inheritances, such as the state parks system and the San Antonio River Walk, owe their existence to the government funding of this era.

Dallas won the bid to host the centennial exposition, and some fifty new buildings went up on 185 acres, each one representing a different aspect of Texas's proud history. President Roosevelt made it known that he planned to attend the exposition. Millions of tourists were expected to descend on the state, and cities competed frantically to draw them in. Organizers envisioned something akin to a world's fair—only the entire world would be Texas.

Texas had changed much since the beginning of the century. It was no longer simply a poor, cotton-growing former slave state. The oil boom had helped ease the worst ravages of the Depression and created a new class of millionaires. Industrial production was rising as people flocked to rapidly growing cities. Texas's political and economic leaders wanted to draw new investment and corporate relocations from Northern states, and they recognized that it would be to Texas's advantage to reshape its image from a failed "Southern" state into a vigorous "Southwestern" one. Such a conceit played right into Dobie's hands.

As the centennial year dawned, Dobie's failure on *Tongues of the Monte* became evident. He was bitter and he blamed his publisher's marketing, particularly the title, which had not been *his* first choice. He also blamed reviewers and the public for not sufficiently appreciating his artistry. There was some merit in his thinking. Even later critics of Dobie, such as Larry McMurtry, concluded that *Tongues of the Monte* was his best work; certainly it was his most adventurous. He remained very devoted to the book and made efforts to get it back in print. When Southern Methodist University Press agreed to republish it in 1942, Dobie gave it a new, more explicit title: *The Mexico I Like.*

Dobie's setback, after the long, steady rise in his fortunes, infected his mindset as he approached the Texas centennial. Shaken from his dream of national success, he scrambled to get his career back on track by retreating into the world he knew best, embracing Texas pride with newfound zeal. He was a vigorous forty-eight-year-old accustomed to a large stage, and he made it clear to all that *he* was the reigning expert on Texas matters. Anyone who didn't go along with him could expect to be verbally tarred and feathered.

He was appointed to a select three-person commission, the Advisory Board of Texas Historians, which made recommendations on how to spend the state's money for history projects. Dobie, as his colleagues at UT already knew, was not cut out for committee work. He quickly began to clash with the others. As he wrote to a friend, "I am in the minority on this Board . . . when you have stubbornness and ignorance and bad taste as well as politicians to contend with, you had as well resign."[2]

The other commission members favored using money to build statues of politicians, whereas Dobie "wanted to honor men who had contributed to the various currents of culture and civilization of the state—cowboys, Texas Rangers, poets and writers."[3]

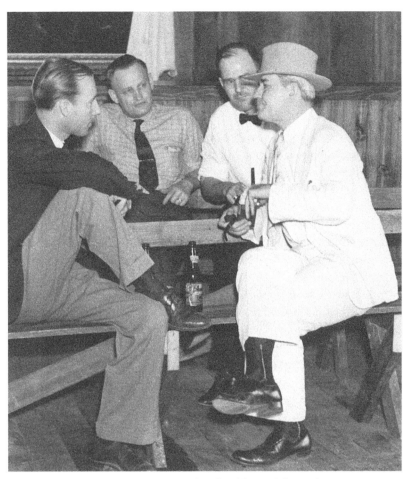

Dobie holds forth at the Texas Centennial, with publicists (left to right) Gene Cooper, Roger Busfield, and Bob Coulter, 1936. Southwestern Writers Collection / The Wittliff Collections, Texas State University–San Marcos.

When the committee proposed erecting a statue in Jones County of Anson Jones, the last president of the Republic of Texas before the office was abolished, Dobie responded, "I know positively that the people away out on the Clear Fork of the Brazos care nothing for a $14,000 statue of Anson Jones." He added, "Not many people anywhere, as a matter of fact, care for Anson Jones."[4] Dobie argued instead—unsuccessfully—for a memorial in honor of Larry Chittenden, the cowboy poet of Jones County.

Before long, Dobie's complaints about wasteful spending found their way into the newspapers. "One may live in the age of the New Deal and still realize that $1,000 is a lot of money," he declared. He threatened to resign from the board, but contented himself instead with issuing a sharply worded "minority report." Reporters soon got hold of Dobie's text, in which he fulminated about people "merely joining in the National Democratic movement to grab from the public barrel while it is open—a move that is making America a nation of sap-suckers instead of upstanding individuals like Sam Houston, Jim Bowie, and other real Texans whom we are supposed to be honoring."[5]

As it turned out, Dobie's battles with the Board of Texas Historians were just a warm-up for the main event to come. The most spectacular of all historic monuments was to be a symbolic tomb, or cenotaph, to be constructed adjacent to the Alamo in homage to fallen Texas heroes. The commission was worth one hundred thousand dollars. It was the centennial's plum prize.

Among those interested in obtaining the job was Pompeo Coppini, an Italian-born artist who had first immigrated to New York City before coming to Texas in 1900. In Texas, Coppini quickly usurped Elisabet Ney as the state's most prominent sculptor and he completed a number of major assignments, including the Littlefield Fountain on the campus of UT. Coppini built a magnificent home in San Antonio and became immersed in local society. By the 1920s, however, he had returned to New York and his stature as an artist went into gradual decline. Still, he retained a number of influential friends in Texas.

When he learned of the Alamo Cenotaph, Coppini began lobbying members of centennial commissions, writing letters emphasizing his Texas roots. Among those he contacted was Dobie, even though Dobie's committee was only responsible for approving funds, and had no say in appointing specific artists. Dobie was no fan of Coppini's work, though he kept his opinion private for the moment.

A centennial sculpture advisory board, consisting of experts in the field, was charged with selecting artists. That committee created a list of twenty-one leading American sculptors to be considered for major projects. A secondary list of twenty-four lesser sculptors was also put together—these were the artists recommended for the less expensive projects, such as the Anson Jones statue. Listed among this secondary group was Pompeo Coppini.

The board's list became controversial, however, when Texas sculptors complained they had been shut out of the major commissions. This appeal drew the attention of politicians and, after some backroom dealings, it was announced that Coppini had won the commission to do the Alamo Cenotaph.

This was too much for Dobie. He went public, criticizing the politicians and describing Coppini as an artist who had "littered up Texas with his monstrosities in the name of sculpture." Dobie blasted Coppini's Littlefield Fountain on the campus of UT, describing it as "a conglomerate of a woman standing up with arms and legs that look like the stalks of a Spanish dagger; of horses with wings on their feet, aimlessly ridden by sad figures of the male sex; and of various other inane paraphernalia. What it symbolizes probably neither God nor Coppini knows." Regarding Coppini's plan for the Alamo Cenotaph, Dobie said, "I had rather have nothing at all than have the monument executed by him."[6]

Coppini took aim at Dobie in return, noting that the author "was entitled to his own opinion in regard to something of which he was absolutely as ignorant as a hillbilly."[7] The Texas centennial, which had been so carefully planned, suddenly erupted with a sideshow.

Coppini's lawyers sent Dobie a letter informing him that his language was "plainly libelous" and that he could expect a $50,000 lawsuit. Dobie wrote back to say that he welcomed the suit, as it "would give me an opportunity to do something towards educating the people of Texas in sculptural taste." Dobie, despite his fame, was not wealthy, and he added, "As a courtesy to you, I suggest that before filing suit for $50,000 you investigate my financial rating."[8]

Although Dobie didn't know it at the time, Coppini did not want his lawyers to threaten Dobie. He considered Dobie a "coyote" and explained in a letter to his law firm that "a suit where my name would be involved would give him a great publicity, which I am not willing to be any part of."[9]

Dobie went on to wage a very public campaign against Coppini. He appeared on the radio, wrote articles, and was frequently quoted in newspapers denigrating the Italian sculptor's work. On one radio program, he told listeners that Coppini could no better capture the heroism of the Alamo heroes than "I, J. Frank Dobie, can write an Italian sonnet." Dobie also said, "A Coppini monument in front of the Alamo would be another massacre—a massacre of good sense and nobility."[10]

Dobie may have won the battle of words, but Coppini eventually won the war. Despite the considerable public opposition Dobie rallied, Coppini secured the commission and completed the cenotaph, which stands on the Alamo plaza today. When the monument was dedicated, Dobie took one last shot, comparing it to a grain elevator and declaring that its only good quality was that "no one can see it from the [front] door going into the Alamo."[11]

★ ★

Another outgrowth of the centennial was the creation of a Texas Institute of Letters "to promote interest in Texas literature and recognize literary and cultural achievement." Naturally, Dobie needed to be included in order to validate the fledging organization. This was easier said than done. After receiving his formal invitation to become a charter member, Dobie responded to the organizer, "I doubt seriously if anything that could be done by any commission would do anything towards producing first rate literature in Texas or elsewhere." He refused to commit himself to joining, but he did add that if such a commission were formed, he would vote against appointing a certain professor from Southern Methodist University who Dobie believed was smug and hypocritical. "In the first place," Dobie wrote, the man "doesn't know anything about Texas literature, and in the second place his mind is so small that anything he fostered would be valueless."[12]

But by September 1936, Dobie had made up his mind: "I have decided to join the organization. I do not like the closed corporation nature of it, however, and I see a few names on the membership roll that seem to me not to belong." However, Dobie refused to nominate anyone else for membership, writing that, "The reason I am joining the organization is not because of any honor I should feel in belonging to it . . . but because I think it has a chance to do some good for the culture of Texas."[13]

Dobie also didn't expect to attend the first meeting, which was scheduled for November in Dallas. But in the meantime, support for the Texas Institute of Letters was gaining momentum. Its first president was Patrick D. Moreland, a published author, but more importantly, the personal secretary to Governor Jimmy Allred. This move was politically astute, and Dobie was sensible enough to get out in front of the parade.

On the occasion of the Institute's inaugural meeting, Governor Allred declared "Texas Literature Week" and issued a proclamation urging Texas citizens "to read the saga of romantic Texas, from the time the Anglo Saxons first crossed the Sabine River, until this our Centennial year."[14]

Dobie on the UT campus in his trademark white suit, ca. 1930s. Southwestern Writers Collection/ The Wittliff Collections, Texas State University–San Marcos.

Dobie not only attended that first meeting, he also gave the main speech. He argued that Texas writers should focus on writing about Texas, and he intoned, "great literature transcends its native land, but there is none that I know of that ignores its own soil."[15]

Dobie's remarks at the meeting were well covered in the press, and he was getting his name into the newspapers for much more than the Texas Institute of Letters and his Coppini feud. Dobie enjoyed casting himself as the conscience of Texas, and in this role he waged several high-profile campaigns. At UT he issued a call for enhancing the university's "Texas Collection," which he complained was being treated as "a kind of subsidiary of the Latin-American collection." He also drew notice to the university's landscaping when it hired a firm from Kansas City that had no familiarity with native vegetation. Dobie sneered about the "graveyard growth" that professional landscapers would try to inflict "unless the owner [of the property] stands guard over it with a shotgun." When his beloved mesquite trees broke through the manufactured veneer and reestablished themselves on campus, Dobie let out a loud whoop for all to hear.[16]

Dobie's biggest target was UT's new skyscraper, which was under construction in 1936 and rose twenty-seven stories high, dominating Austin's skyline. Administrators saw the UT Tower as a tangible sign of the university's increasingly high status. Dobie, however, was disgusted. "For a university that owns 2 million acres of land and has a half section in its own campus, it's ridiculous" to build a skyscraper like they have in New York, he argued. He described the architectural style as "Late Bastardian" and suggested "they ought to lay the tower on its side and put a long [porch] around it." When the building was completed, he refused to move into it, telling reporters "all the offices look like steam lockers in a laundry." He kept his basement office in Old B-Hall.[17]

Dobie's driving habits also made the news. He remained more comfortable on horseback than behind the wheel of an automobile, but when he did drive he was seen as one of "the biggest menaces on Austin's streets." Dobie's friend J. Evetts Haley cracked everyone up by observing, "Frank doesn't drive a car—he just loose herds it!" Once, while driving in Austin, Dobie made an illegal U-turn on Congress Avenue. Bertha told him, "Frank, you can't do that." He shot back, "Rules are for those who need them."[18]

In the spring of Texas's centennial, Dobie came to the attention of the Austin police department; twice for parking violations on Guadalupe Street

next to campus, and once when he ran a stop sign, even though, as he protested, "there was no [other] car in sight."[19]

Dobie "ignored the conventional summons to appear" because "any
man of sense could see that the rule in those instances was stupid." But the
stop sign infraction made things more complicated. He wrote to the judge
that he would pay a fine for the moving violation, but he contended that
he shouldn't have been ticketed for the parking, since there were few cars
around at the time. As in the case of the UT Tower, Dobie believed that
Texas had plenty of wide-open spaces, and that fines for parking threatened
the bountiful freedom that was a Texan's natural birthright. He told the
judge, "If I am fined for parking . . . I will not pay the fine."[20]

When the judge read the letter, he exclaimed to some nearby reporters, "The hell he won't!"[21] The alternative was jail time. Dobie's letter was
leaked to the press and the media had a field day reporting on the impend-
ing showdown between the "maverick professor" and the legal system.
Dobie's move echoed Henry David Thoreau's civil disobedience, in which
Thoreau went to jail rather than pay taxes to support a war he didn't believe in. In Dobie's case, however, the principle had been taken to absurd
lengths. Even he became embarrassed by the publicity, but it was too late
to back down.

Dobie arrived at the court trailed by cheering fans, many of them students from campus. Once inside, he complained to reporters, "I don't see
anyone else up for overparking with his name all over the newspapers."
One of the reporters called out, "That's the penalty you pay for having a
well-known name."[22]

The next day, readers of the *Austin Statesman* opened their papers to find
a banner headline: "Dobie Works Out Traffic Fine: Jail Is Preferred Over
$2 Payment." Underneath the headline was a photo of the famous author,
sitting in the police station with his typewriter.

As it turned out, Dobie didn't have to spend any time in jail. The police
chief allowed him to do some clerical work around the office and give a
talk on Texas history. Dobie also composed a missive about his case, which
he hand-delivered to the chief. When reporters asked about Dobie's latest
letter, the chief refused to make it public. He did tell reporters, however,
that Dobie started off "by quoting Abraham Lincoln."[23]

Dobie's steady buzz of publicity created an inevitable backlash. Several
of his university colleagues "thought he was overplaying the part of the
'cowboy professor.'" Questions were also raised about a man who routine-

ly condemned the mass media—"I damn sure would rather hear a coyote bark than anything I've heard on another man's radio," he once said—but then "could not resist their attractions." As early as 1932, he began appearing on a weekly radio program, "Longhorn Luke and His Cowboys." Many more appearances followed in the years ahead, and his voice became as familiar to radio listeners as his face was to newspaper readers. Despite Dobie's professed devotion to "authenticity," one scholar has noted, his "sense of showmanship led him to perform the role of 'cowboy professor' with a gusto that belied his misgivings about sensationalized portrayals of Southwestern 'folk.'"[24]

★ ★

The pinnacle of the centennial year for Dobie came with the publication of his book, *The Flavor of Texas*, a hearty collection of Texas history tales. This was not a volume for the national market—it was aimed squarely at Dobie's home audience, and it helped reassert his primacy among Texas boosters.

Dobie vigorously promoted the state's Southwestern image, writing that ranching, not cotton farming, "has given Texas more fame to the outside world than any other single element." He described how "many, many Texans died with their boots on," and he praised their adventures as "truly unique in American life."[25]

*The Flavor of Texas* is filled with tales of heroic Anglo martyrdom at the hands of Mexicanos and Indians, and Dobie, caught up in the centennial spirit, asserted that such propaganda deserved inclusion in the American literary canon. He compared a memoir written by the filibustering adventurer Peter Ellis Bean to great European literature, and he predicted that a book about a famed Texas Ranger, *The Adventures of Big Foot Wallace*, would one day "be treasured as one of the classics of the American soil."[26]

Dobie lionized his nineteenth century heroes, claiming that they "did not lie, cheat, steal, oppress the weak, discuss respectable women, or backbite." Dobie was not nearly as generous, however, in his assessment of contemporary Texas. "If I had to divide the population into classes today," he judged, "I should characterize a goodly number as Texians, a very large number as Texans, and finally all too many as just people who live in Texas. The Texians are the old rock itself; the Texans are out of the old rock; the others are wearing the rock away."[27]

Dobie's Texas jingoism also carried an explicit political message. Texans overwhelmingly supported President Roosevelt, but Dobie remained an opponent of the New Deal, which he equated with the evils of modernism. In *The Flavor of Texas*, he contrasted traditional Texas values with "urban centers, machinery, constantly accumulating regulations over all industries . . . and now all that the New Deal implies." Dobie invoked none other than Sam Houston in claiming that real Texans are "against 'swallering that.'"[28]

In his political views, Dobie had a ready ally in his old friend J. Evetts Haley, who chaired the Jeffersonian Democrats, a statewide organization dedicated to defeating Roosevelt in 1936. The Jeffersonian Democrats were proud archconservatives and an early incarnation of what would later become known as the John Birch Society. Haley was Roosevelt's most notorious opponent in Texas, giving barnstorming speeches and radio addresses in which he blamed Roosevelt for everything from Panhandle dust storms to hiring Catholics in the postal service in order "to wipe out Protestantism." Haley also accused the president of "playing ball with negro politicians [and] openly supporting radicals of variegated hues, from pink to red." If Texans voted for Roosevelt, Haley said, "they would be casting a vote for communism." The Jeffersonian Democrats were well funded by industrialists opposed to the New Deal's business regulations, and they published anti-Roosevelt tracts that appeared in nearly every rural Texan's mailbox.[29]

Haley also published a new book in 1936, a biography of cattleman Charles Goodnight that celebrated the robust individualism that was prized during the nineteenth century. According to Haley, "No labor union protested their lot" back in those days. He added, "No welfare worker tore his shirt to better cow-camp conditions; no woman's club proposed child labor laws. . . . Yet somehow they managed to live, and happily."[30]

Despite its polemics, Haley succeeded brilliantly in capturing the old rancher's character, and Dobie praised the book as "the greatest biography of a cowman ever written." In a private letter to Haley, Dobie told him that it "will be read as long as people who speak the English language look over the Plains of the Palo Duro." Haley's book is still considered a southwestern classic.[31]

Haley's political activities, however, raised concerns at UT because he engaged in work for the Jeffersonian Democrats while also traveling throughout the state on university business. As the election drew nearer, he asked for a leave of absence in order to campaign full-time. UT's president signaled his willingness to grant the request, but reminded Haley that his position was not permanent and was only renewed on an annual basis. If Haley was not in the job when the new fiscal year began, there was no guarantee that it would be funded.

Haley had already "been looking for an excuse to leave the University." He wrote to Dobie, "After standing it so long, I rebelled. . . . When I see a bunch of intellectual bastards doing everything they can to destroy the ideals that have made us a virile race . . . I know that I'll finally do violence to somebody if he has enough manhood to resent an insult."[32]

Haley announced to the press that he had been purged from UT by pro-Roosevelt forces, and he went on a speaking tour of the state to emphasize the point. Few of Haley's university colleagues supported him. One who did was Dobie, who wrote to Haley soon after his departure. "There isn't anybody else in Austin whose company gives me the pleasure and rightness that yours gives. I meet many people—and most of them are sawdust." Dobie went on to tell Haley, "I feel very bitter about the way the University has treated you . . . it was clear to me that they were hiding behind technicalities."[33]

Dobie also made his feelings about Haley known to the public. He lobbied strenuously for his friend's rehire in a newspaper column, adding, "I don't believe I could define satisfactorily a representative of Texas, but if I were called upon to pick out a representative Texan from the younger generation, I should pick Haley."[34]

★ ★

Unknown to Dobie, another representative Texan was also coming of age, and this young man would eventually issue the sharpest rebuke to Dobie during his lifetime. He also created the most scathing portrait of Dobie ever to appear in literature, setting the stage for later generations of Mexican American critics to engage Dobie after his death.

Américo Paredes was born in 1915, during the height of the sedicioso uprisings in South Texas. Unlike Dobie, who seemed barely affected by such matters, the events struck close to home for Paredes. His family had arrived in the 1700s, but had lost its lands on the north side of the Rio Grande following the U.S.-Mexican War in 1848. In the years afterward, Paredes's ancestors became known for their rebelliousness, often joining in revolutionary movements.

As a student growing up in Brownsville, Texas, Paredes recalled that he "used to attack the history lessons that the teacher gave us" because the

Américo Paredes,
ca. 1930s. Courtesy of
Alan Paredes and
Vincent Paredes.

accounts were so slanted in favor of the Anglos. Paredes considered himself "an angry young man," yet he also showed great promise as a writer.
While still in high school, he entered and won a statewide poetry contest
sponsored by Trinity University.[35]

In the early 1930s, Dobie came to Brownsville to give a talk at Paredes's
school. Paredes recalled later, "Dobie was constantly in the news at the
time. His books were being highly touted for the truth of their representa-
tions of Texas folklife." Paredes resented how Dobie was always described
as a man who "knew the Mexicans better than the Mexicans knew themselves." In fact, Paredes found much to condemn. "Everywhere everyone
claimed that he was the best authority on Mexico. . . . But he didn't even
know the Spanish language!"[36]

Paredes disliked Dobie's talk, which he found long-winded and condescending. He also took sharp note of Dobie's propensity to mischaracterize
Mexicanos. Under Dobie's guidance, the Texas Folklore Society had published a volume in 1935, *Puro Mexicano*, that supposedly contained authentic Mexican folklore. In fact, some of the accounts were offensive to Mexican Americans.

One contribution—which Dobie did not write, but as the editor, he allowed its inclusion—tells of a "Mexican who slipped into heaven and began stealing things. The Lord knew that the thief must be a Mexican, so he had a fiddler play 'La Cucaracha,' whereupon the thief threw his hat in the air and shouted 'Viva Mexico!' St. Peter kicked him out." As Francis Edward Abernethy noted in his later history of the Texas Folklore Society, the account "sounds more like a gringo's story about a Mexican than a true Mexican folk tale."[37]

After Paredes graduated from junior college in Brownsville, he began working as a newspaper reporter.[38] Paredes was also a musician of some renown, and he hosted his own radio show, which featured the famous bolero singer, Chelo Silva, who later became his wife. During this time Paredes won several more writing contests and he began work on a novel, *George Washington Gómez*, a loosely autobiographical account of his years growing up in Brownsville.

While writing the book, Paredes opened up the newspaper one day and saw a story in which J. Frank Dobie explained to readers how the word "wetback" had come into existence. Dobie said that after illegal aliens swam across the Rio Grande "they would lie down in the sun. And when they awoke, all their clothes were dry except their backs. So anytime you saw a Mexican with a wet back, you knew that he had just swum across the river."[39]

As Paredes later recounted, "Now, notice that Dobie's explanation involves two stereotypes. First, the Mexican is too dumb to take his clothes off before he crosses the river, too stupid to put them on some kind of raft and float them across, which is what they did, of course. And second, as soon as he comes out of the river, what does the Mexican do? He's so lazy he falls asleep in the sun! [laughter] So, that really got to me. Dumb and lazy!"[40]

Recalling his bitterness at Dobie's appearance at his Brownsville high school a few years earlier, Paredes said, "I decided to take advantage of the opportunity to satirize him. I gave the Dobie character [in the novel] the name of K. Hank Harvey and got my revenge by making him look ridiculous."[41]

Indeed, K. Hank Harvey, as Paredes describes him, is a pompous racist known as "the Historical Oracle of the State." Paredes writes, most "early Texas books were written in Spanish, and K. Hank didn't know the language. However, nobody mentioned this and it didn't detract from Harvey's glory."[42]

Paredes described Harvey as "quite a celebrity. He went all over the United States telling his Mexican anecdotes and historical vignettes. And a sizable school grew up around him, a following of newly made 'Texians' who mashed a little Spanish into their conversation for the same reason Mexicans mash chile piquin into their frijoles, for spice and aroma . . . ."[43]

In the novel, Harvey gives a dull, long-winded speech that is memorable only in one regard—it insults Mexican Americans while appealing to Texian pride: "When our forefathers rose on their hindlegs and demanded independence," Harvey rants, "they arose with a mighty shout and forever erased Mexican cruelty and tyranny from this fair land, when they defeated bloody Santa Anna and his murderous cohorts at the heroic battle of San Jacinto, they set an example which the younger, weaker generations would do well to follow."[44]

For a long time it seemed as though K. Hank Harvey would never make an appearance in Texas literature. Paredes finished the book in 1939, but few publishers at the time were interested in a novel about a firebrand Mexican American. Speaking in 1994, Paredes joked that, "the mail took two days to get from Brownsville to Austin, but whenever I sent my manuscript out it was always returned the next day."[45] He set the manuscript aside for decades.

Paredes would eventually make his presence felt, however, and in his own way he became as seminal a figure in Texas literary history as Dobie. He did so by essentially creating the field of Mexican American studies. After serving in World War II, Paredes would come to Austin to attend the University of Texas, and there he would meet up with J. Frank Dobie.

# The Austin Liberals
## 1936–1938

**B**Y 1936 AUSTIN was already enjoying a reputation as something of a Texas oasis. The pleasant environment and the presence of the state's flagship university helped attract a modest coterie of Texas-bred intellectuals. These were not the "sawdust" Dobie referred to in his letter to J. Evetts Haley—by that he meant the bulk of his academic colleagues. These men, rather, were extraordinary individuals in their own right, and as they grew closer to Dobie they inevitably began to influence his thinking.

One such friend was Ralph Yarborough, a young lawyer who had just been appointed District Judge by Governor Allred. Born in East Texas, Yarborough was a populist and one of his favorite sayings was "put the jam on the lower shelf where the people can reach it." He eventually became a prominent politician and the "patron saint of Texas liberals." He was extremely well read in history and literature—more so than many UT professors—and he was considered "a walking encyclopedia." Dobie had little regard for politicians of any stripe, but was impressed to come across one possessing intellectual curiosity, and he and Bertha began joining Yarborough and his wife Opal for occasional dinners.[1]

Mody Boatright, a colleague in the English department at UT, was another important contemporary for Dobie. Boatright was an accomplished

John Henry Faulk with Dobie, ca. 1940s. Southwestern Writers Collection/The Wittliff Collections, Texas State University–San Marcos.

folklorist and also a devout liberal. He grew up on a ranch in West Texas, and Dobie preferred his company to that of other faculty. The two men worked well together, and by 1937 Boatright was coeditor of the Texas Folklore Society publications with Dobie.

Together, Dobie and Boatright encountered a charming rogue of a student in the 1930s named John Henry Faulk, who was raised by freethinking Methodists. Faulk grew up despising racism and embracing liberalism. He had exceptional public speaking skills and he was already developing a reputation as a talented storyteller. He did his graduate work on African American folklore and he taught English at UT after earning his master's degree. He took Dobie to black churches in Austin and introduced him around, doing his best to broaden the older man's views on African Americans. Faulk eventually went to New York and starred on his own radio program, "The John Henry Faulk Show." In the 1950s, during the McCarthy era, he was blacklisted and lost his job. Faulk then became a celebrated fighter for free speech, winning his lawsuit against the blacklisters and publishing a book of his experiences, *Fear on Trial*. Today the main branch of the Austin Public Library is named for him.

Also in Austin was Walter Prescott Webb, who in 1935 published a book on the Texas Rangers, which became a far bigger success than Dobie's *Tongues of the Monte*. Hollywood was already making Webb's book into a movie. In addition to its commercial appeal, Webb's newest work also displayed a formidable intellectual gravitas, as his keen, analytical mind plucked unified themes from a morass of official reports and records.

Webb's racism in *The Texas Rangers* has deservedly come under fire in recent generations. However, Webb's treatment of Mexican Americans was actually far superior to that of most other Texas Anglo historians, even as late as the 1970s. Although Webb's prejudices were clear, he was the first popular historian to report Anglo atrocities—rather than simply considering the massacre of unarmed civilians to be great military victories.

Webb also took care to occasionally present the non-Anglo side of the story—something no other historian chose to do. In his description of Juan Cortina's 1859 border uprising, Webb was far more progressive than Dobie. He reported that landowning Mexicanos were "victimized" by Anglo law, and he described Cortina's proclamation as a "stirring appeal." In contrast to those—like Dobie—who vilified Cortina as a "bandit," Webb concluded that, for an insurrectionist, he had "acted with restraint" and probably destroyed much less property than the Anglos who battled him.[2] Reading Webb's book was undoubtedly a learning experience for Dobie.

Dobie and Webb never shared the warmest of emotional bonds, but Dobie did have tremendous respect for Webb's mind, and considered him "the most active and the most seeing-into-things thinker that the state of Texas has produced."[3]

Webb strongly supported the New Deal, particularly its efforts to improve farmers' lives. In the mid-1930s, he became dismayed when the conservative U.S. Supreme Court struck down several pieces of New Deal legislation, including the Agricultural Adjustment Act. As his friend Joe Frantz later wrote, Webb "went to pieces. The conservatives, it seemed to him, had struck again, and the farmers' opportunity to pull even economically had once more been derailed."[4]

Walter Prescott Webb, ca. 1940s. Southwestern Writers Collection/The Wittliff Collections, Texas State University–San Marcos.

Roy Bedichek, photograph by Bill Shrout, ca. 1940s. Southwestern Writers Collection/The Wittliff Collections, Texas State University–San Marcos.

Within a few weeks, Webb wrote a book as a response: *Divided We Stand: The Crisis of a Frontierless Democracy*. In it, he argued that the South and the West were little more than economic colonies—the source of raw materials that made Northern industrialists rich.

Webb believed that corporations were creating a new feudal system. They had no interest in democracy or the common good, yet they dominated the country's economic life and they controlled many of its elected representatives. The Supreme Court had even granted corporations the same legal status as individual citizens—giving them a protective shield they used to "rape" people, Webb wrote.[5]

Webb's economic analysis mirrored Dobie's own anger over how the Yankees controlled America's literary culture. Yet Webb pointed out something Dobie hadn't considered—that Roosevelt and the New Deal might be on the right side of history. Although Dobie was slow to recognize it, the rise of industrial capitalism in the twentieth century had changed the equation. Mass production did bring about a rise in living standards—at least until the Great Depression struck—but it also concentrated greater power in the hands of fewer people.

Corporate capitalists disguised their expanding powers by claiming the mantle of individualism, even as they dominated the lives of millions of ordinary people. Liberals such as Webb understood from the beginning of the New Deal that Roosevelt's reforms, however imperfect, were aimed at bringing the corporations under some measure of control to ensure the common good, to protect common folks.

One of Webb's insights in *Divided We Stand* carried the weight of prophecy for Dobie and his university. Webb wrote that corporations were turning universities into "technical and personnel bureaus for the corporate overlords. They are teaching people to do rather than to think, analyze, synthesize, and understand."[6]

Webb pointed out that corporate leaders were initiating investigations "to oust university professors who have the intelligence to understand them and the courage to teach young men and women the truths they have discovered. Such professors are usually charged with heresy or communism . . . ."[7]

At the time Webb wrote these words, such academic witch hunts were unheard of in Texas. But soon enough the move would engulf the University of Texas, creating its greatest crisis and ensnaring its "maverick professor."

★ ★

One gathering place for Austin's intellectuals was the Town and Gown Club, where formal presentations—often involving contemporary matters—were followed by discussion and debate. Dobie still had little interest in the modern world and he naturally resisted such functions, but the group's secretary during these years, Roy Bedichek, often cajoled him into attending.

Bedichek was, simply, one of the most interesting and unique people in Texas. A decade older than Dobie, he grew up on a farm and hated picking cotton so much that in 1896 he quit work in the middle of a row and announced his intention to go to the University of Texas. He became a friend of folklorist John Lomax and after graduation helped Lomax collect cowboy songs. But Bedichek wanted to see the rest of America. "I traveled all over this country like a hobo, tramping and working my way," he recalled. He "peeled potatoes on a river boat, gathered berries in New Jersey, assisted a fake divine in Boston, dug coal and explored rivers in West Virginia, cut off hogs' heads in a Chicago slaughterhouse, and homesteaded in Oklahoma."[8]

He also became a teacher, but quit that in 1908 to ride his bicycle across Texas to Deming, New Mexico, where he homesteaded once again. Later he joined the *San Antonio Express* and covered Governor Jim Ferguson's impeachment, drawing the governor's ire for being too aggressive in his reporting.

After getting married and having children, Bedichek settled down in Austin and took a job at the university in 1917. He was not a faculty member, but rather held a staff position as the athletic director for the Interscholastic League, which managed high school athletic competitions. Bedichek tried to "preserve some morality" during an era when it was not uncommon to find bearded men in their twenties joining hometown teams for important football games.[9]

Bedichek often traveled throughout the state for his job, and he preferred camping out rather than taking motel rooms. He endeared himself to the university's budget office, historian Joe Frantz later wrote, because "if it didn't rain, [Bedichek and his assistant Rodney Kidd] could stay on the road for eleven days and turn in a travel voucher for $9. They retreated indoors only when the ground was frozen and the rain was pouring, and they ate at cafes—never restaurants—only when they ran out of grub."[10]

Bedichek was considered an excellent amateur naturalist and he well knew of Dobie's interest in wildlife. During his travels, he collected animal stories and made personal observations that he shared with Dobie. Bedichek also kept an ear out for interesting folk stories to pass along. He sent only worthwhile material, and Dobie happily incorporated nearly every one of these anecdotes and observations into his own writing.

Bedichek was not a professional writer, but his letters to friends showcased a wonderful ability with language, and they also gave glimpses into a mind that was observant, witty, and philosophical. Bedi, as his friends called him, seemed to live out of his time, having little regard for contemporary mores. Well versed in classic literature, he was known to wake up before sunrise in order to read for an hour or so "from the works of Plato or Cicero" before going out to get the morning newspaper. "Only after reading one of the philosophers, he would proclaim, did he have the perspective to deal with the day's news."[11]

He was mostly a vegetarian, refused to use pesticides in his garden, and he ate meat only when cooked over an open fire. He also lectured friends "on the pitfalls of pit toilets and indoor plumbing." He preferred to go out-of-doors. "Nature, he maintained, had designed us to squat, and he functioned best for that particular exercise when he squatted as nature had decreed."[12]

Dobie loved colorful characters, and Bedichek was fascinating. Completely at home in Texas, he was also, unquestioningly, a citizen of the world. He approached everything with an open mind, and before long, he would help open J. Frank Dobie's mind, too.

# Apache Gold vs. Pale Horse
## 1937–1939

**F**OLLOWING THE disappointment of *Tongues of the Monte* and his redemption as a Texas patriot during the centennial year, Dobie's path for his next book couldn't be clearer. It was time to return to his roots, even though, as he confided in a 1937 letter to J. Evetts Haley, "I really don't want to write another book on lost mines; I said all I want to say on the subject, but the material keeps hanging over me and tying me up . . . ."[1]

One of Dobie's great treasure stories, which had not yet been put between hard covers, was the tale of the Lost Tayopa Mine. This was rumored to be the richest in all of Mexico, and was said to have produced a bonanza in the early 1600s. An Indian uprising in 1646 had driven the Spaniards out of the area, and subsequent Apache raids made exploration difficult. All records of the mine's location were lost, but secret maps had a way of turning up—usually in the hands of a dying man.

Back in 1927, Dobie had met with C. B. Ruggles, a Texan who had spent the previous six years looking for the mine. Ruggles and Dobie continued the search, making deep sojourns into the canyons of Chihuahua. Dobie had published stories about their adventures in magazines. Now, he decided, it was time to make this tale the foundation of a new book. He knew that this would basically be a sequel to *Coronado's Children*. In fact, among the titles he considered was *Coronado's Grandchildren*. He found a new, more supportive publisher, Little, Brown and Company, which agreed to bring *Coronado's Children* back into print as part of the deal.

Dobie returned to Mexico for months at a time, tracking down additional detail about the Tayopa Mine and also polishing up numerous other tales. Aware that his book on Mexico had failed, and that contemporary writers in New Mexico were winning attention for writing about Native Americans, Dobie made sure to cast his book in a new light. Instead of referring to Mexicans or Mexico, he presented the book as a series of stories involving "Indians."

Dobie selected an appropriate title, *Apache Gold and Yaqui Silver*, and the book came out in 1939 as Dobie turned fifty-one. Among the book's distinct pleasures were the striking drawings by his new friend Tom Lea, an El Paso artist Dobie had met on a return trip from Mexico. Lea had drawn a portrait of Dobie during that first meeting, and afterwards Dobie told him, "Well, I'm writing a book now, Tom, and I think you could do the illustrations."[2]

Lea was just beginning to make a name for himself as an artist and he found an enthusiastic supporter in Dobie, who introduced him to wealthy patrons and tirelessly promoted him for commissions. Lea's work on *Apache Gold and Yaqui Silver* brought him to the attention of editors at *Life* magazine, who hired him a couple of years later as a war correspondent-artist. Lea's striking World War II illustrations, including most famously "The Two Thousand Yard Stare," documenting a shell-shocked soldier, became part of the war's iconography. Lea eventually became one of Texas's best-known artists, and with Dobie's encouragement he also turned his hand to writing, becoming a prominent American novelist from Texas. Lea and Dobie became the best of friends over the next two decades, though a tragic rupture would eventually destroy their bond.

★ ★

In *Apache Gold and Yaqui Silver*, Dobie serves as an informed tour guide for this new batch of treasure tales. Along the way, readers become aware of all the work he went through to obtain the stories, and how much he knows about the social history that provides the context for their telling. He clearly delights in the adventures, and his sense of joy practically leaps off the page as he describes riding through Mexico: "Whoever follows this trail westward from Miñaca will travel two hundred and fifty miles without seeing a pane of window glass or going through a pasture gate."[3]

Dobie, as always, goes beyond the simple tales in order to provide a compelling portrait of the men who undertake such adventures, extolling their questing spirits, hardiness, and perseverance. In Dobie's previous books, such heroes were always the white men. Yet in *Apache Gold and Yaqui Silver*, he became far more inclusive, thanks in part to his friendship with African American folklorist J. Mason Brewer. In the years since their first meeting, Dobie had become a mentor to Brewer, assisting him with grants, introducing him to others, and writing letters of recommendation. His affection for the man clearly grew, as did his respect for Brewer's scholarship and writing. In 1937, thanks in part to Dobie's help, Brewer received a Rockefeller Foundation Grant, which allowed him to attend graduate school at the Indiana University—a major center for folklore scholarship. There Brewer studied under Stith Thompson, one of America's leading folklorists. Dobie warned Brewer that Thompson's "approach to folklore is purely mechanical and he is not particularly interested in making the folk live in their lore."[4] Brewer completed his master's degree at Indiana and he eventually became a major folklorist in his own right. But as his future writings would show, he remained far more influenced by Dobie than by his exposure to scientific folklorists like Thompson.

Prior to his friendship with Brewer, Dobie had written condescendingly of "niggers" and, like many Southerners, he found Reconstruction a convenient excuse for many of the region's problems. In one of his early articles on the Lost Tayopa Mine, Dobie had mentioned an African American man named Henry O. Flipper, but only briefly, as he turned most of his attention to the white treasure seekers. But as Dobie went back and conducted further research for the new book, he realized that Flipper was not only a key figure, he was an extraordinary person in his own right.

Henry O. Flipper was born into slavery and in 1877 he became the first African American to graduate from West Point. He served admirably as an Army lieutenant in Texas before a superior officer had him court-martialed on a trumped-up charge, which resulted in a controversial discharge that was only overturned decades later.

After leaving the Army, Flipper worked as a mining engineer for several companies in Mexico, and Dobie came to realize that the man knew more about the lost mine than anyone. Further, Flipper's interest in the treasure appeared to mirror Dobie's, as it was more scholarly than acquisitive. Dobie took great pains to be respectful to Flipper in the book, describing him as "a master of the Spanish language and a student of Spanish-American history and laws."[5] Flipper not only comes across as a person of intellectual gravitas, he also emerges as the sanest figure in a book full of half-crazed prospectors. Henry O. Flipper was still alive—eighty-three years old—when *Apache Gold and Yaqui Silver* came out. It must have gratified the old man to see a grandson of the Confederacy, J. Frank Dobie, helping to rehabilitate his reputation.

★ ★

While Dobie's views of African Americans had clearly progressed, his writing style signaled a retreat from the lyricism he experimented with in *Tongues of the Monte*. He became defensive about his writing, and he took pains to inform readers in his introduction to *Apache Gold and Yaqui Silver* that capturing orally told stories in print was not as easy as it looked. "I have an idea that I often know too much for what the average reader regards as good storytelling," Dobie wrote. "In retelling these stories . . . I have naturally omitted many things, made disconnected parts connect, supplied hinges . . . ." After making his case, he stepped back. "How much of an alchemist I am, others must judge."[6]

Most of Dobie's contemporaries judged that he was doing a very fine job, but history has not been as kind. Dobie could put together great sentences, great paragraphs, and he could tell great stories. His books, however, consisted of anecdotes that were loosely strung together without any regard for an overall storyline. As engaging as the individual tales can often be, they inevitably begin to lose their flavor during an extended reading. Thus, most of Dobie's books are best read in bits and pieces, in between chores.

Subsequent generations of critics have condemned Dobie's style, but his seemingly random prose was a deliberate choice, as he sought to capture the idiosyncratic flavor of oral folktales. He refused to allow Bertha or anyone else to corral his writing. He imagined that, in his telling, the stories would spread out before the readers, just as an open range might spread out before a rider on horseback, beckoning the traveler further on. Dobie could not conceive that some readers, like some riders, might find it monotonous to spend days in the saddle amidst little changing scenery.

At the time Dobie's books were published—especially his early works—oral storytelling was still very common, and so to many readers of the day Dobie's folksy, casually ordered writing seemed perfectly natural. To modern ears, however, the same prose comes across as "meandering, sentimental, topically organized, and anecdotal." Yet at the time his books first appeared, few readers paused to quibble over such matters as dramatic structure. Instead, they were largely grateful, as Dobie had nourished the "thousands of people hungry for literature about Texas soil."[7]

\* \*

*Apache Gold and Yaqui Silver* was not the only book released by a prominent Texan in 1939. That same year Katherine Anne Porter published a long-awaited collection of stories titled *Pale Horse, Pale Rider*. Porter's literary reputation had been in ascendancy throughout the decade, but no one considered her "a Texas writer" at the time. She rarely acknowledged her birthplace, and she spent a lot of time "running back and forth between Mexico City and Greenwich Village." With the help of a Guggenheim fellowship she also lived in Paris from 1933 to 1936. When the subject of her background came up, Porter often presented herself as a Southerner, rather than a Texan. As the critic Don Graham has noted, "she wrote about the southern side of the Texas experience," whereas Dobie's work was "almost entirely western in subject matter and mythology."[8]

While Dobie retold folktales, Porter was a different breed of artist. She produced exquisitely crafted short stories that were hailed by literary critics as models of stylistic achievement. The publication of her new book received glowing national attention, and many acknowledged Porter as a master of the American short story. Her national reputation was beginning to eclipse Dobie's and would continue to do so. She eventually won two Pulitzer Prizes, and in the years since her death she has been the subject of numerous biographies and critical studies.

When Porter's Texas background did come up, she practically sneered about her position within Texas letters, telling one interviewer, "I am the first and only serious writer that Texas has produced." She certainly didn't consider Dobie much of a writer, once dismissing him as "a mere chronicler."[9]

In 1939 the Texas Institute of Letters was three years old, and the organization's future was by no means settled. The first president, the well-connected Patrick D. Moreland, was no longer active, and the presidency had been taken over by the organization's founder, William Vann, a professor at Mary Hardin-Baylor College in Belton, Texas. Vann wrote to Porter and invited her to speak at the 1939 meeting. He also notified her that *Pale Horse, Pale Rider* had been nominated for the first-ever Texas Institute of Letters Award for "Best Book."

On September 29, 1939, Porter responded, acidly informing Vann that a writer of her stature not only deserved, but required a speaking fee for all appearances. Porter added that, even if a reasonable fee were forthcoming, she would not attend, as she had no plans to lecture in Texas anytime soon. Further, she seemed to rule out any future appearance at the Institute, telling Vann, "I have a rigid rule against speaking at club luncheons, literary gatherings or associations of any kind whatever."[10]

On November 18, 1939, members of the Texas Institute of Letters gathered in Dallas. There was some disappointment that Porter was not on the program. However, just as he had at the inaugural meeting in 1936, Dobie stepped up to become the Institute's main event. Coincidentally, his *Apache Gold and Yaqui Silver* was also in the running for the Best Book award.

Even before the meeting, some in the Institute feared that Dobie's inordinate influence would result in him winning the prize, despite Porter's obvious superiority as a literary artist. As William Vann recalled in his history of the organization, "The question was raised as to whether judges should be secured from outside the state so as to insure an impartial verdict."[11] But in the end, the Texas Institute of Letters decided to stick with Texas judges.

After Dobie finished his talk, he joined the audience to await the announcement of the award winner. To the surprise of none, yet the chagrin of a few, *Apache Gold and Yaqui Silver* was named the Best Texas Book of the Year. As President Vann explained it later, "While recognizing the fine quality of Miss Porter's writing, the judges felt that because of Dobie's residence in Texas and the indigenous nature of his material, the award should go to him."[12]

In the years since 1939, Dobie's win over Porter has become a landmark in Texas literary history. Porter scholar Sylvia Ann Grider has observed that "the continued critical acclaim of *Pale Horse, Pale Rider*, along with the relegation of Dobie's *Apache Gold and Yaqui Silver* to the status of general Texana or juvenilia, accentuates the injustice of the institute's rejection of Porter."[13]

As Porter biographer Joan Givner once noted, the award signified something beyond literary merit. It served as a validation of Dobie's literary stature within the state. She observed that Dobie would have "won out over Jane Austen, Jean Rhys, Eudora Welty, Marianne Moore, Virginia Woolf, and the entire Brontë clan lumped together. And he would have done so even if these writers had been born in Waco."[14]

*Texas Needs Brains*

# The Longhorns
## 1939–1941

O N SUNDAY, SEPTEMBER 3, 1939, the same day Britain and France declared war on Germany in the wake of its blitzkrieg against Poland, a new syndicated column appeared in Texas newspapers. "My Texas" by J. Frank Dobie debuted in the *Dallas Morning News* and the *Houston Post* and was quickly picked up by newspapers in Austin and San Antonio. The column would appear every week without missing a beat for the next twenty-five years, ending only with Dobie's death.

Dobie took a very personal approach to writing his column, considering his efforts to be a sort of mass letter directed to his many friends and loyal readers. He often shared stories from his ongoing research or reported on interesting anecdotes readers shared with him. The weekly dispatches often served as his first rough draft for stories that he later incorporated into magazine articles and books. Dobie freely shared his opinions, and readers always knew what was on his mind. As his friend Roy Bedichek wrote to him, "I have the advantage in that I get to read a good long letter from you every Sunday morning without having to bother to reply."[1]

Dobie also began appearing on a series of radio programs called "Straight Texas," which featured adaptations of his folktales and were broadcast over the Texas State Network to about two dozen cities in the state. Dobie was not always easy to control during live performances, as he rarely followed the approved script. On one occasion, he paused after delivering his first two lines, leaving dead air as he puffed for a moment on his pipe. Finally, he spoke. "After reading this script, I don't think it explains the story like it should." He proceeded to retell the story, paying no attention to prearranged cues. He sent the production staff into panic, one witness recalled, as "two characters are cut, a tenor loses his only chance to sing on the air, and the engineer in his sound-proof booth is laughing." Dobie finished the broadcast "very pleased with himself." On other occasions he was known to join in with the professional singers, or to create his own sound effects by yelling like a cowboy during stampede scenes.[2]

★ ★

In his early newspaper columns, Dobie's masculine view of Texas was on full display. He wrote about Davy Crockett, razorbacks, rattlesnakes, buffalo hunters, and Jim Bowie, whom he described as "proud, impetuous, daring, plunging, generous, ambitious, the leader of rough frontiersmen and the equal of drawing room gentlemen."[3] But one subject above all others captured Dobie's attention at this time—the Texas longhorn, the subject of the new book he was working on.

Christopher Columbus brought cattle to the New World on his second voyage in 1493, and the Spanish successfully transplanted ranching to the Americas. The cattle quickly adapted to the dry, thorny brush country of northern Mexico and southern Texas. They could survive long periods without water, they could subsist on prickly pear and mesquite beans, and thanks to their long horns they could hold their own against predators. When faced with a challenge, these tough, independent creatures reacted the same way Dobie often did: they snorted and charged.

In the 1800s longhorns were the standard cattle type in Texas. Dobie's father and his Uncle Jim both raised them. Jim Dobie, in fact, was the proud owner of "Champion," a nationally famous longhorn with a reputed nine-foot horn spread. Dobie was an impressionable eleven-year-old when Champion won the blue ribbon at the San Antonio International Fair in 1899.[4]

The rise of national markets in America, however, spelled doom for the longhorn. For one thing, they carried the dreaded Texas Fever, which didn't seem to bother them, but killed every other type of cattle they came into contact with. Northern states imposed quarantines against Texas stock, and Kansas outlawed them entirely in 1885, effectively ending trail drives to that state.

In contrast to the tender meat found on other cattle, longhorns had a reputation for being tough and stringy. As Dobie reported, one Texan who had "eaten a very heavy bait" of longhorn beef was later shot in the stomach. The man miraculously survived, and the examining doctor concluded, "If it had not been for the beef, the bullet would have killed the man, and if it had not been for the bullet, the beef would have killed him."[5]

By the turn of the twentieth century, ranchers were adapting to the new economic reality, and they understood that fat, docile cattle breeds offered more profit. There was no reason to stock longhorns, and as the open range closed off they began disappearing. By the early 1910s longhorns were very rare, existing only in small, scattered groups in remote areas of the Brush Country. By the 1920s they were scarcer than buffalo, and word got out that one had been offered to the San Antonio Zoo as a curiosity item.[6]

Dobie felt a sentimental attachment to the animal. Many others in Texas felt the same way. In fact, the University of Texas began referring to its athletic teams as the "Longhorns" before Dobie ever arrived to campus. Dobie saw in the animals' toughness, hardiness, and independence the very same qualities he prized in heroic, pioneering Texans. The longhorns were "old rock" Texas, and they were disappearing before the onslaught of mass-market modernism.

Dobie's efforts to save the longhorn began early in his career as a folklorist. In 1925 he wrote an article about their fate in the *San Antonio Express* and the following year he published an article on the subject in the cattle rancher's trade magazine, *Cattlemen*. In both pieces Dobie argued for preserving the breed because of its historic significance. He also made sure that the Texas Folklore Society passed a "Save the Longhorn" resolution at its 1926 meeting. By the 1930s, Dobie used his national reputation to widen his preservation efforts, publishing longhorn articles in the *New York Herald-Tribune* and the *Saturday Evening Post*. In his travels as a folklorist, Dobie met and befriended numerous ranchers, each of whom he encouraged to join his efforts. He also made his views known at the annual gatherings of the Old Trail Drivers' Association.

Many viewed Dobie as "the single most important person involved in the Longhorn preservation movement."[7] His own popularity and his enthusiasm for the cause helped turn the longhorns' fortunes around. In 1941 he enjoyed his biggest success, convincing Fort Worth oilman Sid Richardson to fund a "Texas herd" of longhorns, which Dobie arranged to be stocked at two state parks for conservation purposes. Dobie went out to personally select the herd and he maintained a watchful eye over its progress.

142     Dobie's efforts on behalf of the longhorns coincided with his new book project. He planned to take the scattered material he had collected and published on the cattle over the previous fifteen years and rework and expand it. He again enlisted Tom Lea, illustrator of *Apache Gold and Yaqui Silver*, to provide the artwork.

Yet a problem existed. Dobie's publisher was not convinced that a book on cattle would sell and thus expressed reluctance to publish it. Dobie grudgingly agreed about the commercial prospects, writing to Lea, "I doubt the general public will read the book." He could have gone to a regional press, but he was unwilling to surrender his New York publisher and the national status it conferred. He managed to salvage his relationship with Little, Brown and Company by agreeing to take a smaller royalty, eight percent, rather than the standard ten percent. If the book managed to sell more than five thousand copies, the rate would go up accordingly.[8]

While working on the book, he sequestered himself for long periods of time on a ranch owned by the wealthy Sid Richardson, who had funded Dobie's longhorn herds. Dobie also made numerous forays into the field, and he made sure to take along Tom Lea so that the artist could make first-hand observations while working on the illustrations. When he finished the book, Dobie was very pleased and wrote to Lea, "I don't know how it will sell, but I feel confident that it will be read by some as long as LONG-HORN has meaning."[9]

Dobie had every right to be proud of *The Longhorns*. It was his most skillfully written book yet—a vigorous blend of informed, yet highly readable scholarship, collected anecdotes, and personal observation. As a herd, the longhorns were so tough that "on the way to the Pacific they crossed deserts still feared by automobile drivers," Dobie wrote. As individuals, they remained highly distinctive, and Dobie wrote of one steer that "was driven all the way to the slaughterhouse before it broke loose, bailed out of a second-story window, swam a river, and headed back south to the Brasada."[10]

In contrast to all expectations, Dobie's book became a big success. It made several bestseller lists and received strong reviews, including a glowing full-page write-up in the *New York Times* and a story in *Time* that praised Dobie as "the nearest thing the Southwest has to a cultural voice."[11] Dobie's portrait of tough, enduring animals that love freedom and will fight for it struck a responsive chord among Americans as World War II continued to spread its dark shadows across the globe.

# True Patriotism and the Singing Governor
## 1940–1941

**D**OBIE AND HIS FRIEND Tom Lea had camped out in the Brush Country for weeks at a time while trailing longhorns, but it was difficult to avoid thoughts of Europe. After taking Poland, Hitler methodically dismantled Denmark, Norway, Belgium, Luxembourg, and the Netherlands. As the world watched to see what would happen next, Dobie wrote, "The fate of England and France, of the art of living, of all things beautiful and glad in civilization, hangs like a pall over us."[1]

He warned readers of his newspaper column that "Hitler's domination of the world" threatened America's freedom. Just as in World War I, Dobie argued against neutrality, pleading, "in the name of decency and of the civilization of which we are heirs, let us give the Allies at once, all the planes, tanks, guns, ammunition and other materials that they need and we can supply. . . . The Allies are fighting our war."[2]

Dobie's sentiments were not universally popular. Isolationism still retained a hold over millions of Americans who believed that two oceans shielded the country from the world's problems. Pearl Harbor would change things overnight, of course, and Americans overwhelmingly supported U.S. entry into World War II. Yet in Texas, isolationism and even outright hostility toward the federal government remained vigorous during the war years.

By the time liberal governor Jimmy Allred left office in 1938, most Texans still supported the New Deal, especially its provisions that protected farmers and the poor. Roosevelt remained very popular in the state, winning reelection with eighty-seven percent of the vote in 1936. Many of Texas's business leaders, however, had turned against the president. They resented government regulation of the oil industry and they believed that Roosevelt was too sympathetic to laborers. New Deal measures such as the forty-hour workweek, child labor laws, and health and safety codes were all condemned as socialism or communism. Texas conservatives also feared that Roosevelt was too liberal on the race question. His wife Eleanor had openly called for equal rights for African Americans, and Roosevelt himself had expressed support for an antilynching bill.

Texas had escaped the worst ravages of the Depression thanks to the discovery of vast quantities of oil. Yet the petrodollars also widened the gap between Texas's rich and poor, and the new class of oil millionaires threw its political support—and its funding—to opponents of the New Deal.

Into this vacuum stepped a man whose star outshone Dobie's own. W. Lee "Pappy" O'Daniel was a flour company executive who had been born in Ohio, lived in Kansas, and didn't move to Texas until 1925. He quickly grasped the potential of the airwaves and he used the radio to promote his business. He hired a band, The Light Crust Doughboys—that included future legends of Western Swing Bob Wills and Milton Brown—and he served as their announcer, becoming known to listeners as "Pass the Biscuits, Pappy." He cultivated a simple, homespun image that enraptured rural Texans. He also composed "a maudlin bit of homespun balladry," a song called "Beautiful Texas" that became a popular hit among hillbilly bands.[3] Dobie despised the tune.

By 1938 Pappy O'Daniel was Texas's biggest radio star, although many savvy Texans recognized him as a charlatan and musicians such as Bob Wills and Milton Brown had long deserted him. Thousands of listeners wrote in begging him to run for governor, and O'Daniel obligingly took to the campaign trail. He perfected his pose "as a hillbilly" while acting "under the professional direction of public-relations men."[4] Although he had never before evidenced Christian devoutness, he began appearing at political rallies carrying a Bible, and he claimed that his only platform was the Ten Commandments and the Golden Rule. Pappy won in a landslide.[5]

Once in the governor's mansion, O'Daniel's true agenda became clear. He "unveiled a tax plan, secretly written by manufacturing lobbyists, that

W. Lee "Pappy" O'Daniel, the radio personality turned politician. Texas State Library & Archives Commission.

amounted to a [regressive] sales tax."[6] He attacked organized labor and became a consistent opponent of Roosevelt's policies, although he continued to publicly praise the president, knowing of his enduring popularity.

Dobie's liberal friends in Austin had little use for O'Daniel—Roy Bedichek referred to him as a "lick-spittle of the rich"— but Dobie's friend J. Evetts Haley was very close to the new governor.[7] In fact, O'Daniel nominated Haley to a major state board. This came despite overwhelming opposition in the Democrat-controlled Texas Senate, which took a dim view of Haley's record of personal attacks on President Roosevelt. Sure enough, when Haley's name came up for confirmation he was rejected.

Haley's failure to win an appointment only hardened his opposition to Roosevelt's run for a third term. In a letter to Dobie, Haley predicted that Wendell Willkie, the Republican candidate, "will beat the hypocritical egotist in the White House" and he described the "Hitlerized" Democratic convention as "nauseating [even] to a turkey buzzard." After Roosevelt cruised to victory and carried Texas easily, Haley wrote to Dobie, "I doubt not that the final results for us will be disastrous, even to the extent of economic chaos and complete loss of freedom."[8]

Ever since his separation from the University of Texas, Haley publicly railed against "parlor pinks" on campus. He undoubtedly influenced Governor O'Daniel, who soon after taking office launched a campaign to purge UT of its "radical" elements.[9] The university had often been subject to political pressure—for years the state legislature had micromanaged its budget, including faculty salaries, and in 1916 Governor Jim Ferguson had fired several faculty members before getting himself impeached. But during the 1930s, Texas's massive oil revenues—a fair share of which went to the university—helped drive a renewed sense of mission to create a first-class educational institution in Texas.

The university made great strides during these years, raising faculty salaries to become competitive nationally, and it began attracting good students from other states. In 1939 UT hired a promising new president, Homer P. Rainey, who was a native Texan, an ordained minister, and a former pro baseball player. Dobie was among those who approved of the choice, writing to Tom Lea, "This new president of the University seems to be in favor [of] developing native culture . . . ."[10] Rainey was also a staunch defender of academic freedom—a concept that would soon come under attack.

Regents at UT were notoriously prickly, and early in O'Daniel's administration, Roy Bedichek came under fire from Regent Lutcher Stark. Bedichek had issued a controversial new directive setting the age limit for high school players at eighteen. This was designed to prevent the practice of "laying over," in which students deliberately fell short of graduating high school so that they could play another year of football. The rule change affected Stark personally, as his two sons lost the extra year of eligibility they were counting on.

At the next Board of Regents meeting Stark made a motion to eliminate the entire budget of the University Interscholastic League, the agency overseeing high school competition that Bedichek directed. When that failed, he moved to strike Bedichek's salary. This prompted President Rainey to rise and speak in defense of Bedichek, and the majority of regents voted to maintain his position. Some time later, Stark encountered Bedichek and told him, "I'm going to clean you out; I gave you your chance and President Rainey, too."[11]

Governor O'Daniel soon began reshaping the Board of Regents with new appointments. He refused to reappoint J. R. Parten, the chair of the board, to another term, despite the fact that Parten received much of the credit for turning the university's fortunes around. O'Daniel also removed George Morgan, who held a Ph.D. from Columbia University. In their place, he nominated two Republican businessmen well known for their anti-Roosevelt agendas. One was Dan Harrison, an oilman who had actively opposed Roosevelt's reelection. The other was Orville Bullington, who had run for Texas Governor as a Republican in 1932 and charged that Roosevelt's New Deal was being run by Communists. Bullington had also helped establish the Jeffersonian Democrats, the anti-Roosevelt organization headed by J. Evetts Haley. Considering that Texans had just overwhelmingly reelected Roosevelt, most political observers concluded that these two appointees would fail to clear the Senate. Yet during the confirmation hearings, both men appeared conciliatory—unlike J. Evetts Haley. Harrison and Bullington promised that education, not politics, was their only concern, and each was duly confirmed.

Dobie was among those who welcomed the two new regents, who he liked personally and sympathized with politically. Writing to Haley, Dobie said, "I can't abide O'Daniel. He's a sleazy pious fraud. . . . But when he put Dan Harrison and Orville Bullington on that board he wiped out many sins, and often I feel like forgiving all of them just for that act."[12]

Dobie's dislike of O'Daniel was personal, rather than political. It had emerged full-blown on April 21, 1941, the 105th anniversary of Sam Houston's victory over Santa Anna at San Jacinto. Dobie was invited to speak at the San Jacinto monument for the occasion and the well-attended event received statewide press coverage. It was the sort of occasion to which Dobie had become well accustomed in his role as "Mr. Texas."

Texas politics was in a state of limbo that day, as veteran U.S. Senator Morris Sheppard had recently died and people were wondering whom O'Daniel would appoint to serve out the remainder of the term. Political observers knew that O'Daniel coveted the seat, but under Texas law the governor could not appoint himself.

At the San Jacinto event, Dobie had just risen to give his talk when a buzz rippled through the crowd, interrupting his remarks. Governor O'Daniel had been sighted—a surprise appearance—and was making his way to the stage amid cheers and hollers. The governor bounded onto the platform and the crowd roared its approval. He brushed Dobie aside and took center stage to acknowledge the cheers. Once the crowd quieted, O'Daniel made an important announcement: he would appoint Sam Houston's surviving son, the eighty-seven-year-old Andrew Jackson Houston, to serve as the new U.S. Senator. During his brief appearance, O'Daniel erroneously referred to Sam Houston as a hero of the Alamo, but few—aside from Dobie—seemed to mind the mistake. After he finished talking, O'Daniel led the crowd in singing his patriotic tune, "Beautiful Texas."

Political pros understood the rationale for O'Daniel's appointment. Frail old Andrew Jackson Houston would not serve long, and thus the move was a way to keep the seat open until O'Daniel could run for it himself. Indeed, Houston did go to Washington, D.C., over his daughters' objections. There he attended one committee meeting, then died. O'Daniel won the subsequent special election—after some exceedingly suspicious late returns came in that put him slightly ahead of a New Deal congressman named Lyndon Johnson.

When O'Daniel joined the Senate, the major issue was the European war. Britain, alone, had so far managed to stave off a German invasion, and Dobie was among those enthralled by their resistance, writing to Tom Lea, "These days I feel like saluting the British people morning, night, and noon—the most admirable people in the world."[13]

President Roosevelt was doing everything he could to aid Britain while still maintaining America's official policy of neutrality. Yet his efforts were often thwarted by a group of isolationist senators who opposed him. In some cases these isolationists were simply worried about drawing the United States into the conflict. Others, however, were sympathetic to Nazi Germany, and they had many adherents throughout the country, including famed aviator Charles Lindbergh, who had accepted a medal from Germany in 1938 and refused to return it once the war began.

O'Daniel wasn't exactly a fascist, but he threw his lot in with Nazi sympathizers often enough, and in the Senate he joined the isolationist bloc, undermining Roosevelt. Once Dobie realized that O'Daniel was not interested in helping to save Britain, his hatred for O'Daniel transcended the personal and became political.

★ ★

As political divisions in Texas heated up during Roosevelt's presidency, Dobie couldn't help but notice a difference in the way his friends J. Evetts Haley and Roy Bedichek conducted themselves. Dobie remained very close to Haley, and he dedicated a chapter in *The Longhorns* to him. But Haley's correspondence often had a vitriolic, even melodramatic quality. He secured his strong opinions by heaping scorn on those he disagreed with.

This was in stark contrast to the warmly philosophical, intellectually nurturing notes Dobie received from Bedichek. In fact, just a few days after Dobie received Haley's missive denouncing Roosevelt as a "hypocritical egotist," a new letter from Bedichek arrived.

Bedichek was among those who had early recognized O'Daniel's flatulent appeals to Texas pride, and in his letter Bedichek expounded on his idea of true patriotism. He wrote to Dobie, "I mean *patriotism*, that is, love of country (and by *country* I mean country, rocks, soil, creeks, rivers, hills and valleys) not flag and a lot of gaseous intangibles. There is no patriotism without love of your physical environment just as there is no romantic love without a love of the physical body of some individual woman."[14]

Dobie loved that letter, and he referred to it time and time again. When he decided, some months after the San Jacinto incident, to use his newspaper column to go after O'Daniel, he enlisted Bedichek's letter as his reinforcement.

In a soon-to-be-notorious column titled "My Texas, Patriots and Patriotism," Dobie quoted his "wise, good friend" Bedichek, who wrote of true patriotism—and then contrasted that sharply with O'Daniel. "The person in Texas who has done the most mouthing about patriotism in recent times is now our junior senator, Mr. Lee O'Daniel," Dobie wrote. "He hires a band to sing Beautiful Texas, [but he] knows so little about its history that when he speaks off guard he calls Sam Houston the hero of the Alamo. He has prated for more than two years about his love for the aged, the poor, the mothers and the children of Texas, and then, underground, he demonstrates that while he was the poor's elector he was the rich man's governor."[15]

O'Daniel, Dobie wrote, "has never shown an iota of knowledge or care concerning the gravest crisis that liberty and civilization have faced since the Western Hemisphere was discovered." One-time hero Charles Lindbergh "manifestly admires" Hitler's Germany, Dobie wrote, "and now Patriot O'Daniel has joined the . . . Lindbergh Company." Dobie concluded with an "acidic parody" of O'Daniel's signature song: "Oh, beautiful Texas. Oh, buzzard puke and puppy vomit!"[16]

Bedichek wrote to Dobie afterward: "Last night I left the paper with your article in it on the dining-room table and retired to my room to read. Presently I heard my wife in peals of laughter. Inquiring the cause, I found that she had gotten to the climax of your panning of O'Daniel."[17]

Dobie, however, was just getting warmed up.

# The Liberal Hero
## 1941–1943

**L**ESS THAN SIX WEEKS before Pearl Harbor, J. Frank Dobie summoned the first kind words he could ever write about Franklin Roosevelt. In a letter to Tom Lea, Dobie mentioned Roosevelt's recent fireside chat over the radio, and told him that the president, "didn't exactly give us any news, but it was the only speech I have heard him make that I call great, all the honeying and avoiding and concealing gone. . . . Bully for Roosevelt."[1]

Shortly after the United States declared war on December 8, 1941, Dobie wrote to oilman Sid Richardson, "This war makes everything else seem trivial and unreal. I am looking for something to do that's worth doing. It will be morally impossible for me to stay on here teaching school. Uncle Sam won't let me in the army as I'm now 53 years old, but [I'm in good shape] and could do lots of work. I just don't know where to offer myself."[2]

Dobie's attitude contrasted sharply with that of Senator Pappy O'Daniel, who told reporters, "I ain't worried about the war. That's Roosevelt's job."[3] Pappy also drew national condemnation after he gave a radio address in which he appeared to portray Roosevelt's liberalism as a bigger menace than Hitler's fascism.

O'Daniel was gearing up to run for a full term in the Senate in 1942, and Dobie made it his personal mission to make sure he lost. Dobie wrote several columns condemning "the oily skinned senator." In one article he

confided to his readers: "I am a lot more scared of Fascists at home during
this war than I am of Communists."[4]

Dobie's attacks on O'Daniel generated plenty of mail, both positive and
negative, but no reaction pleased him more than the letter he got from
Roy Bedichek, who wrote, "You are really getting in a class by yourself.
. . . This heated political, competitive atmosphere is jarring loose things in
you that have been hanging fire. In this long article this morning you reach
heights . . . that put you along with the very top-notchers." Bedichek also
told Dobie that, while reading the article, "my mind pictured the warrior-
orator of some old Norse tribe standing on a rock with the clan gathered
about him to hear his councils of wisdom and his incitation to heroism."[5]

In addition to his columns, Dobie also made public talks calling for
O'Daniel's defeat. As he wrote to Tom Lea, "I have been working day and
night against O'Daniel, writing articles, making speeches, talking over the
radio. I have lost six weeks of time for what I intended to do, but I just had
to fight for decent leadership, seeing as how I could no longer get in uniform and fight the damned Germans."[6]

A few days later, O'Daniel narrowly won reelection. Dobie wrote,
"Well, Texas elected O'Daniel again. As my mother says, 'What can't
be cured must be endured.'"[7] Nevertheless, Dobie continued to snipe at
O'Daniel in the years ahead, and by 1946 O'Daniel had enough. He announced to the press that he was filing a seventy-five thousand dollar libel
suit against the *Waco Tribune-Herald* because it had printed Dobie's remarks
about him made during a speech. The suit went nowhere, and by that time
many others had come to agree with Dobie's views on O'Daniel. When
O'Daniel left office in 1948, his colleagues in the Senate openly shunned
him and his approval rating in Texas had sunk to just seven percent.

★ ★

Meanwhile, at the University of Texas, the conservative regents O'Daniel
had appointed were beginning to make their presence felt. Orville Bullington, one of the men Dobie had welcomed aboard, recommended budget
cuts for all state universities because they were wasting money on "un-
necessary and even harmful programs and activities." Bullington suggested
that if the "dirt and paint dobbers" wanted to study art, "they should go to
a girls school or to Paris or some other [foreign] seaport."[8]

By 1942, with regents appointed by the new governor—Coke Stevenson—conservatives now controlled the board's majority, and they wast-

ed no time flexing their muscle. In the first meeting after gaining power, the regents handed President Rainey a card containing the names of four tenured economics professors. Rainey was told to fire the men because they had "unsound economic views."[9] The academic witch-hunts Walter Prescott Webb had warned about back in 1937, in *Divided We Stand*, had finally arrived.

Rainey explained that professors could not be fired simply because the regents disagreed with their teachings. Regent Lutcher Stark told Rainey in response, "I am going to fight you like hell." Regent Bullington began complaining that President Rainey "does not believe . . . in our system of government," and he warned that if Rainey were left in office, he would try to hire more "radicals of his stripe."[10]

The regents began looking for ways to eliminate the tenure system. When Rainey protested that such action would prevent the university from attracting quality faculty members from across the country, Regent D. F. Strickland responded that he "was certain they could find good patriotic Texans to teach at the university who were from smaller Texas schools that had no tenure."[11]

At last, Dobie's long-held dream of a more Texas-centric institution seemed to be approaching reality. But the vision was mutating into a nightmare.

The attacks continued. One regent proposed loyalty tests for faculty. After some discussion, that idea failed to pass, not because regents didn't think that loyalty tests weren't a good idea, but because they felt that traitorous professors would probably lie on such tests anyway. However, regents did clamp down on travel to academic conferences, thus limiting professors' exposure to "Bolsheviki" ideas in other parts of the country.[12]

In June 1942, the regents fired four untenured economics instructors who had engaged in "subversive activities." The instructors' crime had been to make public statements in support of President Roosevelt's Fair Labor Standards Act, which mandated overtime pay for hours in excess of forty per week. As Dobie pointed out, such subversion consisted of "views on labor that Roosevelt and millions of other citizens of America hold."[13]

More than any other factor, these attacks on academic freedom caused Dobie to reassess his deeply held, almost instinctive political beliefs. He realized that the greatest threat to individual freedom was no longer the government—it was right-wing business interests. With this insight, fifty-three-year-old Dobie became a political liberal.

Dobie with UT President Homer Rainey. Southwestern Writers Collection/The Wittliff Collections, Texas State University–San Marcos.

He wrote to a friend, "Here in the University we have a fight for academic freedom on, against a board now made up almost entirely of millionaires and corporation lawyers, Roosevelt-haters and new-style fascists. I am expected to take the lead on the side of the liberals, and I am expecting to be called up on the carpet for taking part in politics."[14]

Along with Bedichek and others, Dobie presented a petition to the Board of Regents seeking to overturn the firings of the economics instructors. The petition was ignored. Instead the regents upped the ante.

They summoned several members of the English faculty to explain why suggested reading lists included *U.S.A.* by John Dos Passos. Regents condemned the book as "thinly disguised Communist propaganda [that] repeatedly showed vile contempt for the flag, the church, and the nation's most sacred institutions." They grilled each of the instructors, asking "about his place of birth (non-Texans were immediately suspect), family

154 and educational background, marital status, and whether or not he knew who had placed [the book] on the reading list."[15]

This was altogether too much for Dobie. He blasted the regents in a column that the *Dallas Morning News* considered so inflammatory it refused to print it. Readers in other parts of the state, however, learned from Dobie—and no other major news source—that regents were scheming "to suppress freedom of speech, to get rid of liberal minds, and to bring the University of Texas nearer to the status of fascist-controlled institutions of learning and farther away from the democratic ideal of free and inquiring minds."[16]

For Texas's outmanned liberals, having a figure like Dobie join their side was a cause for celebration. As Bedichek observed in a letter to Walter Prescott Webb, "Whenever by chance, or by the will of God, a little culture is grafted on to that good old Texanese ranch stock, you really have something."[17]

# A Contemporary of Himself
## 1943–1946

The high soul takes the high way,
And the low soul takes the low,
And every man must choose
The way his soul will go.

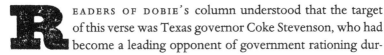EADERS OF DOBIE'S column understood that the target of this verse was Texas governor Coke Stevenson, who had become a leading opponent of government rationing during World War II. By 1943 the tide of the war had begun to turn in the Allies' favor. On the home front, citizens planted victory gardens, held scrap metal drives, and purchased bonds in support of the war. Rationing was a fact of life, but not everyone was happy about it. Governor Stevenson claimed that gasoline in Texas was as necessary as "the saddle, the rifle, the ax, and the Bible."[1] Senator Pappy O'Daniel, too, issued public complaints, criticizing the fact that Texas produced forty percent of the nation's oil yet had to conserve gasoline.

Dobie took on these two Texas statesmen in a column, writing that they "can be counted on to always take the short-sighted view and to prod people into being more grasping for themselves."[2]

Governor Stevenson, like O'Daniel, did not respond publicly to Dobie's attacks. But soon enough Dobie did encounter a public figure spoiling for a fight: newly elected Lieutenant Governor John Lee Smith, whom Dobie described as someone who goes "into a fever of righteous indignation every time he sees, hears or thinks of the word labor union." Shortly after taking office, Smith made headlines by sending a "censorious" telegram to

President Roosevelt, accusing him of hurting the war effort by being "over-zealous in behalf of organized labor."[3]

Texas was perhaps the most antiunion state in the country, and in 1942 it passed a new law that gave the state government veto power over any new union memberships. Dobie told *Time* magazine in response, "A man can come to Texas and without interference invite all the people he wants to join the Republican Party, the Liar's Club, the Association for the Anoint-ment of Herbert Hoover as Prophet, almost any kind of organization ex-cept one. If [this antilabor law] is an index of capitalism's future policy, the people had better begin digging cellars for the revolution."[4]

Dobie criticized Smith in his weekly column, and the lieutenant gover-nor responded with a public letter, telling Dobie that his "terribly mixed" ideas were "in keeping with the mental processes so typical of your long-haired university brothers." Smith argued that labor strikes during wartime were "treason" and he pointed out that strikers had caused the loss of some six hundred thousand working days since Pearl Harbor.[5]

As Dobie considered his response to John Lee Smith, he looked over a recent letter from Roy Bedichek, which discussed a new book, *Patents for Hitler*, written by a German economist who had fled the Nazis. Dobie and Bedichek had already talked about corporations that seemed more inter-ested in maximizing profits than in supporting the war effort, and *Patents for Hitler* detailed how several American companies had entered into en-tangling agreements with Nazi Germany, bound far more by their desire for profit than in their country's national security. When the war came they "were caught with their britches down," Bedichek wrote, and they responded by "yelling 'stop thief' and pointing at Labor and at Bureaucrats and at the New Deal, and at everything else which can possibly take atten-tion off their own nakedness."[6]

Bedichek also expressed a fairly radical critique of the press, telling Dobie that the media are "pretty well subsidized" by these same corporate interests, and thus primed to broadcast "the stop-thief technique."[7]

Dobie raked in Bedichek's thoughts as he gathered his own, and a few days later he published one of the major articles of his lifetime. Taking his title from Walter Prescott Webb's influential 1937 book, Dobie named his essay "Divided We Stand." He exposed the industrialists who "held up emergency defense legislation for months while they worked for tax conces-sions" and "refused to convert from commercial to war production." Some of these "mighty corporations," Dobie wrote, "wanted to do business with Hitler," and he detailed the "stop thief" technique Bedichek described.[8]

Dobie noted that "Hitler banned all labor unions as soon as he came to power," and he argued that the six hundred thousand days lost to strikes that Smith complained about were negligible compared to the two hundred and fifty-one *million* lost days due to industrial accidents.[9] If business interests really wanted to maximize production, Dobie wrote, they should worry less about unions and more about plant safety.

Dobie's assertion that laborers have a right to strike, even during wartime, proved to be a bombshell. Responses raged in the editorial pages of national newspapers, and pro-labor publications across the country picked his article up, reprinting it by the tens of thousands to give away to union members. Dobie, of course, gave the reprint rights away for free and sat back, content in the latest media firestorm he had created.

Many traditionally minded Texans felt betrayed by Dobie's turn towards "communistic" views. Some of the hate mail he received suggested that "he should have died right after the glory he gained" from his early books. One letter writer called him a "yellow-bellied bastard" and added, "I would punch your face in if . . . you weren't a decrepit old fool." Dobie's many conservative friends, however, were inclined to think more generously of him, believing that he simply needed straightening out. John Lomax wrote to J. Evetts Haley, "It's a damn shame that such a lovable person should write himself down as so unbelievably silly."[10]

One consequence of Dobie's newfound politics was that the *Dallas Morning News* often declined to print his columns, and his appearances in the paper gradually dwindled until the column was canceled entirely. Other papers also dropped him. But even as news of such unwelcome developments reached Dobie, additional papers signed on to pick him up, ensuring that throughout most of its twenty-five-year run, his weekly column was available to readers in the state's largest metropolitan centers.

Dobie's emergence as a liberal affected many of his personal relationships. His friendships with oil millionaires such as Sid Richardson cooled off, as did relations with many conservative South Texas ranchers. Robert Kleberg of the King Ranch referred to Dobie as "that academic clown acting like a cowboy." Dobie's correspondence with old friend Kate O'Connor, to whom he had dedicated a chapter of *The Longhorns*, virtually ceased. John Lomax sent Dobie a letter accusing him of "stirring up class feeling." He also told him, "You're disgracing yourself, and you're disgracing Texas. You'll ruin your reputation writing trash like this."[11]

Dobie, however, worked very hard to prevent politics from spoiling his friendships. He "never exacted agreement from anyone as a price of friendship or respect," one friend recalled, and he successfully maintained many relationships. After Ted Dealey, publisher of the *Dallas Morning News*, dropped his column Dobie caught a plane ride to Dallas with the publisher and complained about his treatment. Dealey told him, "Frank, when you deal with Southwestern stories you are great. When you get into politics you are nuts." Dobie responded, "Don't you think I'm entitled to my opinions?" Dealey said, "Yeah, but I don't have to carry them in my newspaper." Still, the two men remained friendly by focusing on their common interest in Texas history.[12]

Even when Dobie was baited by archconservative friends such as John Lomax, he remained calm, responding, "Friend John Lomax, I am not going to argue. Believe it or not, I am coming to where I can state a point of view . . . without feeling combative."[13] However, Dobie's efforts to preserve his friendships would find one notable exception in the years ahead: J. Evetts Haley.

★ ★

Dobie's newfound political zeal soon brought him to the attention of the Federal Bureau of Investigation, which received tips from informants and began compiling a dossier on him. Even before his controversial "Divided We Stand" article, the FBI had received a warning—erroneous, as it turned out—that Dobie had acquired "communist literature over a long period of time and is just about ready to become an active member of the Communist Party."[14]

Dobie was also reported to the Bureau for his failed campaign to convince the University of Texas to offer Russian language courses. Dobie favored teaching Russian for one simple reason: he believed that the Soviet Union was poised to play a larger role in world affairs in the years ahead, and he felt it wise for Americans to learn something of the other country's language and culture. Although Dobie's rationale was based on a reasoned view of world events, several observers saw this as further evidence that he favored Communism. As a consequence, his FBI file became filled with dark references to him as a "Communist who advocated teaching Russian at the University of Texas."[15]

Over the next few years, the FBI seemed content to simply collect information about Dobie, but then one of his weekly articles galvanized the agency into action. On July 6, 1947, Dobie published a column decrying intolerance in which he complained, "Democracy is coming more and more to mean, 'Wear my kind of hat, or get it shot off your head.'" Dobie's column would have likely been overlooked had he not included an unflattering reference to "our Gestapo-flavored FBI."[16]

The San Antonio Field Office immediately forwarded Dobie's article to J. Edgar Hoover, the agency's director, prompting an extensive review of the Dobie files. Senior officials expressed grave concerns about Dobie, but due to his status as a well-known writer, the FBI decided to hold off on taking action against him—at least for the time being.

As much as Dobie had alarmed the FBI and upset Texas's old guard with his endorsement of labor rights and his perceived sympathy for the Soviet Union, he was about to go one step further, into a place few white Texans dared to tread.

World War II ratcheted up pressure on civil rights as minority groups demanded better treatment from the nation whose freedoms they were fighting to protect. The National Association for the Advancement of Colored People pressured for changes in public policy, and the Congress of Racial Equality, established in 1942, took to the streets, staging antisegregation demonstrations in which the protesters carried signs that read "Are You for Hitler's Way or the American Way?" and "We Die Together. Let's Eat Together."[17]

President Roosevelt, in response to a proposed mass march on Washington, issued an executive order forbidding racial discrimination in defense industries and government service. In 1944 the U.S. Supreme Court, which had become more liberal due to Roosevelt's appointments, struck down Texas's "whites-only" primary elections as unconstitutional.

Texas's conservatives were horrified at such developments and feared that African Americans would go so far as to seek equal education. Regent Orville Bullington tried to allay concerns by stating, "There is not the slightest danger of any negro attending the University of Texas as long as the present Board are on the throne."[18]

Racism was so deeply entrenched in Texas politics that even liberal candidates supported segregation, at least publicly, because to do otherwise would be political suicide. One of the few unabashed progressives on race matters was Roy Bedichek, who began lobbying Dobie on civil rights, asking him to be "conscious of how we treat the Negro. Do you remember drinking fountains in every dirty East Texas courthouse labeled 'For Negroes' side by side with those labeled 'For Whites'? Nothing comparable to this exists outside of India."[19]

Thanks in part to his discussions with Bedichek, Dobie began addressing civil rights in his columns. He was somewhat circumspect at the beginning. He published a column, "Commencement Oration on Texas That Nobody Will Deliver," in which he listed a long litany of unpleasant facts about the state. Rather mildly, he included this line: "Annually Texas celebrates the achieving of her liberties, and constantly Texas denies the vote to the Negro."[20]

This observation drew a sharp reaction. One letter writer noted, "Yes, thank Heaven, Texas is a white man's state that will never submit to Negro domination." The writer then took aim at Dobie's position as a college professor, adding, "Here's hoping that my boy will never have to be instructed by J. Frank Dobie."[21]

Such responses appear to have only strengthened Dobie's resolve. He soon began a crusade to educate Texans about civil rights, and in his weekly column he approvingly quoted Booker T. Washington's observation that "it takes two whites down in the ditch in order to hold one Negro there." Dobie also condemned "this fear of educating the Negro," opining that those "places in the United States that produce the most colored ignorance produce also the most white ignorance." He also took the University of Texas to task, noting that it allowed German prisoners of war to sign up for correspondence courses at the same time it "expressly forbids registration of any Negro."[22]

Hate mail poured in to Dobie and newspaper editorial pages filled with letters complaining about him. Yet he also received many letters of support from Anglo Texans who had long believed in equal rights for African Americans, but never before had someone of Dobie's stature to speak for them. Dobie, just as in his folklore, freely adapted these letter writers' thoughts, which gave him ammunition for future columns. The debate was on, but the sides were hardly balanced. White Texas newspapers at the time rarely mentioned African Americans unless they "had committed some sort of crime against a white person." As one reporter recalled, "Anything that could be construed as positive [about blacks] was off limits . . . that was called a 'nigger deal.'"[23] Dobie was essentially the only voice in support of civil rights to appear in white Texas newspapers.

As always, Dobie was not content with simply publishing his opinions. He also made public appearances at rallies and forums, often appearing alongside African American leaders. He reported on such events in his column, praising the "serious, decorous and altogether reasonable" requests for equal rights. "I do not see how any fair-minded person who honestly faces the future," Dobie wrote, can help but "be glad that the Negroes are coming to have a chance in this land so boastful of being the home of the free."[24]

Dobie's activities on behalf of civil rights brought renewed attention from the FBI, which believed that "racial agitation" was a tactic employed by Communist-front organizations, rather than a heartfelt desire among patriotic Americans for a more just society. FBI agents took note that Dobie had "addressed a meeting of the National Association for the Advancement of Colored People in Austin." Even more worrisome to the agency, Dobie served as "Honorary Chairman of the Texas Civil Rights Congress," which the FBI considered to be "dominated by CP [Communist Party] members."[25]

The documents make it clear that the FBI considered Dobie its ideological enemy, yet, once again, the agency decided against further action. However, later events would prompt another review, leading J. Edgar Hoover himself to get involved.

★ ★

In early 1946, a young African American man, Heman Sweatt, challenged segregation in higher education by applying to the University of Texas law school. Sweatt "met all eligibility requirements for admission except for his race," but his application was denied, and the state of Texas frantically set about creating a "separate but equal" law school for blacks.[26] A long legal battle ensued, and Sweatt's lawyer, Thurgood Marshall, eventually won the case before the U.S. Supreme Court, setting the stage for the subsequent *Brown v. Board* decision.

Dobie joined the podium at rallies in support of Sweatt. Much of the talk during these events was intentionally confined to the particular issue at hand—whether or not the young man could be admitted to a specific graduate program at the University. In this way, black leaders sought to tamp down fears of a white overreaction by cautiously proceeding with integration, one step at a time. But by now, Dobie's views transcended such details, and he was never a man for caution in any case. He told one audience, "I am for human justice and decency. . . . I know that keeping one's fellow man, no matter of what color, down in ignorance is evil and undemocratic, and that such injustice results in evil to the oppressors as well as the oppressed." In 1946, speaking before hundreds of people, Dobie called for the complete integration of the University of Texas. "I am for admitting them at once," he said, predicting, "Such Negroes would find a welcome among a surprisingly large portion of students."[27]

Bedichek spoke for many of Dobie's liberal friends when he wrote to congratulate him, telling him how "splendid I thought your speech at the race-meeting was. It was utterly fearless but showed damn good judgment."[28]

Dobie's actions, however, made him even more reviled among conservatives. Members of the Texas legislature rose to denounce him, speaking engagements were cancelled, and more hate mail poured in. There was even talk at the university that Dobie might be fired. But as one conservative faculty member glumly noted, "There are two assumptions to make about Dobie. One is that he is too important to be fired. The other is that he is too insignificant."[29]

# A Texan in England
## 1943–1946

**I**N 1943 DOBIE received a welcome offer from Cambridge University, inviting him to spend a year in England as a visiting professor of American history. He could escape the turmoil in Texas and, at last, contribute to the war effort by assisting the valiant British. The trip was not without risk. German U-boats remained a threat as he sailed across the Atlantic, and in Britain the Luftwaffe still mustered sporadic bombing raids. Air raid sirens punctuated daily life.

Along with Dobie, some one hundred and fifty thousand American soldiers a month were arriving in Britain as preparations intensified for the cross-channel invasion. Relations between America and Great Britain had never been better, and Dobie, despite the lack of sunshine in England, found much to like in Cambridge, a bucolic intellectual community about fifty miles outside of London. The venerable college had been founded in the 1200s, and alongside the picturesque River Cam were centuries-old buildings that had housed some of the world's greatest scholars.

Cambridge welcomed the spirited American with open arms, and Dobie admired the British in return. Their reverence for tradition, counterbalanced by a devotion to free inquiry, exemplified Dobie's idea of a model civilization. The British character, Dobie wrote, has an emphasis "on being, not on possessing . . . on sensitiveness to the beautiful and on cultivated intelligence, not on getting ahead; on rounded natures, in which spirited wit plays."[1]

His weekly columns back home portrayed the English in laudatory terms. Their average student, Dobie wrote, is "better trained mentally, has the fibers in his mind better developed, enjoys the act of thinking more and has more intellectual curiosity than the average American student." Dobie also believed that the typical parliamentarian "is more civilized than the average Congressman." His admiration even extended to British conservatives, who "seem more willing than their stiff-necked American counterparts to accommodate themselves to . . . trends inevitable in society."[2]

His friend Roy Bedichek stepped in to prevent him from slipping into romanticism again. He wrote to Dobie, "You are doubtless seeing England at its heroic best. War has cured unemployment and much of the caste atmosphere I encountered there in 1907." Bedichek told Dobie how he had once worked for a London newspaper, investigating living conditions among industrial workers. "We often found families of 4, 5, or 6 littered in a 16-foot square room two stories under ground. I shall never forget the terrible sights. Never before or since, have I seen humanity so degraded, and I worked once in the West Virginia coal fields."[3]

Dobie acknowledged Bedichek's point, which he incorporated into his expanding awareness. He was ripe for an evolution and England provided the necessary intellectual nourishment as he threw off the shackles of Texas provincialism. Back in the old days, Dobie had written gloriously of Texas cattlemen, portraying them as "old rock" and reinforcing Texans' impression that these pioneers, with perhaps a little help from God, had created the ranching industry. But at Cambridge, an Egyptologist on the faculty explained to him that cattle ranching had been around for thousands of years, as "Egyptian medals and coins depict the whole process of roping and branding cattle."[4]

Dobie appreciated the value of such lessons and in his columns he began condemning Texans' propensity for bragging. He now saw "provincial inbreeding" as "one of the chief impediments to amplitude and intellectual freedom." He was no longer whooping and hollering on behalf of Texas. Instead, he came to serve as the state's chief critic. He acknowledged Texas's economic gains but he also pointed out that it "has not yet produced a poet, novelist, artist, thinker, humanitarian or statesman to be ranked as a great American."[5] This was quite a change for a man who had long argued in favor of Big Foot Wallace's memoir as classic American literature.

Dobie visiting with students in Cambridge, 1944. Southwestern Writers
Collection / The Wittliff Collections, Texas State University–San Marcos.

Dobie's new outlook allowed him to finally shake loose of his attachment to the past. He had grown up believing that he had just missed out
on the world's greatest adventures, but now he understood that it was his
own lifetime that saw "the making of more history—history pregnant with
import and change to the human race—than any other generation during
the last thousand years."[6]

Friends in Texas kept him apprised of political developments, and he
continued to raise hell, even from a distance, about free speech and civil
rights. As the Texas election season geared up in 1944, a group of liber-

als spearheaded by John Henry Faulk and women's suffrage leader Minnie Fisher Cunningham led a movement to draft Dobie into running for governor. He began receiving ten cables a day urging him to join the race. Bertha feared "that his vanity, or his love of the unexpected, might carry him away" and she wrote "strongly urging him to put a stop to the efforts at once." She added, pointedly, that, "his mother was equally opposed to such a theatrical prospect."[7]

Bedichek also opposed the idea, writing to Dobie, "I don't think you could be elected anyway for the simple and sufficient reason that you could not get enough money" from the common folks to be competitive. Bedichek added, "I know you would not want to be obligated to any of the big financial boys for really substantial contributions."[8]

The worst-case scenario, Bedichek observed, would be a Dobie victory. "You are a sort of gadfly, and should continue to function as such politically, and not attempt the actual duties of public administration . . . the politician is essentially a compromiser." Bedichek contrasted Dobie to the current Speaker of the House, Sam Rayburn, who "perhaps never gets what he wants done, but he gets *something* done. A Congress of J. Frank Dobies would get nothing done except a lot of broken heads . . . ."[9]

Dobie decided against the race and remained in Cambridge, where he had become an exceedingly popular figure. "So many people ask me to tea and dinner," he wrote to Bertha, "that I have to keep a calendar. I can never pay the calls back. And the groups that want me to talk are thicker than the invitations to tea." In addition to his classes, public events, and Sunday column, Dobie visited Army encampments to give talks to American soldiers. He also received a steady stream of drop-in visits from Texas soldiers who decided to look him up while they were in England. "Ask me for anything but time," he wrote Bertha, adding that nobody could accuse him of "hoarding myself."[10]

At the end of his year, London newspapers wrote glowing editorials about the visiting American professor and Cambridge University awarded him an honorary degree containing a unique inscription: *De longibus cornibus quod ille non cognivit, inutile est allis cognoscere* (What he does not know about longhorns is not worth knowing).[11]

Instead of returning to Texas, Dobie decided to remain in England. He wanted to travel a bit and he also craved solitude so that he could adapt his many newspaper columns on England into a book. Bertha was by now well-accustomed to this instinct of his, but Dobie's mother was less understanding, and she wrote to tell him "that Bertha was really a wonderful wife to allow [you] to stay away from home for so long."[12]

Dobie's long absences from his wife have created a lot of speculation over the years, particularly since the couple never had any children and they slept in separate bedrooms. One Dobie biographer, Lon Tinkle, noted the existence of a "persistent underground rumor that the Dobies had what the French call a 'white,' that is, unconsummated, marriage." In fact, Bertha's health problems made her unable to conceive, and the couple did consider adopting a child.[13]

Additional rumors have surfaced about the close friendships Dobie enjoyed over his lifetime with younger, pretty women, such as Jovita González in the 1920s. Later, while in England, he became very close to Belinda Norman-Butler, who was twenty years his junior and the great-granddaughter of the nineteenth century British novelist William Thackeray. Another good friend was Isabel Gaddis, the vivacious wife of a South Texas rancher and one of Dobie's former students.

It is undeniable that Dobie felt a keen emotional bond with his female friends—he was subject to infatuation, after all. However, his actions were also undertaken in full view of others, including his wife, and he conformed to propriety at all times. Dobie's main drive seemed to be to create an emotional and intellectual bond with others. In this regard he was a good friend to many women as well as many men.

His frequent long absences from home may have pained Bertha, at least in the beginning. But then she also understood him better than anyone else, and she knew that he needed to balance "strenuous action" with "solitude and repose." It is also true that her husband "was never known to be at peace with himself except when inveighing against something." Given the intensity of life with Dobie, it is entirely possible that on those occasions when he left to take yet another trip, Bertha would sit back, relax, and exhale a long sigh of relief.[14]

★ ★

While Dobie remained in England to work on his new book, attacks on University of Texas President Homer Rainey intensified. Regents had never forgiven him for allowing the school's English professors to teach John Dos Passos's *U.S.A.* over their objections. After Rainey gave a speech suggesting that America could do better at living up to its ideals, the Board of Regents charged him with promoting Communism. The state's politicians also jumped into the fray. East Texas Congressman Martin Dies, Jr., who chaired the House Un-American Activities Committee, made headlines by claiming that UT was home to one thousand Communists. Dies's subsequent investigation revealed exactly zero Communists on campus, but regents remained on the offensive.

Orville Bullington charged that Rainey's lack of moral discipline had turned the campus into "a nest of homosexuals."[15] Once again, an investigation was launched, though the negligible results were equally disappointing to inquisitors.

Most worrisome of all to many of the regents was the prospect of integration, and they feared that Rainey's "radicalism" might inspire him to enroll African American students. Regent D. F. Strickland commented that Rainey was "a little ultra-liberal on the Nigger question."[16] When Strickland heard that a new study called for improving educational opportunities for black Texans, he responded that any African American who wanted a better education should simply leave the state.

The regents began excluding Rainey from their board meetings and a whisper campaign began against the embattled president. Rumors were spread that Rainey's daughter "was having sex with a married black man who was a Communist." Other gossip suggested that Rainey himself "had run a homosexual ring on campus."[17]

Walter Prescott Webb, in contrast to Dobie and Bedichek, preferred to stay on the sidelines during the controversy, commenting that Rainey had not been a particularly great president anyway. Bedichek wrote to admonish him, "The whole point is not the virtue of Rainey but the evil purpose of the gang that has captured the university. . . . Rainey's virtue (you may say it is his sole virtue) is that he sees the point and has enough courage to fight the issue out—and that's enough virtue for me."[18]

Finally, in October 1944, the conflict, which had simmered quietly for so long, broke into the open. Rainey decided to make his case public. He called a faculty meeting and presented a list of sixteen specific instances in which the Board of Regents had obstructed academic freedom. The question, Rainey argued, is "whether or not our state universities can be operated in ways that guarantee their essential freedom from undue political interference."[19] The faculty, including Webb, responded with a standing ovation and gave Rainey a unanimous vote of confidence.

As newspapers rushed to cover the crisis, speculation mounted about the regents' response. The wait wasn't long. The regents quickly called a meeting, and afterward announced that Rainey would be fired for his "attacks upon the board [that] were unprovoked and unexpected and calculated to discredit the board and its members."[20]

The campus erupted in protest and students boycotted classes. The national media arrived as several thousand people marched to the state capitol, where protesters laid a coffin labeled "Academic Freedom" at the doorstep of Governor Coke Stevenson. The fallout damaged the university—and Texas's intellectual life—for years to come. National coverage was ruinous to the university's reputation. As a result of the firing, UT was placed on probation by its accrediting agency and formally censured by the American Association of University Professors.

Dobie was on a ship in the middle of the Atlantic at the time of Rainey's firing and he steamed into Boston Harbor two days later. Everyone in Texas waited to hear from him. Regent Lutcher Stark said Dobie is "beloved by all of us and I don't know anybody who isn't his friend." Yet Stark warned, when Dobie returns from England, "the minute he hits town, the front pages of the newspapers will be black with what Frank Dobie has to say; what can you do about it?"[21]

True to form, Dobie issued waves of fulminations, tossing the word "fascist" around several times. He also chased the regents into their home territory. After making a speech against Regent Strickland to a Rotary Club in South Texas, Dobie gleefully wrote to Bedichek, "I put a cocklebur under Strickland's tail right here in his own pigpen." Dobie, believing that Rainey had been too timid in dealing with the regents, added, "This board of regents won't fire anybody that stands up and fights them."[22]

★ ★

Dobie's book *A Texan in England* appeared soon afterward, just as World War II was ending, and it marked something of a renaissance for him on the national stage. America had outgrown its fondness for tales of buried treasure, just as Dobie himself had. And now, presenting himself as a traditional man forced to evolve in the face of rapidly unfolding events, Dobie's journey to some extent mirrored that of his country. Interest in his views on England ran high, and the *Saturday Evening Post* and *National Geographic* commissioned stories from him. *A Texan in England* received much favorable national attention, including a write-up in *Time* that praised the "mellow, witty impressions of England" written by "the silver-haired, granite-faced, panther-hunting professor."[23]

Dobie's book also received acclaim in Texas, and the Texas Institute of Letters named it the Best Book of the Year. *A Texan in England* became a book for the season, but, alas, it would not endure to become a book for all seasons. Caught up in the events of the day, Dobie had difficulty separating the temporal from the timeless—the same curse that afflicts much of daily journalism. Roy Bedichek, fearless as always, provided the diagnosis, predicting in his own way that the book would become dated. In a letter to Dobie, Bedichek wrote, "I can see that you have worked hard on the original material you turned out for the *Saturday Evening Post* and papers, and you have greatly improved it." However, Bedichek pointed out, the book "still has some of the journalese hanging around in it."[24]

Soon after the publication of *A Texan in England*, the Army asked fifty-seven-year-old Dobie to spend a year lecturing to U.S. servicemen in postwar Europe. He extended his unpaid leave of absence from the university for yet another year and sailed back across the Atlantic. Bertha, as usual, remained behind in Austin, managing his stateside affairs and continuing her work on behalf of Texas gardening clubs. Many years later, after she was buried next to her husband, Bertha's own epitaph would read, simply, "She was ever loyal."

In Europe Dobie became something of an itinerant lecturer for the Army, traveling throughout England, France, and, most significantly, Germany. In his dispatches from that country, Dobie described the "bitterness and resentment" he encountered among many Germans, who seemed to him to not have fully accepted their responsibility for the war. He remarked on the "numerous good-sized towns altogether untouched by any bombs or artillery," making it clear that he believed more devastation would have brought the Germans more fully to heel.[25]

He toured Dachau and told readers of "the ovens, the gas chambers, the iron hooks from which tortured bodies hung, [and] the pits in which hordes of human beings were shot . . . ." He was accompanied by a concentration camp survivor, and the two of them walked past Nazi Storm Troopers being held prisoner. "They glared and with their eyes cursed," Dobie wrote. "No chamber of horrors could cull . . . more baseness, depravity, and inhuman malice . . . than those SS faces. I am not delicate, but I positively shudder now at the remembrance."[26]

He attended the war crimes trials in Nuremberg, where at last he began to feel a sense of justice. "Talking with enlightened observers and watching the tribunal at work is a great tonic," he wrote. "There is no substitute for brains."[27]

Yet one aspect of his experience continued to trouble him: "Why did intelligent, decent Germans allow themselves to be ruled, led by these low-browed criminals, even brought to adore the criminals?" He worried that the same thing could happen in America. In Germany he saw plenty of Americans, including Army officers, who displayed natural sympathies for the fascists. One American colonel, Dobie wrote, would gladly have "millions of people like me and you . . . lie down and look up at him with grateful eyes asking for the orders he would so gladly give . . . and it would be as efficient as any goose-stepping the master race planned."[28]

Dobie knew that his best hope was to reach people through his writing, and so he contemplated creating "a book on the Emancipators of the Human Mind—Emerson, Jefferson, Thoreau, Tom Paine, Voltaire, Arnold, Goethe." As he pondered the idea, a sobering thought came to him. "When I reflect how few writings connected with the wide open spaces of the West and Southwest are wide enough to enter into such a volume," he wrote to a friend, "I realize acutely how desirable is perspective to patriotism."[29]

Dobie also considered writing a new book about what he had seen in Germany, which would be something of a sequel to *A Texan in England*. He already had a fair amount of published material to draw from, including his Sunday columns and an article, "What I Saw Across the Rhine," that he wrote for *National Geographic*. But by now his standards were higher for his own work, and as he reviewed his various dispatches he realized, "I have not learned enough."[30]

He now wanted his writing to help shape humanity's future, rather than celebrate its past. But he was almost sixty years old, and he had been facing in the wrong direction for too long. He wrote a letter to Bedichek that effectively summed up his life's tragic arc: "I am too damned ignorant to be effective in writing about the realities of the present. That is what comes from having spent nearly a quarter of a century of my allotted years doing nothing but soak in the lore of coyotes and cowboys."[31]

Another year abroad further weakened his ties to his home state. He had already resigned as secretary-editor from the Texas Folklore Society and he wrote to Tom Lea, "I find myself moving farther and farther from the range. I mean it no longer pulls at my vitals."[32]

As in his previous trip to Europe, he delayed his departure home, writing to Bedichek, "I hate to contemplate being tied to the pervading air of unreality there. I'll always have roots in Texas, but . . . if I had a hundred or so more years to live, I'd spend most of the time . . . in Europe."[33]

Bedichek wrote back, "Don't, I beg you, become expatriated. . . . Think of your brush country and of the paisano, and of the friendly people who talk with just your own accent, and of the good and noble things your countrymen have done and said."[34]

Dobie did come home, but as he wrote to Bertha, he had no desire to go back to teaching. "I am not resigning yet, however," he told her. "I should force that board of regents to fire me and may do that when I get home." He planned to assist Homer Rainey, who had announced his intention to run for governor. Dobie felt an obligation "not to Rainey but to society and civilization. After that," he promised Bertha, "I am most emphatically through with causes."[35]

# Texas Needs Brains
## 1946–1947

ACK IN AUSTIN, an old pickup truck clattered up to the Dobies' house, picked up the famous author, and made its way to Barton Springs, the spring-fed swimming pool in the heart of the city. Behind the wheel was Roy Bedichek, by then a senior citizen sixty-eight years old, and in excellent health. Bedichek preferred driving the truck, Dobie knew, "so that he can load his camping equipment in it and go camping, anywhere, at any time." Along the way to the pool, Bedichek and Dobie would talk or argue about anything—"religion, politics, education, history, literature, grass, the habits of wild animals . . . everything under the sun and beyond it." The two men "had a compact that whenever either should detect signs of senility in the other he would let him know immediately." One of their friends recalled that in the "heat of argument this privilege was sometimes invoked."[1]

Once at Barton Springs, they made their way to Bedichek's favorite spot—a large limestone boulder overlooking the pool. Dobie originally called it "Conversation Rock." Later it became known as "Bedichek's Rock." Under the hot Texas sun, with the sixty-eight-degree water at their feet, "these two gladiators were engaged in animated conversation." Bedichek continued talking even as he stepped into the water, where he would "sit in the spring and throw a double handful of water over his head, each time exclaiming 'Woof! Woof!'" Dobie would sometimes shake his head at something Bedichek said, and then go dive into the water even as Bedichek tried to finish making his point. Other friends joined them—though not Webb, who was no swimmer—and the conversation continued to flow throughout the day, punctuated by regular dips in the pool. As one university colleague, Wilson Hudson, later recalled, "If there was ever such a thing as a literary salon in Austin, its location was Bedichek's rock."[2]

Afterward, Bedichek and Dobie would return to Dobie's house and sit out in the back yard, under the shade of a great elm tree. Bedichek occasionally drank a beer, while Dobie sipped from the whiskey he was so fond of. Bertha often joined them, and other friends regularly dropped by as evening peacefully descended along the banks of Waller Creek.

Bedichek and Dobie were two of the most well-read people in Texas, and each man's knowledge complemented the other's. Bedichek could quote from Voltaire and Thucydides, expound on the value of organic fertilizer, and dissect the critical differences between free speech and corporate-controlled media. The point of his conversations was never pedantic, rather, it was to probe, with touches of occasional whimsy, as he sought to enlarge everyone's understanding, including his own.

Unlike the other people Dobie had met in his lifetime, he never tired of Bedichek's company. He has "the most richly and variously stored mind I have ever associated with," Dobie wrote, seeing his friend as "a whole man, romantic and naturalistic, intellectual and as physical as Whitman, spiritual and earthy. He is one of the most eager lookers-upon-life imaginable." By this time, Dobie recognized Bedichek as "the dearest comrade of my life."[3]

Bedichek and Dobie continued the humanistic quests they had begun during World War II. They developed a fascination with the Soviet Union, which they hoped could offer a viable alternative to heartless capitalism. The Soviets, Bedichek wrote to Dobie, "set up their acquisitions not on a colonial but brotherhood basis, share and share alike, regardless of race, color, or religion . . . ." When Stalin gobbled up Catholic Eastern Europe it troubled them, but their distrust of a reactionary, pro-fascist Church remained stronger. Dobie excused the Soviet's takeover of Poland by writing to Bedichek, "I am confident that millions liberated from priest domination will in time become free to think and say what they will."[4] It took a couple more years before the two men realized that Communism amounted to a totalitarianism as evil as Fascism.

Bedichek joined Dobie's distrust of mass production and he went even further by criticizing the subsidized scientists whose findings always seemed

Roy Bedichek and Dobie at Barton Springs, ca. 1950s. Southwestern Writers Collection/The Wittliff Collections, Texas State University–San Marcos.

to support industry profit margins. Bedichek cautioned against eating "denatured chickens" and he told Dobie, "We are developing a *priesthood* of positive scientists. They are assuming airs. They put you off with mysterious nods, like the priests of ancient Egypt, or like a physician [to] his countrybumpkin patient, or like a preacher insisting on the reality of the Trinity."[5]

Bedichek's lively inquisitiveness, and his refusal to be cowed by society, found a kindred spirit in Dobie, who wrote to his friend, "Bedi, you'll never grow old in outlook, nor I either. That's the payoff age gives for keeping the mind open. How empty life must be for those old men . . . primarily concerned with keeping their own bowels open and other people's minds closed."[6]

\* \*

Dobie remained on unpaid leave from UT as he began work on a new book. Still, he wanted to instruct students about political issues, and so he published an article, "Texas Needs Brains," in a campus magazine. He explained that liberals are hospitable to "ideas and intellectual activity." Un-like the right-wingers, Dobie told the students, liberals "will not want to annihilate a man who does not agree with them."[7]

Free enterprise, Dobie told the students, should include "freedom of intellectual enterprise." Otherwise it "cannot sustain, much less extend, liberty. . . . Liberty means liberty of mind as much as it means liberty to make a profit." Regarding the prevailing wisdom that successful business-men were better at running civic affairs such as universities and the gov-ernment, Dobie wrote, "The truth of the matter is that the average . . . businessman has no more grasp on the complexities of this world and is no more of a thinker than was Davy Crockett."[8]

★ ★

As Homer Rainey's gubernatorial campaign heated up in 1946, Dobie gave several talks and radio speeches, but he kept the campaign out of his week-ly column. Bedichek, too, signed on for Rainey, although, as he wrote, "I am under no illusions as to the outcome of the race."[9] Dobie, following Rainey's instructions, avoided making personal attacks and instead focused on explaining Rainey's stances on the issues.

Their opponents, meanwhile, were less gracious. One candidate de-nounced Dobie as "the leading exponent of the Darwinian theory of evo-lution in Texas," then added, "I am not surprised that Dobie is making speeches in support of Rainey's candidacy." Another candidate made head-lines by proposing an all-Negro university with Rainey as its president and Dobie as its vice president, since the two men "have proven themselves to be vitally interested in Negro education."[10]

In the meantime, Dobie's old friend J. Evetts Haley crisscrossed the state, giving speeches and publishing articles in support of the regents who had fired Rainey. Haley pointed out that, back in 1936 when his own con-tract at the university had been terminated, "not a one of these liberals beat his sensitive breast, or tore his long hair, or burnt up the printer's ink" in protest. Haley—ignoring the fact that Dobie *had* defended him at the time—wrote, "It is time for J. Frank Dobie and the other purely academic warriors to come out of the convenient brush of generalities and open up at close range with the cold and hard facts."[11]

Haley's righteous wrath became evident in July 1946, when Rainey trav-eled to Amarillo to give a campaign speech before several hundred people on the courthouse lawn. At the end of his talk, Haley stood up and accused

Rainey of "having a dirty mind because he had allowed John Dos Passos's U.S.A. to be taught in an English class at the University of Texas." *U.S.A.* had become a staple at anti-Rainey rallies, where opponents "would put on gloves and use a pair of fire tongs to handle the book in public."[12]

The crowd in Amarillo, which was largely pro-Rainey, began taunting Haley. "He's a Democrat who fought Roosevelt in three elections," one person yelled out. "Who's paying for your propaganda?" another asked. Rainey pleaded for calm as Haley was jostled. Then a fistfight began and the rally erupted into "a near riot," as the *Dallas Morning News* reported.[13]

Dobie and Haley quit speaking to each other during this time. Dobie later wrote a critical essay about Haley, condemning him as a fraudulent "super-patriot . . . holier than Jesus Christ" and pinpointing what he saw as evidence of Haley's personal hypocrisy on certain moral issues.[14] Dobie never published the essay, however.

Dobie and Haley each "said things about the other's character and mentality that left no room for friendly retreat." A decade after the Rainey rally, Haley would run for Texas governor as a segregationist, and during that campaign he argued that the civil rights movement "was part of a Communist plot to overthrow the United States." In 1964, as Lyndon Johnson ran for president, Haley published a controversial book, *A Texan Looks at Lyndon*, that attacked Johnson on all fronts and seemed to even accuse him of committing murder. The book was a big hit among members of the John Birch Society, but by this time most moderate observers agreed with the reviewer who concluded that Haley's political stances represented "unhospitalized paranoia."[15]

Ever since Dobie and Haley went off in their separate political directions, mutual friends sought to reconcile them. After Haley's first wife died in 1958, Bertha convinced Dobie to send a condolence letter. In it, Dobie suggested that Haley stop by next time he was in Austin. Haley showed up, and in the course of his visit delivered one of his trademark political rants. "I kept my mouth shut and never disputed a word," Dobie later told disbelieving friends. "We did not fight; I just let him talk."[16]

After Haley left, Dobie concluded, "I never intend to see him again if I can avoid it. We have buried the hatchet, and we'll let it stay buried. But there's no meeting ground any more for us."[17] Dobie's and Haley's uneasy truce would last a few years until the bitterness broke out into the open one last time.

After Rainey's landslide loss, Dobie turned his attention back to his book in progress about coyotes. Bedichek wrote to him, "You have been losing some of your . . . old audience, and maybe it's time to lure them back within striking distance with innocent tales of coyotes and cowboys. . . . I know your book is going to be a knockout. Let causes rest and do that book."[18]

Bedichek, meanwhile, had his own book forthcoming. For years Dobie, Webb, and other friends had begged him to put his thoughts into a published work. He demurred, claiming that his letters to friends would suffice as his literary legacy. By 1945, however, Webb, with help from Dobie, put a plan into action. They worked to raise the equivalent of Bedichek's annual salary so that he could take a one-year leave of absence to write a book. The idea ran into a few snags. Dobie, as it turned out, "was able to help only a little in raising money for this grant; he had become persona non grata with too many of the wealthy men in the state."[19] Webb, however, performed admirably, and on February 1, 1946, Bedichek began his leave.

He spent much of the next year living alone at Webb's Friday Mountain ranch outside of Austin. He was miles from the nearest telephone and spent his days roaming the hills, cooking his meals in the fireplace, and banging out his manuscript on an old typewriter. He corresponded frequently with Dobie and Webb, each of whom critiqued early versions of his manuscript. When it was done, his two friends helped him find a publisher.

*Adventures with a Texas Naturalist* was published in 1947 as the first-time author turned sixty-nine years old. The book was an immediate hit. Bedichek had created "a kind of miscellany that [gave] to the world some of his anecdotes and thoughts on bird life and animal life, and the foibles of mankind."[20] His wise, philosophic voice guided readers on a journey through nature, distilling his lifetime of careful observation and contemplation while also illuminating his playful habits of mind.

Dobie devoted an entire newspaper column to his review of the book, praising his friend's "intelligence, keen and fresh powers of observation, [and] ample soul." *Adventures with a Texas Naturalist*, Dobie wrote, "may be the wisest and most civilized book that Texas has yet produced."[21]

Even though Dobie was hardly unbiased, his assessment proved to be on target. In the years since, *Adventures with a Texas Naturalist* has become a regional classic. Even later critics who were hostile to Dobie and Webb, such as the novelist Larry McMurtry, praised Bedichek. McMurtry observed that, "Bedichek, the writer, is as easy to like as Bedichek the man seems to have been." Ecologically minded Texans continue to draw inspiration from

Bedichek, and the book has been reprinted several times over the decades, most recently with an appreciative introduction by the noted nature writer Rick Bass. Critic A. C. Greene, in *The Fifty Best Texas Books*, concludes that Bedichek's book "could easily outlive" most of Dobie's and Webb's own work.[22]

☆ ☆

Life for new UT president Theophilus Schickel Painter could not have been easy. The campus was politically divided, the school remained on probation from its accrediting agency, quality faculty members stayed away in droves, and a NAACP lawsuit over Heman Sweatt was on its way to the Supreme Court. And then there was Dobie. After returning from Europe in the wake of Rainey's firing, Dobie told an audience in Austin that any man who accepted the UT presidency would be "a bootlicker or a quisling."[23]

Painter was a conservative drawn from the university's science department and he had a reputation as a supporter of segregation. He encouraged the FBI to come to campus and eradicate "subversion," even as he sought to allay fears that UT planned to purge its liberals. Painter also issued a widely publicized call for "tranquility," which Dobie considered foolish considering the university's new restrictions on free speech. "The liberals already on the faculty can be starved out, kept down," Dobie wrote in a column attacking Painter. "The older liberals will gradually die off; the younger ones will drift to other places. Some can be cowed down. The vital, the vigorous and the proud won't come. The belly-crawlers can be hired for two-bits a dozen. In the end the university will be as tranquil as a machine shop. . . . It will be as tranquil as a henhouse full of setting hens." Those who go along with the new order, Dobie prophesied, will be "as free as any pig that swills slop poured out by its master."[24]

Painter declined to respond publicly to Dobie, although he did make it known that he was considering filing a libel suit in response. Painter then issued a warning to the faculty and staff, telling them that he would not tolerate "any further attempts . . . to besmirch the good reputation of the university."[25]

Dobie responded by calling Painter "a flunky of the Laval pattern," alluding to the French Vichy leader, Pierre Laval, who had been shot by a firing squad after collaborating with Nazi Germany.[26]

This new controversy inspired Governor Coke Stevenson, a man renowned for his reticence, to issue a public call for Dobie's firing. "If I were a member of the board of regents," Stevenson told reporters, "I would remove Dobie without batting an eye." Stevenson dismissed concerns that such an action would turn Dobie into a martyr, adding, it is "just a question of eliminating a disturbing influence."[27]

The Board of Regents did not take immediate action against Dobie. Instead, it implemented a new rule: future leaves of absence were restricted to one year only.[28] Alert observers understood that the policy was aimed at Dobie, who was well into his third consecutive year away from teaching duties. A showdown loomed.

In April 1947, Dobie applied for another year of unpaid leave so that he could finish his book on coyotes. It was also true that Dobie suffered terribly from "Cedar Fever," the winter allergy outbreak that afflicts many Austinites. For years he had made himself scarce during pollen's peak months, sometimes turning his classes over to Bertha. He had long arranged his university schedule so that he could teach his "Life and Literature of the Southwest" course in the spring, after the pollen had died down.

His request made its way through the university's bureaucracy, receiving approval every step of the way. Then it reached President Painter's office. Soon thereafter, Dobie opened his morning newspaper and read the news that Painter had denied his request.[29] Dobie could have returned to teaching in the fall on the president's terms, but he refused to back down.

As the new semester arrived Dobie turned fifty-nine and his name was removed from the school's budget. His thirty-year association with UT came to an end. Condemnation of the university poured forth from all quarters, even from newspapers that had opposed Dobie politically. Many articles pointed out that two of Dobie's years of leave had been spent on behalf of the war effort. The national media also weighed in, seeing this as the latest manifestation of political meddling at Texas's largest university.

In Austin, a torchlight procession of some two hundred students made its way across campus towards the Dobie home. Dobie and Bertha were returning from dinner with Ralph and Opal Yarborough, and Bertha recalled, "It was a great dash to get the house open, lights on, my hat off, and be, the two of us, on the side porch steps" to greet the students, who were chanting "We Want Dobie!"[30]

One of the students read a speech, and Dobie thanked them for their concern. He explained, "I do not wish to discuss what brought this about. The last several days have been emotional and a man can't always trust his mind when he is emotional." The students sang "Auld Lang Syne" and quietly left as the small grass fires started by their torches were put out.[31]

*Elder Statesman*

# Coyote Wisdom
## 1948–1953

**T**HE DOBIES HARDLY relied on Frank's university salary to survive. In addition to the twenty-seven hundred dollars his newspaper columns brought in annually, Dobie could usually count on another thousand or two from magazine publications, and several hundred dollars from book royalties and lectures. His family's ranch held oil leases that Dobie's mother shared with the children. Dobie had also made many outside investments over the years. He played the stock market, invested wisely in Austin real estate, and gambled with cattle. Dobie's cattle dealing was his most risky venture; he often borrowed large sums of money and he wrote to friends that he would either "make a wad" or lose "everything I have." He kept hoping to make enough money to start his own longhorn herd, but market fluctuations kept him from obtaining that dream. A far more sober, and lucrative, investment, was the farm in the Lower Rio Grande Valley that he and Bertha owned an interest in. At the time he lost his job the farm was bringing in some three thousand dollars a year.[1]

Dobie's separation from the University of Texas did nothing to diminish his national reputation. In fact, it enhanced it, as people in more liberal parts of the country viewed him as a martyr for free speech. Universities offered him visiting professorships and lecture opportunities abounded. He took

Dobie in his study, photograph by Bill Malone, ca. 1950s.
Courtesy of the Malone family.

to the road regularly, often with Bertha, to make speaking appearances at colleges, writers' conferences, or wherever book folk gathered. His genius for making friends opened up all kinds of trails for him. He was invited by Robert Frost to help celebrate the poet's eightieth birthday in New York. He also broke bread with literary luminary Carl Sandburg in Washington, D.C., and Edward R. Murrow featured him in his popular "This I Believe" series. Readers of Dobie's weekly columns were not kept ignorant of such developments.

Dobie was also appointed to serve on an advisory committee for UNES-CO, the cultural arm of the newly created United Nations. He traveled to Washington, D.C., and New York for hearings, and was feisty as usual in his committee work. Knowing that many Texans bitterly opposed the UN, Dobie argued in his columns for giving the organization a chance. "Logic and history prove that [the UN is] entitled to as much support as the men of war and politics," he wrote.[2]

Dobie also received an appointment to the History Book Club, where he served alongside prominent historians, such as Arthur Schlesinger, on the editorial committee. "All I had to do," Dobie wrote, "was glance through a few books a month and write a letter or two to [the] chairman of the board." This sinecure paid another twenty-four hundred dollars annually.[3]

Dobie and Bertha spent a summer in Colorado, where he taught writing, and then a winter in southern California, where the Huntington Library gave him a twenty-four-hundred-dollar grant to conduct research there for a future book on mustangs. During a lecture tour in New England, Dobie wrote to Bedichek, "It does me good to get out of Texas. I think it must be the damned, provincial-minded, fearing-of-intelligence newspapers there that depress me. Anyhow, I'd just as soon live in New England for a while. . . . I wonder why and how I used to think that I could not live happily anywhere but in Texas and wanted no intellectual pabulum but Texas and surrounding territory. Intensity can make a fool of a man."[4]

He continued to publish in mainstream magazines such as the *Saturday Evening Post*, the *American Mercury*, and *Holiday*, which sent him back to England in 1949 for a follow-up story on Cambridge. He also published in academic journals such as the *Yale Review* and the *Southwest Review*. Translated editions of his work were produced by the United States Information Agency for distribution in the Soviet Union and its satellite countries.

Undiscriminating about where his byline appeared, Dobie also wrote for pulp magazines such as *Ranch Romance* and *Zane Grey's Western Magazine*. Best of all for Dobie was the June 1952 issue of the *Atlantic Monthly*, one of the country's most respected magazines. The *Atlantic*'s cover featured a Norman Rockwell-esque painting that depicted a grinning J. Frank Dobie, at home in the brush country. Inside was his story "My Horse Buck."

News of his *Atlantic* cover made the papers in Texas, and, indeed, Dobie's genius for publicity continued unabated. Even the *Dallas Morning News*, which no longer ran his column, carried some sort of update on the colorful author every few weeks. One typical example came when Dobie arrived in the city, bearing a dogwood tree to help christen a local bookstore's new location. Such canned events were the media's staple, Dobie knew, and he made sure that a reporter was on hand for the occasion. The newspaper obligingly reported, "With the aplomb that only Dobie can muster, he delivered [a tree that was] only mildly shaken by its plane ride."[5]

Although Dobie did not possess a record player and he continued to denounce the electronic media, he narrated some of his tales for spoken word record albums. Television was a more difficult medium to crack. He once wrote, "Not three people in a million will be any happier inside themselves because of . . . television sets." Still, he allowed TV production companies to dramatize his stories, and he also narrated a television documentary on Texas for NBC in the mid-1950s. But Dobie's own appearances were hardly successes. Historian Joe Frantz saw Dobie interviewed on the "Today Show" in New York, and he recalled that it "was a disaster." The interviewer "had the New York entertainer's feeling for the quick line, and Dobie was rambling as Dobie did with such relish." The interviewer "kept interrupting, trying to squeeze out the point ahead of time. Dobie ignored him. Dobie was never invited back, and shouldn't have been. He belonged to the campfire and a ring of silence, where a man lets his words and thoughts lie on the wind a while before moving on to the next stanza."[6]

\* \*

Dobie continued to be active in politics, although he cut back considerably on the time he invested in such matters. "If you work for causes," he later observed, "you've got to be leading society around every two or four years."[7] Shortly after his separation from the university, he agreed to become the editor of the financially troubled *Texas Spectator*, a crusading liberal weekly established in 1945. His halfhearted tenure lasted only a few months, and the *Spectator* folded the next year.

In the 1948 presidential election Dobie opposed Harry Truman, whom he considered "a very mediocre person in intellectual powers." Instead, he supported the third-party candidacy of leftist Henry Wallace, who had once been Franklin Roosevelt's vice president and spoke of creating a friendship with the Soviet Union. Dobie considered Wallace "a true friend of the common people," and he was named the Texas chair of the Wallace campaign.[8]

He quickly ran into another political buzz saw. Wallace was very controversial in Texas and even many liberal Democrats distanced themselves from him. Lyndon Johnson, the former New Dealer who was running against Coke Stevenson for the Senate that year (and would later win by the notorious eighty-seven-vote margin), denounced Wallace as an appeaser, "a farmer planting strange seeds in our soil, seeds of fear, of false hope, dragon seeds of ultimate destruction."[9]

Dobie had accepted the Wallace chairmanship on impulse. He wasn't that devoted to the candidate—certainly not enough to get drawn into another round of political squabbles. He called the media to announce that, while he personally supported Wallace, "I'm not having a doggone thing to do with this campaign." His affiliation, Dobie told reporters, was "strictly honorary." With that, Dobie made a conscious decision to withdraw from the ever-present political battles that raged in Texas. He would, however, find a few choice occasions in the future to fully engage the opposition.[10]

★ ★

Dobie's turn towards liberal humanism had come too late for him to invent an entirely new career for himself as a writer. His books would continue to be about the past, and they would remain centered in the Southwest. But his work now contained a crucial difference—it was written from the perspective of someone who was aware of the present and who thought about the future, a man who wanted to guide others towards the liberated mindset he himself had achieved.

Unlike the revered longhorn, Dobie's new book, *The Voice of the Coyote*, published in 1949, addressed a species that was widely considered vermin, particularly among rural people in the American West. Yet as he worked on the book, Dobie developed a sympathy for the animal, which he described as a feeling "that has grown until it lives in the deepest part of my nature."[11]

Dobie's political thoughts were clearly expressed in this new work, as he used the coyote to score jabs against his opponents. He admired how coyotes "often exhibit extraordinarily individualistic conduct," and he praised their ability to adapt to change, contrasting them against "the haters of Franklin D. Roosevelt [who] have never comprehended that he did not make change as much as meet it." Dobie also pointed out that coyotes demonstrated altruistic behavior, and were not simply the "fang and claw" stereotypes that have been "overemphasized by a society devoted to propagating the philosophy of greed under the guise of free enterprise."[12]

He became a fierce advocate for coyotes, calling for their preservation in the face of widespread extermination campaigns then under way. He detailed the cruel methods employed in killing the animal, and he provided anecdotal and scientific evidence to back up his assertion that the highly intelligent creatures deserved human admiration. Dobie also suggested, decades before the term "eco-tourism" entered the language, that preserving the coyotes' home range would provide more economic benefits than trapping and killing them. "If chambers of commerce in Western states that strive for tourist money had imagination," Dobie wrote, "they would arrange hearing places for those who would like to hear coyote voices . . . and they would both lure and educate tourists . . . ."[13]

Dobie collected much of what humans have observed about coyotes over the generations, and for the first time he included Native American folktales as part of his work. By now, he no longer saw Indians as enemy savages, but rather, he professed his admiration for "Indian harmony with nature."[14]

*The Voice of the Coyote* received the usual accolades, regionally as well as nationally. *Time* magazine called it "the final word on its subject, and very nearly one of those classic studies that seem to sum up everything that was written before it." Yet national reviewers also voiced, for the first time, criticisms about Dobie's writing style. His habit of piling on anecdote after anecdote, without any regard to the book's overall structure, resulted in "a lack of focus . . . a discursiveness," one reviewer ventured. Dobie's "material is so voluminous," another reviewer observed, that it would benefit from more "classification and organization." The mixed reviews were evidence that a younger generation—which had not been raised on oral storytelling—was coming of age, and this new generation would be far less enamored of Dobie's casual, folksy approach to writing.[15]

Elder Statesman
1951–1958

B Y EARLY 1951, J. Frank Dobie was sixty-three years old, his mother had been dead for two years, and the Dobie children realized that the time had come to sell the family ranch in Live Oak County. The land had never been particularly profitable as a cattle ranch, but it did show some promise for oil exploration, and the family retained half the property's royalty interests after selling out to a group of Houston businessmen. The buyers told Dobie that he was welcome to return for a visit anytime, but he knew "that an end has come to something of a lifetime. I could not feel thus towards any other plot of ground on earth. . . . Something irreplaceable has passed from me."[1]

Dobie's friend and one-time mentor John Lomax had also died, and Dobie mourned the fact that so much of Lomax's unique character was forever lost. He wrote to Roy Bedichek, "I was thinking what a pity it will be if we do not sometime for our own delectation set down the warty realities, along with hearty and not-warty other realities about Lomax."[2]

Bedichek was already into his seventies, and mortality was beginning to hang over both men, although, as Bedichek observed, they "should not repress the aspiration to be happy in old age." Dobie's weekly columns began to take on a nostalgic tone as he increasingly revisited his past. He wrote of his boyhood in the Brush Country, his mother and father, his teaching at Alpine, his experiences during World War I, and the transformative effect of listening to Santos Cortez tell stories on his Uncle Jim's ranch in 1921. Dobie also told readers, "I have never gone in for ancestor worship," and then proceeded to relate what he had learned about the first Dobies to come to Texas. All of these were pieces of an autobiography that he was beginning to assemble.[3]

Although he was once again turning his gaze to the past, Dobie's perspective was now too informed to allow him to descend into mere sentimentality. In fact, he expressed regret about his earlier self, admitted to readers that "a long time ago" when he was a graduate student at Columbia, he had been ill equipped to appreciate other cultures. "It is depressing to me," he wrote, "to think about what a damned fool I have been in the past."[4]

With the season of pause and reflection came the career-spanning accolades. The Texas Institute of Letters named him its first-ever Fellow and in 1950 created a Distinguished Achievement Award, which it split between Dobie and Katherine Anne Porter—who did not show up to claim her half of the prize. Dobie's alma mater, Southwestern University in Georgetown, staged a grand "Dobie Day" celebration in 1952, which was broadcast live on statewide radio. A laudatory article in *Arizona Highways* bestowed on him the title "Mr. Southwest." In 1955, the Texas Folklore Society honored Dobie with a tribute dinner that featured testimonials from Bedichek, Webb, and others. Webb stole the show by delivering a mock-serious speech in which he praised Dobie's "unfailing spirit of obedience, his submissiveness to authority. He likes all the people in high places," Webb said to laughter, "and he is especially fond of regents."[5]

★ ★

In 1953, Dobie and Bertha used some of the proceeds from the sale of his family ranch to purchase a new spread, a 746-acre ranch about thirty-five miles west of Austin in the hills overlooking the Colorado River. Dobie named it Cherry Springs and set about restoring the native grasses and stocking it with a few head of cattle. The ranch proved to be not only a great weekend escape for the Dobies and their friends, it also served as a writing retreat for him, a place where he could get back in touch with the natural rhythms that pulsed so closely to his own heart. One friend observed that Dobie seemed "most happy . . . when he is on his ranch."[6]

Despite no longer being on the front lines of the state's political battles, Dobie still made his opinions known when he felt the stakes were high enough to warrant comment. He became one of the few Texans to force-fully challenge Wisconsin Senator Joseph McCarthy in 1952, when the right-wing senator, funded generously by Texas oilmen, was at the height of his powers and was considered by many to be "Texas's Third Senator."

Dobie also aided the *Texas Observer*, a new liberal weekly founded in 1954. He not only penned articles for them, but also made financial contri-butions to the publication. Dobie also supported UT's campus newspaper, the *Daily Texan*, when its young editor, Willie Morris, battled against cam-pus censorship. Dobie famously observed during that crisis that the univer-sity's regents "are as much concerned with free intellectual enterprise as a razorback sow would be with Keats's 'Ode on a Grecian Urn.'"[7]

Dobie remained a strong supporter of his friend Ralph Yarborough, who became Texas's liberal standard-bearer during the 1950s. When Yar-borough ran against McCarthyite Allan Shivers for governor in 1954, he sought to outflank Shivers on the right by claiming a stronger fealty to seg-regation. Dobie wrote to Yarborough, "I think you underrate people. . . . I know you are not going to emulate McCarthy, but why don't you stand up straight for the best traditions of the Democratic party?"[8]

After Yarborough lost that race, Dobie visited the campaign headquar-ters in Austin. Yarborough recalled that Dobie's "presence carried with it an aura of inspiration, an uplift of spirit. Cheers and laughter returned, and as Dobie smiled his greetings with that white mop of hair waving, it sud-denly seemed as if the burden of defeat and debt had been lifted . . . ."[9]

Within a few years, Yarborough's persistence paid off, as he won a spe-cial election for U.S. Senator in 1957 and was reelected to a full term the following year. Dobie campaigned on his friend's behalf, denigrating Yar-borough's millionaire opponent Bill Blakely as a drugstore cowboy trying to "buy his way into the Senate."[10]

After Yarborough won, Dobie asked his newly elected friend to consider becoming a statesman rather than a politician. "I think that if you throw in with the Old South reactionaries on the race question," Dobie wrote, "you will be going against the tides of history."[11]

Yarborough did renounce his earlier segregationist stands, and he be-came, along with Lyndon Johnson, the only senator from the south to vote in favor of a civil rights bill. Yarborough was also instrumental in making Padre Island a national seashore and he preserved parts of the rapidly dis-appearing Big Thicket as a national forest. As a special favor to Dobie, he helped get a commemorative stamp issued for Charles Russell, Dobie's favorite western artist. Yarborough also saw to it that Dobie was appointed as an Honorary Consultant in American culture to the Library of Congress. Dobie, in turn, praised Yarborough as "perhaps the best-read man that Texas ever sent to Washington."[12]

☆ ☆

In 1952, when he was sixty-four, Dobie published *The Mustangs*, a book about the free-running horses of the American West. The book was written during the McCarthy era, which led Dobie to celebrate the horse's "spirit of freedom" during "a time when so many proclaimers of liberty are strangling it."[13]

*The Mustangs* covered familiar territory for many readers, yet it also showed evidence of Dobie's continued evolution as a thinker and a writer. For the first time in any book, he meticulously footnoted his sources, and he proudly told friends that he felt like he could finally qualify for a Ph.D.

Dobie's work on *The Mustangs* also gave him more regard for "pure" historians, those devoted to "naked collection of documented facts." While these types of scholars "may not open windows," Dobie wrote, neither do they "shrink intellects." Nevertheless, he made an eloquent argument that historians should aim higher: "Excellence in historical writing," he observed, "comes only when interpretative power, just evaluation, controlled imagination and craftsmanship are added to mastery of facts."[14]

Dobie did his best to meet such standards. He explained how the horses came to the American West by tracing their origins back to Spain and the Arabian Peninsula, and he explored their effect on Native American and cattle cultures. Along the way, he told stories about notable horses and famous horse people. His range of knowledge, as always, was extremely impressive.

Dobie continued his passion for making humanistic points within his books, writing, "The easiest tag for the lax-minded has always been color, and from the remotest times to the present, superstitious beliefs pertaining to horse colors have been as common as those pertaining to man colors." Dobie then quoted an old saying about horses, which he makes clear should also apply to people: "A good horse can never be of a bad color, no matter what his coat."[15]

*The Mustangs*, like so many of his other books, received rapturous reviews, and it came to be seen as the definitive work on the subject. Dobie's admirers considered it his best book ever. Still, a pattern was emerging in

his books on animals, and within a few years, one observer, Martin Shockley, would draw attention to this habit of Dobie's in a humorous way. Introducing Dobie at a meeting of the Texas Institute of Letters, Shockley
remarked:

> I came to Texas with about the average ignorance and prejudice. I had
> always considered the coyote a pesky varmint, a cunning chicken thief,
> a sneaky villain best seen over the sight of a .30-30; then I read a book
> by Frank Dobie and learned that the coyote is a noble creature with a
> proud and independent spirit and a fierce love of freedom.
>
> I had always considered the longhorn a stupid cow critter, all bone,
> gristle, and stringy meat, mean, vicious, and hard to handle; then I read
> a book by Frank Dobie and learned that the longhorn is a noble crea-
> ture with a proud and independent spirit and a fierce love of freedom.
>
> I had always considered the mustang the sorriest specimen of horse-
> flesh, hammer-headed, wall-eyed, ewe-necked, sway-backed, bushy-
> tailed, ornery and dangerous; then I read a book by Frank Dobie and
> learned that the mustang is a noble creature with a proud and indepen-
> dent spirit and a fierce love of freedom. Now they tell me Mr. Dobie is
> writing about rattlesnakes, and I anticipate an agonizing reappraisal.[16]

★ ★

While Dobie's engagement in specific political issues waned, he continued
to develop as Texas's leading free-range thinker. He never challenged the
world's greatest philosophers in this regard, but instead came across as
something of a wise village elder. His wisdom was hard won, it was honestly dispensed, and it inspired readers. As Yarborough later wrote, Dobie's
life "evolved into a quest for justice for all men, for freedom of the human
mind from fears and superstitions, for a just sense of values in life. With his
voice and his pen he was a freedom fighter for mankind."[17]

One of Dobie's favorite targets was organized religion. He reminded
readers that Jesus Christ and Martin Luther were nonconformists, and in
response to an announced drive to put more "spirituality" into Christmas,
he wrote, "They may as well put on drives to have newspaper editorials be
humorous. Like humor and intelligence, spirituality comes from within.
The way towards it is the way of contemplation and serenity . . . the very
opposite of organized 'drives.'"[18]

Dobie also criticized public prayer, and said of football coaches who led their teams in prayer before games, "Who believes that God cares whether one bunch of young apes or another has the most success with an inflated pig bladder?"[19]

During the devastating drought of the 1950s, many Texans prayed for relief. Governor Allan Shivers, perhaps hoping to remind voters that God, rather than himself, was responsible, proclaimed a day of prayer to break the drought. Dobie responded by ridiculing the notion, wondering why Shivers, "as a very astute real estate trader," did not buy a bunch of dry worthless land in West Texas, and "take along a colony of believers, and lead them in prayer" to refashion the desert into a Garden of Eden.[20]

After the Soviets launched Sputnik and seemed to have surpassed the United States in science, many Americans called for imposing reading regimens in order to catch up. Dobie wrote, "I consider such reasoning puny and lopsided. Books, and therefore libraries, contain the inherited wit, wisdom, humor, life . . . of all the centuries during which man has left a record of what he's thought and done. . . . The great reason for reading books and for valuing libraries is to live life more abundantly, to think more justly, to be in love more delightfully, and to use the sputniks more wisely when we get them."[21]

As Dobie's outlook broadened he began to rethink his views of early Texas history, becoming something of a prototype for the revisionist historian. He wrote columns debunking frontier heroes and he pointed out that the celebrated Battle of San Jacinto was, in fact, "a massacre after the first eighteen minutes. . . . The 600 dead Mexicans never were buried, to match Goliad. Neither old Sam Houston nor anyone else could control the San Jacinto soldiers."[22]

Dobie's continuing disgust with Texas bragging led him to point out that many of the state's most famous brags weren't even original to Texas, and had in fact been borrowed—plagiarized, as Dobie put it—from other states.

In a Texas Independence Day column, Dobie announced that he would write about "the most admirably independent man that, to my limited knowledge, history records." Was this Davy Crockett? Sam Houston? No. Instead, Dobie spent the remainder of his column sketching the life of Socrates.[23]

Dobie's most famous crusade during the 1950s was his series of attacks on professional educators, whom he considered "the chief practitioners in the unctuous elaboration of the obvious." He wrote, "Dullness is their trade, it is safer than vitality." He called for abolishing college education courses and he described how "fifty years ago I started looking for students with first class minds who voluntarily and with enthusiasm and appreciation took courses in education I have found not one to this day." He added, "but I've encountered many first class students who would not go into teaching because they would have to take those stupefying courses before they could be certified."[24]

Dobie pointed out that UT offered 351 different courses on education and judged that, "They are all to make teachers more banal-minded . . . ." Educators, Dobie said, "are johnny-on-the-spot with Rotary Club optimism, football teamwork, Dedication-to-America Week, and such as that: but many of them don't know . . . knowledge." Taking into account "their contribution of flabbiness rather than of fiber to the minds of tens of millions of Americans during the twentieth century," Dobie wrote, "I accuse them of having been far more lethal enemies to society than all the Communists dreamed up by the late Senator Joe McCarthy . . . ."[25]

Dobie's exhortations for intellectual rigor were not just public posturing; they also reflected his deepest-held principles. He constantly lobbied other writers to speak the truth in their work. When William Vann began writing a history of the Texas Institute of Letters, Dobie counseled him: "Put in human details, put in differences of opinion that have shown up, put in the evolution of the character of the membership." Later, Dobie took Vann to task, writing to him, "It still sticks in my gorge that you expurgated, excised, cut out, [without] consultation, a sentence of mine critical of the Texas Philosophical Society." Dobie ended his letter with this intonation: "Fear of realities and fear of grappling with the facts will weaken any writing."[26]

When a college student approached Dobie and said that she was writing her master's thesis on him, he told her: "Now—people—writers come to me. They want me to approve what they are going to say about me. That's nonsense, you know. You can write what you damn please about me— otherwise it's no use your writing at all!"[27]

# Literary Dictator
## 1952–1960

O N THE EVENING of December 12, 1953, J. Mason Brewer, who had once worked as a porter at Austin's Driskill Hotel, integrated the building in grand style, appearing at a banquet in his honor wearing a tuxedo.[1] The occasion was the publication of his book *The Word on the Brazos*, the first-ever work by an African American scholar to be published by a white Texas press.

Brewer had long ago compiled what his friend Dobie considered "a remarkable collection of Negro folktales, very skillfully told," yet he had never been able to publish a book of his work.[2] When the director of the newly reconstituted University of Texas Press asked Dobie for some publishing recommendations, the old man's first suggestion was a book by Brewer.

Dobie wrote the preface for *The Word on the Brazos* and served as the master of ceremonies at the banquet, which also featured a talk by Hodding Carter, the Pulitzer Prize–winning Mississippi newspaperman. The hotel had almost cancelled the integrated gathering after receiving several threats. Further complicating matters, Dobie recalled, were "certain messages" received by the dinner's sponsor, Mrs. O. H. Davenport, "from the professional 'Daughters'—daughters of this, and daughters of that." Dobie remembered that Mrs. Davenport had said in response, "I told them to kiss me where I couldn't, and I didn't mean my elbow."[3]

Dobie was also president of the Texas Institute of Letters that year and he made sure that the organization inducted Brewer as its first black member. Brewer went on to publish four more books, becoming one of the nation's leading chroniclers of African American folklore. Although he had studied "scientific" folklore at Indiana University, he preferred, like Dobie, to "improve" the stories for retelling. Scholars affiliated with the American Folklore Society did not approve, and a review of Brewer's book in the journal wondered "how much of [the] art lies in the narrators, and how much in the rewriter?"[4]

Brewer's work has remained historically important, even as debates have arisen, just as with Dobie's protégé Jovita González, over how much of this "folklore" was calculated to be subservient to Anglo hegemony. Both Brewer and González underreported the active spirit of resistance within their respective communities. Some critics have blamed Dobie for this, rather than considering the effects of Texas's prevailing social conditions at the time. No evidence suggests that Dobie ever sought to restrict anyone's thinking. Further, his encouragement of Brewer and González—often in the face of opposition from other Anglos—made it possible for them to publish their work in Texas. Prior to Dobie's efforts, African American and Mexican American intellectuals often fled the state and ended up in New York City or on the west coast. The very presence of Jovita González and J. Mason Brewer helped inspire succeeding generations to continue the struggle to improve Texas, rather than to simply abandon it.

★  ★

Dobie's weekly column offered the best possible exposure for up-and-coming writers, and his attention—or neglect—could make or break a book. He received constant solicitations from writers, publishers, agents, and the media. Ambitious young writers were expected to pay a call on Dobie. It was a rite of passage.

Many writers were also personally indebted to Dobie. He allowed them to use his ample personal library for research, and he took time to give constructive readings of hundreds of manuscripts, although his brutal honesty scared off many would-be writers. He also helped secure publishers, offered sage advice, and for those he believed in most strongly he contributed prefaces and introductions for their published works. As one of the beneficiaries of Dobie's attention, Wayne Gard, later wrote, "Probably Dobie has helped more younger writers than has any other current American author."[5]

Dobie reading to Caroline Wardlaw, ca. 1950s. Southwestern Writers
Collection/The Wittliff Collections, Texas State University–San Marcos.

Dobie was a born mentor, and bringing along young writers was akin to teaching classes full of bright, highly motivated students. Dobie also understood that he had an obligation. "Many have helped me," he said, and so "I like to help others." He aided men more often than women, but that was because of the type of writing he was interested in, rather than any gender preference. One of his most accomplished protégés, in fact, was Elithe Hamilton Kirkland, author of the Texas historical novels *Love Is a Wild Assault* and *Divine Average*. He also mentored other Mexican American writers, including Fermina Guerra, a student of his at the University of Texas in the 1940s. She considered him "one of those rare persons who possesses the qualities of a true friend," and under his direction she wrote several very fine historical sketches of the South Texas border country, many of which focused on women's lives.[6]

Dobie's willingness to assist a good writer or a good cause was part of the Texas ethos he was raised with. Unlike the rivalries and backbiting found in many literary communities, Dobie was straight up, always, and those he aided believed that Dobie was "free from the professional jealousy that affects" other writers.[7]

Dobie's own literary tastes were very distinctive, even narrow, and he had little inclination to recognize or appreciate work that fell outside his boundaries. As the literary scholar Don Graham has pointed out, Dobie "completely failed to recognize or relate to the real triumph of Modernism in the revolutionary works of James Joyce, Ernest Hemingway, William Faulkner" and others such as Katherine Anne Porter. As another critic, James Ward Lee, has observed, Dobie instead "liked books about cowboys . . . Texas Rangers, mustangs, humble Mexicans, ranch life, and buried treasure."[8]

Dobie's humanistic progression led him to a broader understanding of the world, but as far as his native Southwest was concerned, his reading habits were little changed from earlier years, and he was ill equipped to recognize that a major evolution was underway in Texas literature.

Since World War II, writers began focusing less on Texas history and instead novels became the state's dominant literary expression. Dobie had often been critical of regional fiction, believing that, "Actualities in the Southwest seem to have stifled fictional creation." He asked readers of his column, "How many novels, all of them feeble, have been written about the Alamo, about the Texas pioneers, early Texas trails? Not one of them has ever been able to match non-fictionalized reality."[9]

Yet a younger generation of novelists was publishing significant works that documented vital aspects of Texas's present. Among these was George Sessions Perry's *Hold Autumn in Your Hand*, an account of a year spent sharecropping that won a national award in 1942. Perry was among several young Texas writers turning heads in New York. Many were addressing previously uncharted topics: civil rights, politics, crime, and the state's oil boom. In contrast to the lingering romanticism of Texas historians, many of the novelists were clear-eyed in their observations, and they employed modern literary techniques such as realism and irony.

By 1949 the state's literary culture reached a new milestone, as over one hundred books associated with Texas were published. The annual Texas Institute of Letters banquet featured the chief editor of MacMillan Publishing in New York, and boosters grew so heady with his presence that some, such as book critic Lon Tinkle of the *Dallas Morning News*, began to compare "the development of Texas literature with that of [ancient] Greece."[10]

Dobie welcomed the idea of books that addressed contemporary themes and he recognized that the Southwest had "become predominantly urban." Yet in reality, he mostly ignored or discounted the new novels. Regarding Perry's *Hold Autumn in Your Hand*, Dobie believed that the author had "played with present-day life rather than grappled with it."[11]

Instead, Dobie used his newspaper columns to praise work such as *The Iron Mistress*, a novel about Jim Bowie and his famous knife. Dobie asserted that it was "the best historical novel published dealing with the Texas scene and with historical characters." *Time* magazine, meanwhile, panned it as a "creaking fictional makeshift." The novel is all but forgotten today.[12]

One writer much favored by Dobie was his good friend Tom Lea, the gifted artist who had illustrated *Apache Gold and Yaqui Silver* and *The Longhorns*. With Dobie's encouragement, Lea turned his hand to writing, and in 1949 he published his first book, a novel titled *The Brave Bulls*. Dobie praised its "economy, the clean-limbed saliency, and the strength," and he concluded that "clarity of both purpose and execution are constant in all of Tom Lea's work."[13]

Dobie was by no means alone in his opinion of Lea, who enjoyed rousing national success. *The Brave Bulls* was favorably reviewed, sold very well, and was made into a film starring Anthony Quinn. Lea's second novel, *The Wonderful Country*, which came out in 1952, made an even bigger impression, and the film version of that novel starred Robert Mitchum.

Lea quickly established himself as Texas's premier novelist and his stature began to rival Dobie's. His books sold more copies, and he even beat out Dobie in winning a Texas Institute of Letters Award for Best Book. Dobie, however, seemed proud, rather than jealous, of his younger friend's accomplishments, and he predicted in a column, "at no distant date Tom Lea will be recognized as the most original and the most potent creator, without exception, that the expanses of Texas can claim."[14]

Dobie was often generous with praise for friends, but friendship by itself didn't guarantee an unblemished review. One of his cohorts in Austin, Hart Stilwell, helped edit the liberal *Texas Spectator* and was often good company. In 1945 Stilwell published *Border City*, a well-received novel that drew attention to discrimination against Mexican Americans in South Texas. Dobie's brief comments on the novel were studiously neutral. Two years later, Stilwell published a thinly disguised memoir, *Uncovered Wagon*, that has since become part of the Texas canon, listed in such volumes as A. C. Greene's *Fifty Best Texas Books*. The best thing Dobie could say about the book in his short review was that it is "the most pitiless piece of realism that has ever come out of Texas." Then, hoping to elaborate, he added, "In places it is terrible."[15]

Another young writer Dobie was friendly with, Fred Gipson, had once been a student in his class, and later went on to win great acclaim with his novel *Old Yeller*. Writing of Gipson's early efforts, *Hound Dog Man* and *The Home Place*, Dobie praised Gipson's genuine characters, but then counseled that the books "lack the critical attitude toward life present in great fiction . . . ."[16]

A cousin of Dobie's, Frank Goodwyn, wrote *The Magic of Limping John*, a charming fictional adaptation of Mexicano folktales. Dobie faulted his cousin for not having "achieved objective control over imagination or sufficiently stressed the art of writing." Even Dobie's praise of Walter Prescott Webb's *Divided We Stand*, which had influenced him greatly, was blunted by his observation that the book's last chapter was "half-hearted" and "altogether unconvincing."[17]

Most of Dobie's friends were taken aback by his criticisms, although, once their trauma subsided, they recognized that his remarks were perfectly in character for a man who demanded intellectual integrity. "Hell," Dobie once wrote, "when I want to say something I say it out, and I don't go around behind tree stumps to get it suggested."[18]

Tom Lea and Dobie in El Paso, 1953. Special Collections,
University of Texas at El Paso Library.

\* \*

In 1952, Dobie issued a new edition of his *Guide to Life and Literature of
the Southwest*. This volume, he noted, was "Revised and Enlarged in Both
Knowledge and Wisdom." As with the first edition, Dobie refused to copyright the book. In his preface, he backtracked from the bold claims he had
made for the region's literature in his earlier guide, instead suggesting that
people in the Southwest would benefit more from reading *The Trial and
Death of Socrates* than "all books extant on killings by Billy the Kid."[19]

Dobie granted that the hundreds of the books recommended in the
guide had given him pleasure and enriched his own work. Yet he also observed, "they increasingly seem to me to explore only the exteriors of life
. . . ." Having to "reread most of them would be boresome, though *Hamlet*,
Boswell's *Johnson*, Lamb's *Essays*, and other genuine literature remain as
quickening as ever."[20]

Despite Dobie's revised preface, the guide itself followed the same well-worn reading trails he had marked out decades earlier. The chapter on "Range Life" dominates the book, and other chapters were devoted to increasingly arcane topics such as stagecoaches and the pony express.

Back in 1942, a reviewer of his first edition pointed out that he had ignored much of "the literature of the Old South in the Southwest and the distinguished body of New Mexico Indian material." The reviewer also noted that he "decidedly undersells the poetry, drama, and fiction of the Southwest."[21]

Those looking for improvements in this new edition were disappointed. The inconsequentially updated chapter on Southwestern fiction ignored a dozen or more notable newer novels, although Dobie found room to list his own books of folktales. The "revised" guide proved that, as Southwestern literature continued to expand, Dobie did not keep up with new developments.

A list of excluded authors would be very long indeed, but one worth mentioning is Karle Wilson Baker, a pioneering woman of Texas letters. Her novel of the oil patch, *Family Style*, had been a national bestseller and she was also "the best-known and most frequently anthologized poet from Texas in her lifetime."[22] In 1938 she became president of the Texas Institute of Letters and in 1952 she became the Institute's third Fellow, following Dobie and Webb in receiving that rare honor. Surely Dobie's guide, which included Eugene Cunningham's *Triggernometry* and Jack Thorp's *Pardner of the Wind,* could have found a place to mention Baker's work.

One could argue, however, that being ignored by Dobie was preferable to being recognized by him. In mentioning the New Mexico writer Mary Austin, who was now dead but had been a friend of his, he informed readers that she "seems to be settling down as an expositor. Her novels are no longer read."[23] In fact, Austin remains more popular than ever. Many academics study her work, and her fiction is available in modern editions for contemporary readers.

Dobie's critics have claimed that his omissions and failures are evidence of "his almost total ignorance of literary matters. He became a literary dictator without taste and without serious study," James Ward Lee wrote. "He knew nothing about literature . . . ." In fact, a more generous—and realistic—assessment is provided by Frank Wardlaw, a former director of UT Press, who observed that Dobie's "judgment is not, of course, infallible, and he has blind spots where certain kinds of books are concerned (haven't

we all?), but his mind separates the genuine from the spurious almost un-
erringly and he never hesitates to express his opinions forthrightly."[24]

As evidence of this, one can point to a book review that Dobie came
across in 1959. It was written by a young man named Larry McMurtry,
who was still in college, had not yet published a book, and was not yet
known. Dobie clipped the review and mailed it, along with a handwritten
note, to the current president of the Texas Institute of Letters: "This newspaper critic can think; he can write; he knows. Who is he? Better regard
him for Texas Institute of Letters."[25]

Dobie's imperfect literary instincts are best represented in his separate
reactions to two different writers who came of age in Texas during the
late 1950s. One was John Graves, who wrote *Goodbye to a River*, an elegiac
journey down the Brazos that weaves together history, folklore, ecology,
personal observations, and philosophical ruminations. Graves was one of
those writers who paid a call on Dobie, and Dobie effusively praised the
young author in his column, noting that while reading the book, "I realized that I've been waiting for it a long time."[26] Dobie's early assessment of
Graves proved to be correct, and *Goodbye to a River* has become one of the
most beloved Texas books ever published.

Around the same time, Dobie sent a letter to Texas Institute of Letters president William Vann, protesting the Institute's induction of a writer from Wharton, Texas. "I feel I have a right to veto the nomination of
Horton Foote," Dobie wrote. Of the future Pulitzer Prize–winning play-
wright, he observed, "I've seen [his plays] and don't think anything at all of
them."[27]

# End of an Era
## 1955–1959

**T**HROUGHOUT THE 1950S the friendship between Roy Bedichek and J. Frank Dobie strengthened. The men remained fixtures at Barton Springs during Austin's summers, and on the wall of Dobie's bedroom hung a photograph of his dear old friend, sitting in a rocking chair. When Bedichek turned seventy-nine in 1957, Dobie gave him a book on Socrates and inscribed it to "the wisest and justest and best man that I have ever known." Dobie continually lobbied Bedichek to work on an autobiography, and when the older man demurred, Dobie lamented in a newspaper column how Bedichek, "despite his superb books . . . has never approached a record of himself."[1]

Dobie mentioned Bedichek often in his columns, trying to capture some aspects of the man he described as "a Priest of 'Living in the Open.'"[2] Whenever Bedichek published a new book—he would publish three more after *Adventures with a Texas Naturalist*—Dobie became positively rhapsodic in his praise.

Dobie's other great friend during these years was Tom Lea, whose successful novels brought him to the attention of the fabled King Ranch, which was looking to commission an authorized history as it prepared to celebrate its one hundredth anniversary. The job paid one hundred thousand dollars—an astonishing sum for the time—along with all expenses.

Dobie and Roy Bedichek, ca. late 1950s. Southwestern Writers Collec-
tion/The Wittliff Collections, Texas State University–San Marcos.

The chosen author would travel to visit the King Ranch's vast holdings not
just in Texas, but also in Cuba, Brazil, and Australia.

Many believed that Dobie was the perfect choice. He had grown up
nearby, his brother worked as a foreman for the King Ranch, and Dobie
had already proved himself to be the leading interpreter of South Texas's
ranching culture. But as Lea recalled, the Kleberg family, who owned the

ranch, was "very much against Frank. I'm not sure what the origin of the trouble was except for Frank's great liberal politics. . . . So that's why I, and not Frank, got the job."[3]

Dobie likely would have refused the commission even if it had been offered to him. The King Ranch was famously protective of its image, and Dobie would never subordinate his independence for an "authorized" history. However, he did encourage Lea to take on the job, and after Lea had been working on the project for four long years, Dobie began to express regret. He wrote to Lea, "I am not a constitutional brooder, but in these last several months I have at times come near brooding over my responsibility for your getting into the King Ranch book." Dobie worried that Lea's long association with the ranch would subvert his artistic integrity. The next year, as Lea neared completion on the book, Dobie wrote to him, "I wonder if you are satisfied that, through the facts given, you have arrived at the truth. I believe that all great acquirers of material things . . . are greedy to the superlative degree."[4]

* *

While Lea was engaged burnishing the King Ranch's legend, Dobie's lifelong paternalism towards Mexicanos was set for a rude awakening. A young scholar at the University of Texas was putting the final touches on his dissertation, a piece of brilliant folkloric scholarship that would single-handedly upend the Anglo establishment, creating shockwaves that continue to register today.

Américo Paredes, who had earlier written the unpublished novel that featured an unflattering character based on Dobie, had decided for his dissertation to take on a topic that Dobie had often written about: the case of Gregorio Cortez, the subject of Texas's most famous manhunt. In Dobie's earlier accounts of the episode, he had incorrectly described Cortez as a bandit, and in 1923 he wrote that Cortez had been hanged after his capture. Later, in his Texas centennial publication, *The Flavor of Texas*, Dobie correctly noted that Cortez had not been hanged, but rather pardoned by a Texas governor. But then Dobie added—again incorrectly—that Cortez later "became a horse thief and was killed out near El Paso."[5]

Paredes's account, titled *"With His Pistol in His Hand": A Border Ballad and Its Hero*, explained the other side of the story. Cortez was no bandit, but rather a peaceable man who simply fought to protect his rights "with his pistol in his hand." He was not hanged, nor was he a horse thief. Cortez's

Américo Paredes, photograph by Walter Barnes Studio, ca. 1958. Southwestern Writers Collection/The Wittliff Collections, Texas State University–San Marcos.

case became symbolic of an entire people, and Paredes staked out an alternative view of the Brush Country's history, one that challenged the notions promulgated for years by Dobie, Walter Prescott Webb, and others.

By the time Paredes finished his dissertation, he and Dobie came to know each other and developed a modest friendship. "I got to like him very much," Paredes recalled. He added later, "He was a loveable old guy, but

to me, as far as his knowledge of Mexicans, he was a loveable old fraud."
Paredes and his wife visited the Dobie home several times, and the conversations there never ventured into contentious territory. The two men also
exchanged pleasant letters about Mexican American folk songs and other
topics of mutual interest.[6]

In Paredes's dissertation, Dobie received his share of criticism, as the
younger scholar sternly corrected Dobie's errors about Gregorio Cortez.
Paredes also condemned Dobie for his previously held belief that "ancient
war propaganda directed against Mexicans" was among "the best writing
done about Texas until recent times."[7]

Still, Dobie got off extraordinarily easy, especially compared to Walter
Prescott Webb, who was pilloried. Paredes quoted Webb's racist remarks
about Texas Mexicans, including the eminent historian's aside that his comments were made "without disparagement." Paredes responded, "Professor Webb does not mean to be disparaging. One wonders what his opinion
might have been when he was in a less scholarly mood and not looking at
the Mexican from the objective point of view of the historian."[8]

Paredes also took on the Texas Rangers, whom Webb had done so much
to lionize. Satirizing the often-inflated claims made on behalf of the Rangers, Paredes observed, "If all the books written about the Rangers were put
one on top of the other, the resulting pile would be almost as tall as some
of the tales they contain."[9]

Paredes's ironic jabs and finely honed sense of outrage were bolstered
by his extensive, well-documented research. His combination of scholarship and lively writing set a standard that has rarely been matched in the
half century since, and his work made it clear that previous depictions of
Mexicanos by Anglo American writers had grossly misrepresented his people's history. Paredes's weapon was his pen, rather than a pistol, but there
was no mistaking the fact that he had launched a revolution.

In 1956 Paredes's dissertation director recommended that UT Press
publish the work as a book. Frank Wardlaw, director of the press and a
good friend of Dobie's, was inclined to do so, despite the political fallout
that was sure to follow. Yet a problem existed. The press's titles needed to
be approved by a faculty advisory committee, and the chair of the committee was none other than Walter Prescott Webb.

Webb, contrary to legend, did not oppose Paredes's book. Instead, he
agreed that "a study and service like this was long overdue." As Wardlaw
reported to Paredes, Webb "has always considered it a weakness of his

book on the Texas Rangers that he was unable to give the Mexican attitude toward the Rangers, and their side of the border conflict, with any degree of thoroughness."[10]

Still, Wardlaw felt that the book had too much "bitterness and partisanship," and so he asked Paredes to tone down his criticisms of Webb. Paredes refused. Grudgingly, UT Press issued the book in 1958, eschewing the customary publicity and autograph party. Still, word of Paredes's book managed to get around, and before long a Texas Ranger showed up at UT Press's office, asking how to find the author because he wanted to "shoot the sonofabitch who wrote that book."[11]

Dobie's personal copy of *"With His Pistol in His Hand"* is interesting for its annotations, for they indicate how much Dobie's core viewpoints had changed. On page twenty of his book, Paredes wrote, "The picture of the Mexican as an inveterate thief, especially of horses and cattle, is of interest to the psychologist as well as to the folklorist. . . . The 'cattle barons' built up their fortunes at the expense of the Border Mexicans by means which were far from ethical. One notes that the white Southerner took his slave women as concubines and then created an image of the male Negro as a sex fiend. In the same way he appears to have taken the Mexican's property and then made him out a thief." In the margin next to this paragraph Dobie wrote, "Just about the truth."[12]

Paredes's book, which occasioned little notice upon its publication except among a few angry Rangers, nearly disappeared without a trace. And it might have, the author later noted, if Mody Boatright and J. Frank Dobie hadn't stepped forward. The two men helped keep the book in print by distributing copies to some four hundred members of the Texas Folklore Society. About the only copies that sold for many years, Paredes recalled, "were those that went out to [folklore society] members. It wasn't until the Chicano movement in California discovered the book in the 1970s that it really took off."[13]

With the emergence of Chicano literature, Paredes became the godfather of the movement, and *"With His Pistol in His Hand"* its cornerstone. The book has gone through twelve printings and is one of UT Press's bestselling titles ever. It was also made into a film in 1983, *The Ballad of Gregorio Cortez*, starring Edward James Olmos. It remains an extremely influential work, and is a standard text in several college courses.

Paredes founded the Center for Mexican American Studies at UT in the early 1970s and he continued to produce compelling scholarship throughout his career. Meanwhile, amidst his personal papers lay the manuscript for his unpublished novel *George Washington Gómez*, which he had written back in the 1930s and contained the unflattering "K. Hank Harvey" character based on Dobie. By the late 1980s, Paredes retired from teaching and began looking over his old manuscripts. In 1990, as Paredes turned seventy-five, Arté Público Press published his fifty-year-old novel.

Paredes decided to let *George Washington Gómez* stand as it had originally been written, and this literary time capsule provided a fascinating historical portrait of the Lower Rio Grande Valley, anticipating themes not addressed by Texas historians until decades later. The book also showcased Paredes's formidable writing talent and received many glowing reviews. *George Washington Gómez* has since become recognized as a significant Texas novel. One consequence of the book's popularity is that its contemptuous depiction of "K. Hank Harvey" has given rise to a stereotyped image of Dobie as a racist.

Paredes seemed somewhat apologetic afterward about his portrayal. "I was pretty harsh on Dobie in the novel," he said. Paredes noted, however, that this was "because I didn't know him when I was writing [it]." Paredes seemed to recognize that, despite Dobie's flaws, his intentions were often good. Soon after Dobie died in 1964, Paredes wrote kindly about him in the *Journal of American Folklore*. He also sang a corrido composed in Dobie's honor at the following meeting of the Texas Folklore Society. Nonetheless, Paredes's books have contributed significantly to a negative image of Dobie among Mexican Americans. Just as Dobie once dismissed all rebellious Mexicanos as bandits, he is now dismissed as a reactionary racist. The world may progress, but the misunderstandings remain.[14]

★ ★

Tom Lea finished his book *The King Ranch* around the same time UT Press was making preparations to publish Américo Paredes's dissertation. Lea's own work came out to over eight hundred pages. It was originally planned for private distribution only, but the King Ranch, sensing its commercial possibilities, sold the rights to Little, Brown and Company in New York. Anticipation swelled as people eagerly awaited the first-ever history of Texas's most famous ranch, written by one of the state's most famous writers.

Dobie was asked to review the book for the *New York Times*, and he wrote to Lea, "Nobody should review a book by a dear friend, but . . . I'll write you after I have read the work, and then you can compare what I say with what comes out in print."[15]

Tom Lea, ca. 1950s. Southwestern Writers Collection/The Wittliff Collections, Texas State University–San Marcos.

A month later, Dobie sent Lea his response. In contrast to Lea's novels, which Dobie saw as "models of economy," he viewed the King Ranch book as overwritten and overgenerous in its praise of the King and Kleberg families. He detailed a number of problems and concluded that the book, "never seemed to me to have been spun out of your own insides." At the end of his letter, Dobie made an apology of sorts. "If I were not so proud of you—and you know it—and didn't love you so much—and you know it—I never would have blurted out so much so savagely."[16]

Two weeks later, on Saturday, September 14, 1957, the city of El Paso celebrated the publication of Tom Lea's new book by staging a "Tom Lea Day," with a testimonial dinner at the city's country club. The event drew hundreds of people from all over the country, including writers, artists, movie directors, King Ranch executives, and at least one U.S. Senator. The city of Juarez, across the border, also participated by staging a grand bullfight in Lea's honor.

Frank and Bertha Dobie came to El Paso for the event, although they declined to attend the bullfight. As Dobie told a friend, "Beauty is not justified through violence."[17] Dobie did join the others in praising Lea at the testimonial dinner, but one thing he did not discuss was his review in the *New York Times*, which was scheduled to run the following morning.

Lea's book became an instant success. The initial printing of twenty thousand copies sold out the first day, and the publisher quickly ordered another twenty thousand rushed into print. Newspaper reviews were effusive. Walter Prescott Webb, writing in the *Dallas Morning News*, praised it as a "powerful portrait . . . a most creditable job writing history. The book deserves and will win prizes."[18]

In the *New York Times*, Dobie was gentler to Lea than he had been in his private letter, but his criticisms nonetheless emerged full force. "Sentimental praise and family-album minutiae weaken some parts," Dobie wrote. He also charged that Lea carried "glory too far" by suggesting that the King Ranch had been the birthplace of the modern ranching industry. Millions of Spanish Mexican cattle had been raised in South Texas, Dobie observed, "before King owned an acre or a cow."[19]

Dobie's reading of Paredes also influenced his view of *The King Ranch*. Paredes made him aware, at last, of the extent of Mexicano enmity towards Anglo landowners. Dobie now understood that the King Ranch and the Texas Rangers who worked on its behalf were accused of illegally dispossessing Mexicano land grant families. Lea's book said nothing about such matters; instead it studiously praised the King Ranch's business model. Dobie judged that "certain facts are omitted" in Lea's history, and he criticized the "rhapsodic treatment of relations between King Ranch vaqueros and owners," which he found "suggestive of Marse Chan and Old Black Joe Days."[20]

Dobie concluded his review by taking a swipe at Lea for going on junkets at the King Ranch's expense. The book, he wrote, "may not satisfy social scientists, but it is not social scientists that the King Ranch invites to go hunting along with United States Senators."[21]

Back in El Paso, when Lea finished reading the review, he tore it up. "It burned me," he said later. "I was pretty upset. It just made me goddamn mad that Frank had been here [for Tom Lea Day] knowing that he had written it and that it had been printed."[22]

★ ★

On the way home from Tom Lea Day in El Paso, Dobie, less than two weeks away from turning sixty-nine, began feeling uncharacteristically tired. When he and Bertha arrived in Austin, he refused to see a doctor. In this regard, he agreed with his friend Roy Bedichek, who did not believe in medicine. Bedichek liked to say, "A man ought to have as much sense as a cow. If a cow gets sick she quits eating and goes off and lies down." During one of their friendly arguments on the subject, Dobie had riposted, "I've skinned quite a few cows that never got up after lying down."[23]

A steady rain began to fall, heralding the end of a drought that had devastated Texas for much of the 1950s, but Dobie felt "draggier and draggier." Finally, one week after his review of Lea's book appeared, he told Bertha that he was driving out to their place at Cherry Springs, and that he "would be back in two or three days." Out on the ranch, he found the five-inch rain gauge full. He lit a fire, ate, and went to bed. The rain continued. The next day he felt even worse, and breathing became difficult. "Not long before sundown my head went swimming," he recalled. By late evening, he made it to the hall telephone, cranked the handle, and then passed out. Luckily the single telephone line was shared by the community, and the sound of the operator responding to the empty receiver woke up several neighbors. People checked on each other, and when they found that Dobie did not answer, someone went to his house. He was rushed to the hospital in nearby Johnson City and from there taken by ambulance to Austin in critical condition. He was diagnosed with pneumonia, which had seriously damaged his heart. No one was sure if he would live. Newspaper headlines carried the news across the state, and the hushed reports read like previews for his obituary.[24]

"While I was way down there so deep in the well everything in the world that passed into my consciousness seemed sharply etched, very fragile, and as sensitive as I was," Dobie recalled in a newspaper column dictated from his hospital bed. He began thinking of people he knew. "The image of Tom Lea came before me—not as artist or writer, but as a friend."[25] Many, many friends and admirers sent Dobie messages of goodwill. Lea, however, was not among them.

Dobie never missed a column during this period, thanks to help from Bertha. This was not a new development. She observed later, "Some columns were made, as a housewife may make a soup, of scraps and leavings." She recalled how, at times, Dobie's ideas for columns grew so weak that a friend once wrote, "You seem hard up for something to put in the Sunday papers, so I thought I would give you an item." That item, Bertha said, "duly appeared."[26]

Dobie spent six weeks in the hospital, and life became very different for him after his discharge. His heart and lungs were so damaged that he could not climb the stairs of his home—and his study, complete with his library, was on the top floor. Nor would he ever be able to swim in his beloved Barton Springs again. The steps down to the pool were too much for him to muster. His diet was closely monitored and he was "forever bereft of the exuberant energy that characterized him before."[27] He spent the next few months confined to a downstairs room in his home, where Bertha set up a makeshift study for him.

★ ★

Cherry Springs became another casualty of Dobie's illness. He wrote to a friend, "Well, I've sold the place. . . . It got so I had to get somebody to drive me out to it, and I couldn't take care of it. I feel lost without it." The following year, however, he and Bertha found another retreat, just eighteen miles west of downtown, where a series of lovely hills sheltered Barton Creek as it wound its way towards its rendezvous with Barton Springs. Sitting on the property was a modest house with interior walls over one hundred years old. The land was in good shape and wildlife abounded. This was "not an estate, not a ranch, not a farm," Dobie explained. "It is merely a place of some acres in the hills west of Austin." He named it "Paisano," Spanish for roadrunner, the Brush Country animal that had become his totem animal. The word also denotes "Fellow Countryman."[28]

As Dobie slowly recovered some semblance of his strength, he returned his attention to working on his autobiography and planned books on rattlesnakes, panthers, and cattlemen. Bedichek reported on his progress in a letter to a mutual friend. "I saw Dobie just a few minutes ago," he wrote, "and he is getting better. I found him working feverishly and directing the work of two secretaries. Physically he is still weak, but mentally he is as keen as ever."[29]

Bedichek's own health remained excellent as he turned eighty. He continued to go on camping trips, swim regularly in Barton Springs, and engage in animated conversation with friends. By May 1959, at eighty-one years of age, he completed his fourth book, which would be published as *The Sense of Smell*. On Wednesday, May 20, he took one of his grandchildren swimming in Barton Springs. The next morning he worked around the house a bit, and then asked his wife if they could have lunch a little early, as he was due to drive Dobie and another friend out to Paisano that afternoon. Mrs. Bedichek asked him if he wanted to wait for the cornbread she was preparing. "Oh, I'll wait," he said. "I need Southern corn bread." He took a seat in a chair, fell asleep, and quietly died.[30]

In the tributes that followed, Walter Prescott Webb composed a letter to his deceased friend. "Dear Bedi," he wrote, "You will be interested, and perhaps amused, to learn that you took a good deal of the sting out of your going by the manner of it. Those of us who listened to your vociferous comments on this subject know that you went exactly the way you wanted, as if you had designed it with the skill and determination you used in designing your own life. Few people are able to call their own shots as you did, right up to the end."[31]

*Twilight*

Bertha and Frank Dobie, portrait by Christianson-Leberman, ca. 1960s. Southwestern Writers Collection / The Wittliff Collections, Texas State University–San Marcos.

# One Touch of Nature, Plus
## 1960–1962

**I**'VE BEEN COMPOSING something quite ribald," Dobie wrote to a friend. His "scandalous subject" was a collection of the bawdy folklore that he had collected over the years, along with several new essays celebrating "naturalness" in writing. He had come a long way since his early days as a literary moralist. He set aside his other book projects to work exclusively on what he called "One Touch of Nature, Plus." He cheerfully informed a newspaper reporter of his intentions, saying, "If that book gets published, I will no longer enjoy the society of the respectable."[1]

Throughout most of his life, publishers would not print books that contained proscribed words or focused overtly on sex. D. H. Lawrence's *Lady Chatterly's Lover*, originally privately printed in 1928, only appeared legally in 1960 after an exhaustive legal process. One of the few modern novelists Dobie admired was Henry Miller, who seemed to Dobie to be completely natural, devoid of pretense—but Miller's masterwork, *Tropic of Cancer*, could not be legally published in the United States until a Supreme Court decision in 1964. Dobie had obtained and read copies of both books long before they received the courts' official sanction.[2]

Censorship, Dobie felt, was closely aligned with hypocrisy. In one essay for this new book, he described how Honoré de Balzac's *Droll Stories* "centers around a woman made for love—a woman of positive virtues who was

enjoyed by a bishop and other clerics. Then they burned her for 'sinning.'"
Dobie wrote, "If I could, I'd put . . . beautifully printed copies of it in all
Sunday Schools and other school libraries. . . . Religiosity over [sex] and
creed has produced more hypocrisy and more cruelty than all other factors
of life combined."[3]

Throughout his life Dobie had come across numerous accounts of
"earthy" folklore considered too risqué for his books. These included humorous tales of Sam Houston's defecation practices, stories of penis-swal-
lowing snakes, dirty limericks about virgins, and coarse jokes on such topics as the Texan who raped a grizzly bear. Dobie had also made numerous
personal observations that he had never been able to share. He had grown
up hearing "obscene" rhymes that were common among rural schoolchildren, but these had never been properly recorded and were in danger of
vanishing.

The time had come, he felt, to draw this previously expurgated material
out. He was partly influenced by the censorship battles raging across the
country as America entered the 1960s. "I am in permanent rebellion against
censors and censorship of the language, especially," he wrote to a friend. He
composed several essays noting how particular words, "piss" among them,
had been used in language and literature for centuries, yet had been sup-
pressed in recent decades. Modern college dictionaries did not even contain
the word "piss," Dobie snorted, although the word appeared—both as a
noun and a verb—in the original *Dictionary of the English Language* compiled
by Samuel Johnson back in 1755.[4]

"Piss" was perhaps the most overlooked area of Southwestern folklore,
Dobie felt. He collected several accounts, including the observation that
Kickapoo Indians would test their blood sugar by urinating near sugar ant
mounds and then gauging the ants' reaction. Dobie also described vaqueros who treated horses' eye infections by urinating on their hands, then
rubbing the liquid into the afflicted horse's eye. In *The Voice of the Coyote*,
Dobie had described how some hunters would "urinate all around a deer
carcass left out on the ground overnight" to protect it from coyotes. For
this new book, he was more direct: "I myself have pissed a ring around a
carcass to keep coyotes off until I could come back with a horse to carry the
carcass in."[5]

Dobie, doubtful of the book's appeal to mainstream publishers, wrote
the following:

I am not at all positive of what kind of reception this narrative essay of
mine in naturalness will receive,

I don't expect any of those publishing houses that specialize in
Bibles, cookbooks . . . Zane Grey's novels, college dictionaries that
don't even contain the word piss, in short all respectable publishers, to
publish this slight offering. I imagine it'll be published without any publishing imprint and sold under the rose.

As I compose it, I am nearing my 70th birthday, but I have no idea
of surrendering to the Philistines. I've always craved an abundance of
life. This is one more cry for it, and also a blow for freedom in speech.
. . . I'm going down the road and don't feel alone. It seems a sort of
merry way to me. As François Villon would say: "Return we to piss."[6]

Bertha did not approve of her husband's project, and she strove mighti-
ly to redirect his attention to other matters. He finally agreed to set it aside,
and the book was never published. The manuscript disappeared for a number of years but is now available to researchers.[7]

Dobie's increasingly "scandalous" nature was evincing itself in other
ways. He had long despised preachers "parroting their mummery" and his
tolerance for such activity diminished as he grew older. Even those minis-
ters he personally liked were not immune from his attacks. One, Edmund
Heinsohn, visited him after he became ill, and as Heinsohn was about to
leave, Dobie stopped him. "You seem to be a pretty intelligent sort of fellow," he said. "That being the case, how can you preach the kind of stuff
you preach?"[8]

Roy Bedichek had been equally distrustful of Christianity, as was Walter
Prescott Webb. Bedichek once told an interviewer, "I don't have what's
commonly called religion. I think I must have a kind of nature religion. I
feel sometimes that . . . life in every manifestation is a . . . part of God. . . . Of
course, I have no thought that there is anything after a person dies . . . ."[9]

Webb was "a freethinker, an infidel, as I am," Dobie noted. Webb had
little regard for most preachers. Of one, he had commented, "Hell, he's
the kind who, if he ever visited a whorehouse, would ask for a ministerial
discount!" Webb considered one preacher in particular "lazy," and when
that man asked Webb to give a sermon on the cowboy's religion, Webb,
much to the astonishment of his friends, agreed. On the appointed Sunday
morning, he "arose in the pulpit, looked out over the congregation, [and]
said that he had been requested to talk about the religion of the cowboy.

Then he grinned his rail-splitting grin and said, 'The cowboy didn't have any religion.'" Then he sat down.[10]

Dobie's feelings about religion led him to create a scene at the funeral of his best friend, Bedichek. Historian Joe Frantz, who was present, recorded what happened:

> Dobie grunted and heaved through the whole service. Without bothering to lower his voice, he kept a drumfire going . . . .
>
> "Cant! Pure cant!" he would say in a voice that could be heard several rows away.
>
> "Hush, Frank!" Mrs. Dobie would jab him, as if he were a kid who wouldn't behave in church.
>
> "Mummery!"
>
> "Hush, Frank!"
>
> "I don't care," he'd whisper. "Ed Heinsohn ought to be ashamed for saying such things when Bedi can't answer back."
>
> On the way from the church, Dobie announced to all who would listen: "When I die, I don't want my body inside any damned church where some preacher can insult my mind."[11]

Dobie's disruption of Bedichek's funeral was nothing compared to the stir he created later in the *Texas Observer* when the editors published a special issue on Bedichek. Dobie's remembrance appeared on the front page, and in celebrating his friend as "The Natural Man," Dobie described how Bedichek's elimination habits symbolized his independence. "It did him good . . . to walk out and empty his bladder on the ground instead of having to go in the house and empty it into a mechanical contrivance," Dobie wrote, adding, "I've heard him say that sometimes . . . he would dig a hole in the ground out in the yard near . . . his study—and excrete into it, covering the place with dirt like a cat. It gave him a satisfaction to fertilize the ground."[12]

The Bedichek family was devastated. This was not the eulogy they had expected. His widow, Lillian, called *Texas Observer* editor Ronnie Dugger to complain. Dugger sought to defend Dobie, writing to Mrs. Bedichek, "I printed Mr. Dobie's article the way I thought it should be printed, which was the way Mr. Dobie wrote it."[13]

Later, when Senator Ralph Yarborough moved to reprint the Bedichek issue as a special pamphlet, Bedichek's family demanded that Dobie's "excretory references" be deleted. The essays on Bedichek were later assembled into a book, *Three Men in Texas*, that also contained essays on Dobie and Webb. Dobie's comments about Bedichek's excretory habits were duly omitted from that volume.

\* \*

Tom Lea's silence ever since Dobie's review of *The King Ranch* made its message clear. It was "just the correct thing," Lea felt. "It got old Frank a bit." Finally, however, the two wives set about making things right, and Lea's wife, Sarah, arrived in Austin for a visit the following year. Dobie wrote to his old friend afterward, and quoted Matthew Arnold's observation that all explanations are tedious. "Now all I'll say is that I never did intend to question your integrity," Dobie explained.[14]

Later Lea traveled to Austin, where Dobie "gave me an abrazo [hug] and was very happy that we let bygones be bygones." Bertha told Lea that her husband had "suffered over" the review. "And I was glad he suffered," Lea said later. "I could never figure out how a friend would do that." The two men continued to exchange occasional letters in the years ahead, but their relationship was never again close.[15]

\* \*

In early 1961 Senator Clinton Anderson of New Mexico contacted the Federal Bureau of Investigation on a routine matter. The University of New Mexico wished to honor J. Frank Dobie, but wanted a background check to avoid any political embarrassment. Anderson's request sparked a new review of the FBI's files on Dobie.

Agency officials were clearly disturbed by what they found. Dobie belonged to numerous liberal organizations, including the National Committee to Abolish the Poll Tax, the Civil Rights Congress, and the National Federation for Constitutional Liberties. Though tens of thousands of law-abiding U.S. citizens supported these causes, the FBI considered the organizations to be Communist fronts, and supporters of such organizations were branded as Communist sympathizers.

Further arousing suspicion, Dobie had helped initiate an amicus curiae brief to the U.S. Supreme Court, urging it to declare the Internal Security Act of 1950 unconstitutional. The FBI did not seem mollified by the fact that this onerous act had only been passed over President Truman's veto, or that the president had declared it a great "danger to freedom of speech, press, and assembly," or that much of the act was later overturned by the courts and by Congress.[16]

The FBI's view of Dobie darkened even further when it learned that he had signed a petition in support of the scientists who had urged the cessation of nuclear testing. Making matters worse, he had also signed a petition to abolish the House Un-American Activities Committee. Finally, and perhaps most damagingly, this new review brought up Dobie's newspaper column from 1947, in which he had criticized the FBI's "Gestapo tactics."[17]

A memo containing all of this information about Dobie began circulating among senior agency officials. Once the FBI's second-in-command, Clyde Tolson, received the information, he wrote a note in the file to his colleagues: "I am curious as to why we have not investigated this man." Another official noted below Tolson's addendum, "I am too."[18]

The FBI memo stressed that Dobie needed to be brought to heel for his "propensity for signing appeals supported by the communist movement." Officials added their handwritten annotations to the document. One wrote, "Seems to me we should build a fire under an 'educator' such as this." Underneath that, another official wrote, "I certainly concur."[19]

It is impossible, nearly half a century later, to discern exactly what FBI officials meant when they spoke of the need to "build a fire" under Dobie. However, it is easy enough to surmise, considering that the agency, under J. Edgar Hoover, had become quite adept at harassing political opponents.

Beginning in 1956, the FBI instituted a Counter Intelligence Program, which directed its agents to "expose, disrupt, misdirect, discredit, or otherwise neutralize" its targets. This was done through a variety of nefarious methods. The FBI smeared people by planting false stories and forging correspondence. They also interfered with jobs and tried to break up marriages. Obvious surveillance was used as an intimidation tool, as were break-ins and vandalism. Agents also planted false evidence in order to obtain arrests. While these activities were ostensibly directed towards "subversives" who threatened national security, the process invariably ensnared many law-abiding citizens—those whose sole "crime" was that their political beliefs did not match those of the FBI.[20]

A few days after the memorandum on Dobie made the rounds, FBI Director Hoover issued a directive to the San Antonio office. Hoover provided a list of Dobie's "questionable" activities and he concluded, "In view of the above information, you should review your office indices and check confidential informants and established sources to determine additional subversive data relating to Dobie." Well aware of Dobie's status as a public figure, Hoover counseled, "In your contacts you should be most circumspect in view of subject's prominence so that no embarrassment is caused to the Bureau."[21]

In the spring of 1961, FBI agents set out to secretly investigate Dobie. From sympathetic administrators at the University of Texas they obtained his personnel files from the university. They also checked the Dobies' credit history and spoke to officials at the Austin Police Department and the Department of Public Safety. A prominently placed undercover informant within the Communist Party told them that he only knew Dobie through the newspapers, and he had "never known Dobie to have any connections with the Communist Party."[22]

The heart of the investigation consisted of interviews with people who knew Dobie personally, but were politically opposed to him. One informant, who had clashed with Dobie at UT, called him "an exhibitionist. He loves to make statements and get his picture in the paper." The informant added that, "we all agreed he was one of the sorriest teachers we ever had. He would come to class wearing cowboy boots and wearing a big hat. On some occasions he would bring a guitar or some other musical instrument for the purpose of entertaining the students. The students loved him because many times he did not do a great deal of worthwhile teaching."[23]

Other informants were similarly harsh in their assessments. One described Dobie as someone who wants "to stick his nose in a lot of things just for publicity." Another, who worked in the Office of the President at UT, stated that "he is the type of person that enjoys the limelight; however, very few people take him seriously."[24]

Despite the personal and political antipathy expressed toward Dobie by these informants, they were unanimous in the view that he did not represent a subversive threat to the United States. As one informant said, "I do not feel that Dobie would do anything to injure the United States."[25]

In its report, the FBI field office concluded, "In view of information and results of investigation . . . it is believed no further investigation in this case is warranted and is so recommended. It is noted that Dobie is 73 years old, in ill health, and the possibility exists that Dobie could become aware of the inquiry being made concerning him and would attempt to embarrass the FBI."[26]

With that recommendation, the San Antonio office of the FBI sent a memorandum to Hoover announcing that "this case is being placed in a closed status." The agency, as it turned out, would not build a fire under him after all. From all available evidence, it appears that Frank and Bertha Dobie never became aware of the FBI's investigation.

      ★ ★

By early 1962, the seventy-three-year-old Dobie "was still under doctor's orders to take daily rests and avoid activity."[27] But as a new political issue arose in Texas, the old lion roused himself for one final battle. Many of the same forces that had led to Homer Rainey's ouster from UT and to the rise of McCarthyism in Texas were again on the move. This time, the idea was to cleanse Texas entirely of "subversive" thought by eradicating any school textbook that deviated from "Americanism"—as defined by Dobie's old friend J. Evetts Haley.

Haley led a group called "Texans for America" that waged an energetic campaign of intimidation against teachers, school boards, universities, writers, and politicians. The sixty-one-year-old Haley was already drawing plenty of media attention for a high-profile case against the federal government (which he lost) and for getting into yet another fistfight during a political argument—this time inside the office of a West Texas college president.

Haley also led a campaign against the Supreme Court in the wake of its *Brown v. Board* decision. At a "National Indignation" convention in Houston, Haley told the crowd that one of his colleagues "has turned moderate" because "all he wants to do is impeach [Chief Justice Earl] Warren [but] I'm for hanging him." *Life* magazine was already referring to Haley as a "crackpot." In Texas, however, he retained plenty of followers as the state's conservative zeal hardened in opposition to John F. Kennedy's presidency.[28]

Haley's group had already forced the withdrawal of books such as *The Grapes of Wrath* from school libraries in West Texas, and he denounced textbook writers who "play down the Constitution and . . . play up Negro Communists." His organization opposed any favorable mention of the income tax, social security, the United Nations, farm subsidies, the Marshall Plan, federal funding for schools, UNESCO, or integration.[29]

Texans for America also demanded that textbooks delete any reference to people whose "loyalty to America" was in question. Such names included Albert Einstein, William Faulkner, Ernest Hemingway, Willa Cather, Langston Hughes, Carl Sandburg, and several others. J. Frank Dobie also appeared on the blacklist.[30]

Haley argued during a press conference that "using books by writers with subversive connections gives them status in the eyes of children, even though the immediate reference might be innocuous." On the same occasion, one of Haley's followers criticized Dobie's belief that free speech extended even to Communists, and asked, "Do you think this man is worthy of being presented to our children?"[31]

Dobie roared to life in his columns, and he also published commentary in magazines and journals. In his most widely distributed response he wrote, "Censorship is never to let people know, but always to keep them in ignorance; never to bring light and aliveness, but always to darken and dull; never to make free souls expand, but to suppress and confine them."[32]

In March 1962, the Texas Legislature called a public hearing on the issue, and defying his doctor's orders, Dobie led a delegation from the Texas Institute of Letters to testify at the state capitol. J. Evetts Haley also appeared, and he and Dobie shook hands and sat side by side, waiting their turns to speak as an overflow crowd looked on from the galley.

Dobie was direct, as always. He thundered at Haley during his testimony, "A censor is always a tool. . . . Not one censor in history is respected by enlightened men of any nation. . . . Any person who imagines he has a corner on the definition or conception of Americanism and wants to suppress all conceptions to the contrary is a bigot and an enemy of the free world."[33]

When Haley's turn came, he avoided taking on Dobie and confined his attacks to a Southern Methodist University professor. Then the committee announced a dinner break and Dobie left the building to go home. Haley returned afterward to continue his testimony. This time he lashed out at Dobie personally, calling him "a member of a number of subversive orders and movements," who associated with "long-haired, super-intellectuals, super-sophisticates . . . the authentic liars of Texas."[34] Dobie was stunned. "I didn't think he would attack me personally," he told a reporter. "He hates, hates, hates."[35]

After the hearing, one of the legislators who supported Haley issued a statement to the press. "There is one thing we can be thankful for, that we have only one J. Frank Dobie . . . ." The legislator expressed his fond hope that Dobie's "kind do not multiply faster than the Good American people can keep them in control."[36]

Sunset
1962–1964

**D**OBIE'S ENERGIES ebbed and flowed, and he told a reporter after his seventy-third birthday, "When the juice is turned on I do fine." Young newspaper reporters across the state were assigned to write feature stories on the man they knew only as a wise old liberal, a "sage of the sagebrush." Their stories often emphasized Dobie's faith in the younger generation. "I think we're getting better," Dobie said. "I'm an evolutionist. Evolution doesn't go backward." When the first appearance of the mop-topped Beatles aroused controversy, Dobie suggested that they were preferable to the John Birch Society. The Beatles, Dobie observed, "add a lot to life. I don't see anything bad about them."[1]

Dobie was not supposed to drive. Doctor's orders. But on a Friday night in November 1962, he was behind the wheel of his Ford station wagon when he ran a stop sign and crashed into a car driven by Polk Shelton, Jr., a twenty-year-old University of Texas student. Shelton was thrown from his car and wound up with an injured leg, a concussion, and a deep gash that ran from the top of his forehead down to his right eye. Dobie suffered a head injury and lay gasping from a fractured neck that collapsed his windpipe. An emergency tracheotomy saved his life. He couldn't speak for several days afterward and remained in intensive care. Finally, after about two weeks, "he talked his way out of the hospital."[2]

Dobie was never entirely well again. Even getting out to Paisano became difficult. He abandoned four of the five book projects he had underway and decided to focus on just one, a series of portraits of Southwestern characters he called "Cow People."

★ ★

After Roy Bedichek's death, Dobie seldom saw Walter Prescott Webb. "Bedi was the peg on which a number of my happiest associations with Webb hung," Dobie noted.[3] In March 1963, Webb was driving back to Austin from a book signing event in San Antonio with his wife, Terrell Maverick Webb, when he fell asleep at the wheel. The car rolled several times and the couple was thrown clear. His seriously injured wife survived the crash. Webb died instantly.

Dobie approved of Webb's exit, just as he had of Bedichek's. "Any man who has seen and been a part of life wants to leave it before decomposing into a senile vegetable," he wrote afterward. "Webb died standing up. . . . In a flash he passed from wisdom and happiness to whatever death means." Later he amended his sentence, replacing "whatever death means" to "the finality of death."[4]

★ ★

Dobie had not published a book of new material in over a decade, not since the appearance of *The Mustangs* in 1952. In the meantime, he recycled his earlier work for anthologies, although he carefully rewrote the old pieces, making them more direct and evocative than they had been in the original telling. He was gaining greater control over his writing as he grew older.

In the summer of 1963 he decided to escape the Texas heat by going to Berkeley, California, to work on *Cow People*. He returned to Austin on his seventy-fifth birthday. Bertha and a group of reporters and photographers met him at the airport. When asked about his birthday plans, Dobie said, "I don't see anything to celebrate until I finish this manuscript."[5]

The Kennedy assassination brought home the ugliness of Texas's right-wing extremism, as there were even reports that some schoolchildren in Texas had applauded when informed of the president's murder. The assassination struck Dobie as the culmination of all the right-wing hatred he had seen building over the years. He reacted by publishing a long essay in the *New York Herald-Tribune*. In contrast to his earlier views, in which he expressed hope that humankind was getting better, an air of resignation hung over him, as though nothing could be done to cure humanity from "radical conservatism."[6]

Dobie found himself in Dallas a few months later for the Texas Institute of Letters annual meeting in March 1964. Katherine Anne Porter, at last, was scheduled to attend and give the major address. However, she became ill at the last moment and cancelled. Dobie, as always, stepped in as the replacement. The trip, however, drained much of his remaining strength.

He was being forgotten already. A committee of scholars and critics selected works for Lyndon Johnson's "White House Library," which was said to "provide a basic library of all American writing." None of Dobie's books were listed, "although a dozen inferior books by other Texans were," an outraged newspaper columnist wrote.[7]

Lady Bird and Lyndon Johnson arranged to set things straight. An invitation was issued to visit the White House, but Dobie turned it down, citing his poor health. Then Johnson called, and not even Dobie could resist his arm-twisting. A few days later Dobie and Bertha were flying to Washington, D.C. Dobie reported to readers of his newspaper column about his experiences, and he described the president in glowing terms, gauging that Johnson's interest in helping the poor and improving education proved that he was no longer solely about "egotism and ambition," but rather compassionate about "the human race itself." Dobie also praised Lady Bird, describing her honest and caring interactions with others, and he predicted that she would become known as one of the great first ladies in American history. He summed up his and Bertha's experience by writing, "We came away from the White House realizing more than ever that the friendliness and hospitality of the First Lady of the land and her husband are sincere."[8]

The trip further weakened Dobie, and back in Texas he was hospitalized for another five weeks. His heart was deteriorating and his lungs were filled with fluid. The doctor removed enough liquid, Dobie wrote to a friend, "to swim a catfish." He added, "I dictate this from the hospital but expect to be out soon. All I need is energy. That is all the people in the graveyards need."[9]

A few weeks later, President Johnson announced that J. Frank Dobie was being awarded the Presidential Medal of Freedom, the nation's highest civilian honor. The ceremony would be held in September.

Dobie completed work on *Cow People* but was too weak to go to Washington and claim his medal from the president. Bertha went instead, and Johnson bestowed it to her with a kiss, which he said "was strictly for her."[10] She returned home to present the medal to her husband.

Harry Truman and Dobie visit with Lyndon Johnson in the Oval
Office, 1964. Southwestern Writers Collection/The Wittliff Collections, Texas State University–San Marcos.

A few days later, on the morning of September 18, 1964, the mailman
delivered the first copy of *Cow People*, which had been rushed to him by
his publisher. Dobie looked over the volume with great satisfaction. It was
a handsome book and the portraits he assembled contained some of the
strongest, most disciplined writing he had ever achieved. He no longer romanticized the old-timers; instead he saw them for what they were—fellow
humans who were tough and admirable in some ways, limited in others.

Later that afternoon, during his customary siesta, he died of a heart attack in his sleep.

At his funeral, a friend observed, "His shaggy head was always a little
ahead of his body. Those of us who had the privilege of knowing him well
could always say: There freedom walks, there freedom thinks, there freedom
talks, there freedom teaches, there freedom acts, there freedom hopes."[11]

# Dobie's Legacy

**S**ATURDAY, DECEMBER 14, 1985: Frank had been dead twenty-one years, Bertha eleven. Both were buried in the Texas State Cemetery. Their house and its contents were left to a devoted nephew, Edgar Kincaid, Jr., who had lived in the home until he died in 1985.

A cold front was blowing through and the temperature dropped to twenty-five degrees as people began forming a line outside the Dobie home at dawn. The previous day's *Austin American-Statesman* announced an estate sale, set to begin at 9:00 a.m. Among the items advertised were Dobie's desk, rare and inscribed books from his personal library, fine art, rawhide chairs, Bertha's custom made china, "plus many miscellaneous household items and appliances."[1]

The University of Texas, just across the street, had earlier purchased the entire writing office of California pulp writer Erle Stanley Gardner, creator of the Perry Mason series. Gardner's study had been stripped clean, "right down to the carpeting," and transported to Austin, where it was reassembled and opened to the public as an exhibit.[2] The Gardner collection was part of the Harry Ransom Humanities Research Center, named for the university chancellor who began the world-renowned collection during the 1950s. Ransom was a personal friend of Dobie's and he ensured during his tenure that the bulk of Dobie's library and writing archives came to UT.

Not everything, however, was turned over to the university. The Dobies kept many of their books, including those Frank had inscribed to Bertha. Dobie also retained many of his personal papers. Among them were
voluminous research files for his books in progress, as well as many letters
to Bertha—those he sent during World War I and during the time he spent
as foreman of his Uncle Jim's ranch. Dobie also hung onto much of his correspondence with Roy Bedichek, spanning a thirty-five-year period, and he
kept several diaries, including a journal from his student days at Columbia
that he publicly claimed to have destroyed.

The University of Texas, however, expressed no interest in the material. One person waiting in line at the estate sale told newspaper columnist
Mike Cox, "If Harry Ransom were still alive, he would have written one
check for the house and all the contents and this place would have been run
by the university as a Dobie museum." Even those who were making off
with the Dobies' possessions seemed uneasy about the sale. One man, carrying an armload of artifacts down the stairs, paused to tell Cox, "In a way,
I feel like a grave robber."[3]

* *

The university's reluctance to step in and save Dobie's archives was undoubtedly influenced by the decline in his literary reputation. The attacks
on Dobie's writing began even before he died. The *Texas Observer* published a special issue on him in 1964 that included essays from a number of
friends and admirers. In an essay ostensibly praising him, one contributor
wrote, "There are dozens of people in Texas who are far better craftsmen
than Frank Dobie when it comes to putting down one word after another.
. . . ." The next year, Winston Bode's *A Portrait of Pancho* appeared. Even
this appreciative biographer noted that Dobie had "never been a master
architect at literature" and that a "reader has to strain to keep the thread"
in Dobie's books.[4]

A few years later, in 1968, Larry McMurtry made it official. Dobie, he
wrote, was "a hasty and impatient writer" and "his prose reflects his own
ambivalence toward literary activity." In 1981, McMurtry ratcheted up the
criticism, describing Dobie's books as "a congealed mass of virtually un-
differentiated anecdotage: endlessly repetitious, thematically empty, struc-
tureless, and carelessly written." Around the same time, academic critic
James Ward Lee judged Dobie's writing as "stilted and awkward" and at-
tributed Dobie's success to "his cleverness as a self-promoter, his untiring
ambition, some facility as a journalist, and the fact that Texas can always

use an 'interpreter' to the nation." In 1981, Gregory Curtis, the editor of *Texas Monthly* magazine, concluded, "Dobie, it seems clear enough now, was the author of bedtime stories for boys in junior high."[5]

By the 1990s, feminist critics were condemning Dobie as a paternalist and Chicano scholars were excoriating him as a perpetrator of racist histories. Dobie's association with Walter Prescott Webb has been most unfortunate in this regard, as he often gets lumped in with the historian. Dobie's literary stock plummeted to the point that one scholar described it as "a heap of rusted, abandoned scrap metal."[6]

Yet even as Dobie fell out of favor among scholars and critics, he has remained an important influence on Texas culture. A major part of the Dobie legacy is his 254-acre country place, Paisano, in the hills west of Austin. After his death a group of friends worked to preserve the home and land as a writers' retreat. Houston oilman Ralph Johnston purchased the property and safeguarded it while a fund-raising campaign was waged. The first contribution came from Lyndon and Lady Bird Johnson, and all proceeded smoothly from there. By 1967 the first writer moved in.

The Dobie-Paisano Fellowship, jointly managed by the Texas Institute of Letters and the University of Texas at Austin, has become the state's premier artist-in-residence program. It provides recipients with a six-month stay along with a modest living allowance, and it has nurtured many of the state's best-known writers in their early years, including Stephen Harrigan and Sandra Cisneros, the award-winning Chicana writer who noted that "Dobie Paisano is what altered my destiny, what allowed me to decide not to march out of the state."[7]

Dobie also has several schools named for him, including elementary, middle, junior high, and high schools in Dallas, Austin, San Antonio, and Houston. Adjacent to the University of Texas at Austin stands Dobie Mall, and, above that, Dobie Tower, a twenty-seven-story mirrored glass skyscraper that Dobie would have hated.

Perhaps the single best monument to Dobie is the statue outside Barton Springs swimming pool in Austin—*Philosopher's Rock*. Created by Glenna Goodacre in 1994 with funds raised through the efforts of Austin writers, this larger-than-life sculpture depicts Roy Bedichek and J. Frank Dobie, shirtless, in swim trunks, sitting on "Bedi's Rock" as they engage in animated conversation. Off to the side stands Walter Prescott Webb, in long pants, gamely barefoot, cigarette in hand, joining the fray. The statue is entrancing. Children love to climb up and sit in Dobie's lap.

*Philosopher's Rock*, the statue outside of Austin's Barton Springs by Glenna Goodacre. From left to right: Bedichek, Dobie, Webb. Photograph by Belinda R. Vega.

★ ★

The estate sale at the Dobie home in 1985 turned out to have a happy ending, thanks to the intervention of Bill Wittliff, who befriended Dobie in the early 1960s as a college student. Dobie had encouraged the young man's interest in the Southwest and once sent a note telling him, "I believe in you!" During Christmas 1963, Dobie invited Wittliff over to his house and "presented him with two grocery bags full of books, pamphlets, and things from his desk, all signed and inscribed." In 1964, after graduating, Wittliff and his wife Sally founded a fine book publishing company, the Encino Press, specializing in Texas and the Southwest. Dobie helped launch the press by giving the Wittliffs permission to publish one of his long essays in book form, royalty-free.[8]

By the 1980s the Encino Press had won over one hundred awards for design and content, but Wittliff's main source of income had become screenwriting. He had written and produced several films, including the classic television miniseries adaptation of Larry McMurtry's *Lonesome Dove*. Wittliff worked to decentralize Hollywood by making use of Texas locations and Texas talent whenever possible. In this way he helped build a native Texas film industry—one that expresses authentic, rather than manufactured, values. Dobie would have been very proud of him.

The day before the Dobie estate sale, Wittliff received a phone call from Willie Belle Coker, Dobie's one-time secretary who had inherited the house from Edgar Kincaid, Jr. She invited Wittliff over for an advance look, thinking that he might be interested in Dobie's old mesquite desk. Wittliff did purchase the desk, and while he was writing a check for it he noticed about thirty boxes stacked in a corner.

"That's what's left of Dr. D's writing archives," Coker told him.

Wittliff said, "Oh, those will be going to the University."

"Well, they know about them," she said, "but no one's called and no one's come over. The papers in those boxes are going to be sold in the estate sale tomorrow."[9]

Wittliff pulled his checkbook back out. He called his wife to make sure this new check would clear the bank, and then he purchased the boxes, which contained the entirety of Dobie's remaining literary archives—the manuscripts, letters, and diaries—along with the books Frank had inscribed to Bertha.

At the next day's sale, buyers carted off the Dobies' household artifacts, but Wittliff had saved Dobie's personal papers from being scattered to the four winds. Later, when Wittliff "realized the magnitude of what he had bought, he decided that it was too important to be in private hands and decided to place it in a library."[10] The Ransom Center at UT proved to be uninterested, and so, in 1986, with a gift of J. Frank Dobie papers, Bill and Sally Wittliff founded the Southwestern Writers Collection at Texas State University–San Marcos. The collection has grown and flourished in the years since.

★ ★

In 1986 the Dobie house went up for sale. The leading bidder was the Southland Corporation, which planned to raze the building and install a 7-Eleven convenience store on the site. At this point Dudley Dobie, Jr., a cousin of Dobie's, stepped in along with his wife Saza. The couple used their life savings to purchase the home and to have it completely renovated and restored. They also set about securing historical designations, including National Historic Landmark status.[11]

Meanwhile, the writer James Michener settled in Austin and became a major benefactor to the University of Texas. Michener also shared a very special connection to J. Frank Dobie. Back when he was a beginning writer and was plagued by self-doubt, Michener received a welcome letter of encouragement from Dobie. Michener eventually sold some seventy-five million copies of his novels and became one of America's most successful writers. But he never forgot the good deed Dobie had done for him.

By 1995, Dudley and Saza Dobie had ensured the Dobie home's preservation, but they had wearied of living on what had become a busy six-lane thoroughfare. They let it be known that they were interested in selling the house. At this point, Michener stepped forward. The Dobies agreed to deed the property to UT as a combination gift and sale, and Michener pledged fifteen million dollars to the university. The Dobie house is now home to the James A. Michener Center for Writers, one of the country's elite graduate writing programs. Literary discussions with writers from all over the world take place in the upstairs room that once housed J. Frank Dobie's study.

★ ★

In retrospect, it seems inevitable that Dobie's literary reputation would go into decline. He died in 1964, just as the greatest generational schism in American history was unfolding. It was only natural that many of his critics, who came of age in the 1960s, would want to make their mark by toppling the figure who cast the largest shadow over them. As later generations of feminist and Chicano scholars came to the forefront, the dead old white man proved to be an equally tempting target.

Dobie's critics have raised valid concerns about his writing, but they have also failed to recognize its virtues. The sheer volume of his work— over eight hundred magazine articles and nearly thirteen hundred newspaper columns in addition to his many books—made it inevitable that he would leave mountains of slag behind. Yet his writing should not be discarded, as portions of it capture vital aspects of Texas and the Southwest. Reading through Dobie's books today is akin to panning for gold on a proven claim. The reader will encounter plenty of sludge, but also glittering chunks of literary ore that can be found nowhere else.

As the writer John Graves has pointed out, Dobie's work is "uneven to be sure, often casual in expression, sometimes romantic or sentimental."

Yet Graves adds, Dobie's writing contains insights "into human matters that still move my imagination, and most of his material, historic or folkloric or whatever, I still find compelling stuff."[12]

Américo Paredes summed up Dobie's contributions by quoting approvingly a remark of John Lomax's: "No Texas library—pretty soon it will be no library in the world—can be called a complete library without a set of the Dobie folklore books. All the contents may not accurately be called folklore but there is a world of priceless stories about the basic beliefs, manners, customs, and legends of the people of Texas and her neighboring states."[13]

Many readers still find value in Dobie, and nearly all of his books remain in print. His work continues to influence those who make literary, rather than scientific, use of folklore. Dozens of novelists—including the region's greatest writers—have mined his folkloric accounts for use in their own fiction. Larry McMurtry's *Lonesome Dove* owes much to *The Longhorns*, Bud Shrake's *Blessed McGill* details a search for the Lost Tayopa Mine, and Cormac McCarthy's *Blood Meridian* utilizes portions of Dobie's writing on scalp hunters.

Dobie's many contributions to Texas culture seemed outsized in his time, but they have become subtler as the years have passed, and his hardwon achievements are now taken for granted. First and foremost, he was a catalytic force. As a champion of regionalism, Dobie not only changed people's attitudes within the Southwest, he also broadened the outlook of those in other parts of the country. Further, by making Texas a legitimate setting for literature, he inspired countless writers to recognize that their native soil could be the seedbed for literary expression.

Dobie was also decades ahead of his time in his view that historical writing should explain what life was like for common people, rather than focusing on a few "great men." This "social history" Dobie practiced has now become a standard approach, and the historical profession is much the richer for it.

Perhaps Dobie's most important influence on scholars is his insistence that their work be made accessible to readers. Prior to his time, college professors made few attempts to share their research with the public. Subsequent writers may have transcended Dobie's ability to present scholarship in an engaging manner, but he is the one who led the way.

In contrast to most other Anglo Texans of his time, Dobie encouraged Mexican Americans and African Americans to fully participate in the state's intellectual life. He had the courage to stand up to governors, senators, and his own university—not to mention risking the loss of his readership—in order to promote civil rights. For many progressive Texans in the 1940s and 1950s, Dobie was the sole public figure to express their values.

Most remarkably, Dobie refused to accept himself as a finished person. Though early circumstances had shaped him into a narrow-minded pastoralist, he willed himself into a profound transformation. He used his abundant gifts to guide humanity towards its noblest instincts, and along the way he discovered the greatest treasure of all—he became a liberated mind.

In the interest of readability, all citations that occur within a given paragraph have been combined into a single endnote, which appears at the end of the paragraph.

A LIBERATED MIND

1. J. Frank Dobie, *A Texan in England* (Boston: Little, Brown, 1945), 26.
2. Lyndon B. Johnson, taped telephone conversation with Marshall McNeil, April 11, 1964, sound recording, Tape WH6404.08, Citation No. 3008, Miller Center of Public Affairs, University of Virginia.
3. Don Graham, *Giant Country: Essays on Texas* (Fort Worth: TCU Press, 1998), 110.
4. Ronnie Dugger, *Our Invaded Universities: Form, Reform and New Starts* (New York: Norton, 1974), 55; Ramón Saldívar, *The Borderlands of Culture: Américo Paredes and the Transnational Imaginary* (Durham: Duke University Press, 2006), 117; Lon Tinkle, *An American Original: The Life of J. Frank Dobie* (Boston: Little, Brown, 1978), 146.
5. Wilson Hudson, "Love and Life of Freedom," *Texas Observer*, July 24, 1964, 5; J. Frank Dobie, *Some Part of Myself* (Boston: Little, Brown, 1967), 237.
6. Robert L. Dorman, *Revolt of the Provinces: The Regionalist Movement in America, 1920–1945* (Chapel Hill: University of North Carolina Press, 1993), 120.
7. Larry McMurtry, *In a Narrow Grave* (Austin: Encino Press, 1968), 46.
8. J. Frank Dobie, *Coronado's Children: Tales of Lost Mines and Buried Treasures of the Southwest* (Dallas: Southwest Press, 1930), 60.

9. Vivian Richardson, "J. Frank Dobie Digs for Texas Legends," *Frontier Times*, 1926, 38.

10. Dorman, *Revolt of the Provinces*, 309; "Grab-Bag Centennial Negates Virtues That Made Texas Great, J. Frank Dobie's Report Argues," *San Antonio Express*, October 8, 1935.

11. J. Frank Dobie, "Soldiers in England Air Views on Contrasts in British and U.S. Ways," *Austin American-Statesman*, May 7, 1944.

12. Joe Goulden, "J. Frank Dobie Explains His Convictions on Life," *Dallas Morning News*, November 13, 1960; Dobie, *Some Part of Myself*, 6.

CHAPTER 1: ALONG THE RAMIRENIA

1. Álvar Núñez Cabeza de Vaca, *La relación y comentarios*, http://www.library.txstate.edu/swwc/cdv/book/40.html.

2. David Montejano, *Anglos and Mexicans in the Making of Texas, 1836–1986* (Austin: University of Texas Press, 1987), 52.

3. Dagoberto Gilb, ed., *Hecho en Tejas: An Anthology of Texas Mexican Literature* (Albuquerque: University of New Mexico Press, 2007), 11, 14.

4. Dobie, *Some Part of Myself*, 121.

5. Ibid., 18.

6. Ibid., 58.

7. Tinkle, *An American Original*, 10.

8. J. Frank Dobie, "Possessed by Books," *Austin American-Statesman*, November 11, 1961.

9. Tinkle, *An American Original*, 3; Dobie, *Some Part of Myself*, 31, 13.

10. Dobie, *Some Part of Myself*, 31.

11. Ibid., 118.

12. Tinkle, *An American Original*, 7; Dobie, *Some Part of Myself*, 60.

13. Dobie, *Some Part of Myself*, 8.

14. Ibid., 64.

15. Ibid., 22.

16. J. Frank Dobie, *The Mexico I Like* (Dallas: Southern Methodist University Press, 1942), vii.

17. J. Frank Dobie, *Tongues of the Monte* (Boston: Little, Brown, 1935), viii.

18. Montejano, *Anglos and Mexicans*, 82.

19. J. Frank Dobie to Jovita González, January 11, 1927, J. Frank Dobie Papers, Harry H. Ransom Humanities Research Center, University of Texas at Austin; hereafter cited as Dobie Papers, HRC; Dobie, *Some Part of Myself*, 64, 31.

20. Dobie, *Some Part of Myself*, 26.

21. James McNutt, "Beyond Regionalism: Texas Folklorists and the Emergence of a Post-Regional Consciousness" (Ph.D. diss., University of Texas at Austin, 1982), 182.

CHAPTER 2: THE EDUCATION OF A BRUSH COUNTRYMAN, 1904–1912

1. Dobie, *Some Part of Myself*, 69–70, 118.

2. Ibid., 135, 122.

3. Ibid., 131, 129.

4. Ibid., 134.

5. Ibid.

6. Ibid., 137.

7. Ibid., 140.

8. Ibid., 140–141.

9. Ibid., 144–145, 145.

10. Tinkle, *An American Original*, 20, 19.

11. Ibid., 18, 24.

12. Ibid., 18.

13. Ibid., 122; Judson S. Custer, ed., *Dobie at Southwestern University: The Beginnings of His Literary Career, 1906–1911* (Austin: Jenkins Pub. Co., 1981), 53.

14. Custer, *Dobie at Southwestern University*, 48, 49.

15. *Handbook of Texas Online*, "Literature," http://www.tshaonline.org/handbook/online/articles/LL/kzl1.html.

16. Dobie, *Some Part of Myself*, 169.

17. Ibid., 169–170.

18. Ibid.

19. Ibid., 171.

20. Ibid., 173.

21. Ibid., 174; Catherine Supple and James Supple, "J. Frank Dobie at Columbia University, 1913–1914: His Letters and Diary," *Southwestern American Literature* (Fall 2006): 17.

22. Dobie, *Some Part of Myself*, 176.

23. Ibid., 177.

24. Roy Morris, Jr., and Roy Morris, *Ambrose Bierce: Alone in Bad Company* (New York: Oxford University Press, 1999), 249.

25. Custer, *Dobie at Southwestern University*, 57.

CHAPTER 3: FROM TEXAS TO NEW YORK, 1913–1914

1. Supple and Supple, "J. Frank Dobie at Columbia University," 21, 15.

2. Kevin Hill and Jim Stewart, "Greetings from Frank Dobie," in *2001: A Texas Folklore Odyssey*, ed. Francis Edward Abernethy and Shannon R. Thompson (Denton: University of North Texas Press, 2001), 102; Dobie to Bertha McKee, April 19, 1914, Dobie Papers, HRC.

3. J. Frank Dobie, "In New York or Amarillo, 'The People' Live," *Austin American-Statesman*, April 11, 1954.

4. McNutt, "Beyond Regionalism," 176.

5. Dobie, *Some Part of Myself*, 151.

6. Paul Clois Stone, "J. Frank Dobie and the American Folklore Movement: a Reappraisal" (Ph.D. diss., Yale University, 1995), 98.

7. Dobie, *Some Part of Myself*, 219.

8. Stone, "J. Frank Dobie and the American Folklore Movement," 95. A fascinating record of Dobie's time in New York can be found in the diary he kept, which is held at the Southwestern Writers Collection/The Wittliff Collections, Albert B. Alkek Library, Texas State University–San Marcos. See also Supple and Supple, "J. Frank Dobie at Columbia University."

9. Stone, "J. Frank Dobie and the American Folklore Movement," 96; Dobie to Bertha McKee, May 5, 1914, Dobie Papers, HRC.

10. Dobie, *Some Part of Myself*, 185; J. Frank Dobie, *Tales of Old-Time Texas* (Boston: Little, Brown, 1955), vii.

11. Supple and Supple, "J. Frank Dobie at Columbia University," 22.

12. Dobie, *Some Part of Myself*, 187.

13. Tinkle, *An American Original*, 58, 60–61.

14. Hill and Stewart, "Greetings from Frank Dobie," 102.

15. Dobie to Bertha McKee, April 19, 1914, Dobie Papers, HRC.

16. Dobie to Bertha McKee, March 15, 1914, Dobie Papers, HRC.

17. Tinkle, *An American Original*, 29.

CHAPTER 4: FIGHTING CONFORMITY, COURTING BERTHA, 1914–1916

1. Tinkle, *An American Original*, 29; Dobie, *Some Part of Myself*, 213.

2. Dobie, *Some Part of Myself*, 213; Tinkle, *An American Original*, 35.

3. Tinkle, *An American Original*, 38; Dobie to Bertha McKee, undated, Dobie Papers, HRC.

4. Tinkle, *An American Original*, 36.

5. Ibid., 43.

6. Ibid., 45, 39; Dobie to Bertha McKee, January 12, 1915, Dobie Papers, HRC.

7. Dobie, *Some Part of Myself*, 213, 215.

8. Tinkle, *An American Original*, 59.

9. Ibid., 52.

10. Ibid., 59.

11. McNutt, "Beyond Regionalism," 214.

12. Hansen Alexander, *Rare Integrity: A Portrait of L. W. Payne* (Austin: Wind River Press, 1986), 29; J. Frank Dobie Papers, Southwestern Writers Collection/The Wittliff Collections, Albert B. Alkek Library, Texas State University–San Marcos; hereafter referred to as Dobie Papers, SWWC.

13. Dobie to Ella Byler Dobie, November 20, 1915, Dobie Papers, HRC.

14. Dobie to Bertha McKee, November 20, 1915, Dobie Papers, HRC.

15. Dobie to Bertha McKee, November 28, 1915, Dobie Papers, HRC.

16. Tinkle, *An American Original*, 54.
17. Ibid.
18. Dobie to Ella Byler Dobie, September 26, 1915, Dobie Papers, HRC.
19. Tinkle, *An American Original*, 10.
20. Ibid., 60.
21. Ibid., 59, 60.
22. Ibid., 61.

CHAPTER 5: THE GREAT WAR, 1915–1919

1. Dobie, *Some Part of Myself*, 224.
2. Clipping enclosed in a letter from Dobie to Bertha McKee, November 28, 1915, Dobie Papers, HRC.
3. Dobie to Bertha McKee, April 19, 1914, Dobie Papers, HRC.
4. Dobie to Bertha McKee, undated/postmarked August 13, 1915, Dobie Papers, HRC.
5. For a full discussion of the Plan of San Diego, see Benjamin Heber Johnson, *Revolution in Texas: How a Forgotten Rebellion and Its Bloody Suppression Turned Mexicans into Americans* (New Haven: Yale University Press, 2003).
6. McNutt, "Beyond Regionalism," 186.
7. Dobie, *Some Part of Myself*, 225; Tinkle, *An American Original*, 75–76.
8. Tinkle, *An American Original*, 73.
9. Ibid., 76; Dobie, *Some Part of Myself*, 228.
10. Dobie to Bertha Dobie, undated/postmarked February 1917, Dobie Papers, SWWC.
11. Tinkle, *An American Original*, 76.
12. Ibid., 79–80.
13. Ibid., 82.
14. Stone, "J. Frank Dobie and the American Folklore Movement," 320.
15. Ibid., 88, 90.
16. Ibid., 85.
17. Ibid.
18. Ibid., 86, 91, 92.

CHAPTER 6: A RANGELAND EPIPHANY, 1920–1921

1. Nathan Miller, *New World Coming: The 1920s and the Making of Modern America* (New York: Scribner, 2003), 63.
2. Nolan Porterfield, *Last Cavalier: The Life and Times of John A. Lomax, 1867–1948* (Urbana: University of Illinois Press, 1996), 60.
3. J. Frank Dobie, "The Cowboy and His Songs," *Texas Review* (January 1920): 169.
4. Dobie, *Some Part of Myself*, 233.
5. Tinkle, *An American Original*, 97.

6. Ibid., 100; Dobie, *Some Part of Myself*, 233.

7. Tinkle, *An American Original*, 97.

8. J. Frank Dobie, "Luck Is Just Being Ready for a Chance," *Austin American-Statesman*, November 10, 1957.

9. Dobie to Bertha Dobie, November 6, 1920, Dobie Papers, HRC.

10. Dobie to Bertha Dobie, September 11, 1921, Dobie Papers, HRC, as quoted in McNutt, "Beyond Regionalism," 187. Although McNutt cites this letter from the Dobie Papers at the HRC, I was unable to locate this letter within the Dobie Papers. Several other letters written to Bertha from the Los Olmos Ranch do exist within the collection, but none of them refer to the Texas Rangers' raid.

11. Tinkle, *An American Original*, 102.

12. Dobie, *Some Part of Myself*, 234.

13. Ibid., 232.

14. Richardson, "J. Frank Dobie Digs for Texas Legends," 38.

15. Dobie, *Some Part of Myself*, 236.

16. Ibid.

CHAPTER 7: THE MAKING OF A FOLKLORIST, 1921–1923

1. Dobie, *Some Part of Myself*, 236.

2. Tinkle, *An American Original*, 99.

3. Dobie, *Some Part of Myself*, 238.

4. George Sessions Perry as quoted in *Moody Heritage Museum Hall of Honor, Historical Sketches: J. Frank Dobie, May 1, 1988* (Georgetown, Texas: Southwestern University).

5. Dobie, *Some Part of Myself*, 232; Richardson, "J. Frank Dobie Digs for Texas Legends," 38.

6. Stone, "J. Frank Dobie and the American Folklore Movement," 342; Dobie, *Some Part of Myself*, 240.

7. J. Frank Dobie, "La Canción del Rancho de Los Olmos," *Journal of American Folklore* (April–June 1923): 192.

8. McNutt, "Beyond Regionalism," 190. Dobie had titled his article "La Canción del Rancho de Los Olmos." As Boas pointed out in his letter to Dobie, the title incorrectly used the feminine article, "La," instead of "El" for the noun "canción."

9. Stone, "J. Frank Dobie and the American Folklore Movement," 401–402.

10. Francis Edward Abernethy, "Texas Folklore Society History, 1909–1997," www.texasfolkloresociety.org/History.htm.

11. Stone, "J. Frank Dobie and the American Folklore Movement," 325.

12. J. Forrest McCutcheon, "James Frank Dobie–Texan: An Appreciation," privately printed, 1932, copy held in the Dobie Papers, SWWC; J. Frank Dobie, Mody Boatright, and Donald Day, eds., *Backwoods to Border, PTFS XVIII* (Austin: Steck Company, 1943), x.

CHAPTER 8: THE RISING STAR, 1923–1926

1. Tinkle, *An American Original*, 107, 105.
2. Ibid., 106.
3. McNutt, "Beyond Regionalism," 222.
4. Dobie, "Luck Is Just Being Ready for a Chance."
5. Porterfield, *Last Cavalier*, 260.
6. Dobie, "Luck Is Just Being Ready for a Chance;" Alexander, *Rare Integrity*, 31.
7. Hilton R. Greer, "Secretary of Texas Folk-Lore Society Gathers Notable Collection of Legends," *Dallas Morning News*, June 1, 1924.
8. Review of *Legends of Texas*, edited by J. Frank Dobie, *Journal of American Folklore* (January 1926): 91.
9. Francis Edward Abernethy, *Texas Folklore Society, Volume 1, 1909–1943* (Denton: University of North Texas Press, 1992), 128.
10. Tinkle, *An American Original*, 201.
11. Rollo K. Newsom, email to author, September 26, 2007; Francis E. Abernethy, "Reader's Report" for the author's first draft for this book, submitted March 2008.
12. Alexander, *Rare Integrity*, 37.
13. Ibid., 41. For a fuller account of L. W. Payne's efforts on behalf of Dobie during this period, see chapter four of Alexander's *Rare Integrity*.
14. Stone, "J. Frank Dobie and the American Folklore Movement," 392.
15. Winston Bode, *A Portrait of Pancho* (Austin: Steck-Vaughn Co., 1968), 34.

CHAPTER 9: VOICES OF THE SOUTHWEST, 1926–1930

1. Dobie, "Luck Is Just Being Ready for a Chance."
2. Scarborough published the novel anonymously. See *Handbook of Texas Online*, "Scarborough, Emily Dorothy," http://www.tshaonline.org/handbook/online/articles/SS/fsc1.html.
3. For a fuller discussion of Katherine Anne Porter's Texas roots and influences, see Mark Busby, ed., *From Texas to the World and Back: Essays on the Journeys of Katherine Anne Porter* (Fort Worth: TCU Press, 2001).
4. For a fuller account of the New Mexico literary scene during this era, see Lois Palken Rudnick, *Utopian Vistas: The Mabel Dodge Luhan House and the American Counterculture* (Albuquerque: University of New Mexico Press, 1996).
5. McNutt, "Beyond Regionalism," 195.
6. J. Frank Dobie, "Texas-Mexican Border Broadsides," *Journal of American Folklore* (April 1923): 185.
7. McNutt, "Beyond Regionalism," 249.
8. José Limón, *Dancing with the Devil: Society and Cultural Poetics in Mexican-American South Texas* (Madison: University of Wisconsin Press, 1994), 66; McNutt, "Beyond Regionalism," 251.

9. Jovita González and Eve Raleigh, *Caballero: A Historical Novel* (College Station: Texas A&M University Press, 1996), xxii.

10. Limón, *Dancing with the Devil*, 61.

CHAPTER 10: REGIONALISM GOES NATIONAL, 1929–1930

1. Jeanne Douglas and Liz Wharton, "Maverick Professor," *Saturday Evening Post*, September 11, 1943, 15.

2. Bode, *A Portrait of Pancho*, 161.

3. Dorman, *Revolt of the Provinces*, 73.

4. Hudson, "Love and Life of Freedom," 5.

5. In recent years, John Young's heirs successfully petitioned the University of Texas Press to have Young listed as the primary author of this book, relegating Dobie to secondary status, despite the abundant evidence to the contrary. See Don Graham, "Who Wrote *A Vaquero of the Brush Country*? A Strange Case of Demoted Authorship," *Southwestern American Literature* (Fall 2006): 71–77. An excellent analysis of the book can be found in Mark Busby's article, "J. Frank Dobie's *A Vaquero of the Brush Country*: A Reevaluation," *Cross Timbers Review* 3.1 (1986): 5–11.

6. J. Frank Dobie, *A Vaquero of the Brush Country, Partly from the Reminiscences of John Young* (Dallas: Southwest Press, 1929), xi, 237.

7. Dobie, *Some Part of Myself*, 182; Dobie, *A Vaquero of the Brush Country*, x; Dorman, *Revolt of the Provinces*, 120; McNutt, "Beyond Regionalism," 71.

8. Dobie, *A Vaquero of the Brush Country*, x–xi.

9. McNutt, "Beyond Regionalism," 204.

10. Dobie, *A Vaquero of the Brush Country*, 46, 50.

11. Ibid., 46.

12. Ibid., 50.

13. Ibid., 62–63.

14. Armando C. Alonzo, *Tejano Legacy: Rancheros and Settlers in South Texas, 1734–1900* (Albuquerque: University of New Mexico Press, 1998).

15. Advertisement for *Coronado's Children*, by J. Frank Dobie, *New York Times*, February 15, 1931; Dobie to J. Evetts Haley, June 16, 1929., J. Evetts Haley Papers, Haley Memorial Library & History Center, Midland, Texas; hereafter cited as Haley Library.

16. Tinkle, *An American Original*, 127.

17. R. L. Duffus, "Lost Treasure in the Southwest," *New York Times*, February 8, 1931.

CHAPTER 11: DOBIE IN BLOOM, 1930–1934

1. A. C. Greene, "The Fifty Best Texas Books," in *Range Wars: Heated Debates, Sober Reflections, and Other Assessments of Texas Writing*, ed. Craig Clifford and Tom

Pilkington (Dallas: Southern Methodist University Press, 1989), 2.

2. "Dobie Works Out Traffic Fine: Jail Is Preferred Over $2 Payment," *Austin States-man*, April 3, 1936.

3. Tinkle, *An American Original*, 142. Now, decades later, it is difficult to determine the extent of Bertha's teaching. No records have been located indicating how often she substituted for her husband, and it is likely, as the scholar Mark Busby has pointed out, that neither Bertha nor Dobie wished to draw attention to the somewhat unusual situation, considering that UT was paying for him to teach the classes, rather than her.

4. Michael C. Steiner, "Regionalism in the Great Depression," *The Geographic Review* (October 1983): 442.

5. Ibid., 432.

6. McCutcheon, "James Frank Dobie—Texan."

7. Bill Warren, "Books," *Austin American-Statesman*, June 27, 1971. Clipping in the Bertha McKee Dobie Papers, A. Frank Smith, Jr. Library Center, Southwestern University, Georgetown, Texas; hereafter cited as BMD Papers, SWU.

8. Ibid.

9. Ibid.

10. J. Frank Dobie, *The Voice of the Coyote* (Boston: Little, Brown, 1949).

11. Bertha McKee Dobie, "On Waller Creek," typescript, BMD Papers, SWU.

12. Bertha McKee Dobie, "Notes on Gardening," typescript, BMD Papers, SWU.

13. Mody Boatright, "A Mustang in the Groves of Academe," *Texas Observer*, July 24, 1964, 13; Bode, *A Portrait of Pancho*, 37.

14. Winston Bode, "Pancho and the Patio," *The University of Texas: Alcalde*, December 1965, 15; Tinkle, *An American Original*, 171.

15. J. Frank Dobie, course papers for "Life and Literature of the Southwest," Dobie Papers, HRC.

16. J. Frank Dobie, *Guide to Life and Literature of the Southwest: with a Few Observations* (Austin: University of Texas Press, 1943).

17. Dobie, course papers for "Life and Literature of the Southwest."

18. Ibid.

19. Ibid.

20. Joe B. Frantz, *The Forty-Acre Follies* (Austin: Texas Monthly Press, 1983), 176.

21. Walter Prescott Webb, *The Great Plains* (Boston: Ginn and Co., 1931), 125–126.

22. Walter Prescott Webb, *The Texas Rangers: A Century of Frontier Defense* (Boston: Houghton Mifflin Company, 1935), 138, 128, 14.

23. Abernethy, *Texas Folklore Society, Volume 1*, 154; J. Frank Dobie, ed., *Tone the Bell Easy, Texas Folk-Lore Society, Number X* (Austin: Texas Folk-Lore Society, 1932), 10.

24. Abernethy, *Texas Folklore Society, Volume 1*, 154.

25. Dobie, *Coronado's Children*, 143.

26. J. Frank Dobie, ed., *Publications of the Texas Folk-Lore Society, Number V* (Austin: Texas Folk-Lore Society, 1926), 4.

27. J. Evetts Haley to Dobie, October 24, 1927, Dobie Papers, HRC.

28. Dobie to J. Evetts Haley, May 2, 1928, Dobie Papers, HRC.

29. Ibid.

30. J. Evetts Haley to Dobie, June 7, 1928, Dobie Papers, HRC.

31. J. Frank Dobie, "Picturesque History of Texas Ranch Is Related with Accuracy and Flavor," review of *The XIT Ranch and the Early Days of the Llano Estacado*, by J. Evetts Haley, *Dallas Morning News*, April 28, 1929.

32. J. Evetts Haley to Dobie, February 28, 1937, Dobie Papers, HRC; J. Evetts Haley to Dobie, March 2, 1937, Dobie Papers, HRC.

33. Stacey Sprague, "James Evetts Haley and the New Deal: Laying the Foundations for the Modern Republican Party in Texas" (master's thesis, University of North Texas, 2004), 60, 40, 44, 49.

34. George Norris Green, *The Establishment in Texas Politics: The Primitive Years, 1938–1957* (Westport, Conn.: Greenwood Press, 1979), 3.

35. Tinkle, *An American Original*, 140.

CHAPTER 12: INTO MEXICO, 1933–1935

1. Boatright, "A Mustang in the Groves of Academe," 12.

2. Dobie to Tom Lea, May 7, 1938, Dobie Papers, HRC.

3. Tinkle, *An American Original*, 140; Dobie, *Tongues of the Monte*, 28.

4. Dobie, *Some Part of Myself*, 249.

5. J. Frank Dobie, "Saltillo Diary," Monday, August 21, 1933, Dobie Papers, SWWC.

6. Dobie to Edgar Kincaid, February 16, 1933, BMD papers, SWU.

7. Tinkle, *An American Original*, 135.

8. Limón, *Dancing with the Devil*, 50; McNutt, "Beyond Regionalism," 193.

9. Américo Paredes, *A Texas-Mexican Cancionero: Folksongs of the Lower Border* (Urbana: University of Illinois Press, 1976), 71–72.

10. Dobie, *Tongues of the Monte*, 264; George Carmack, "A Lifetime of Love Between Texas Creeks," *San Antonio Express-News*, September 29, 1973, clipping, BMD papers, SWU.

11. Dobie, *Tongues of the Monte*, 264.

12. Tinkle, *An American Original*, 135.

13. McNutt, "Beyond Regionalism," 205.

14. Dobie, *Tongues of the Monte*, 44.

15. Ibid., 84; Dobie's immigration visa, 1932, Dobie Papers, SWWC.

16. Dobie, *Tongues of the Monte*, 239; C. G. P., "Tall Tales from the Wild Country of Northern Mexico," *New York Times*, November 10, 1935.

17. Henry Smith, "In His Most Recent Book Frank Dobie Uses Past Experience as

Divining Rod to Discover the Spirit of Mexican Life," *Dallas Morning News*, October 20, 1935.

18. Tinkle, *An American Original*, 143.

CHAPTER 13: THE FLAVOR OF TEXAS, 1936

1. For a fuller discussion of the Texas centennial, see Kenneth B. Ragsdale, *The Year America Discovered Texas: Centennial '36* (College Station: Texas A&M University Press, 1987).

2. Page S. Foshee, "San Antonio, the Centennial, and the Cenotaph: Grounds for Controversy: J. Frank Dobie and Pompeo Coppini" (master's thesis, Texas State University–San Marcos, 1993), 45.

3. Ragsdale, *The Year America Discovered Texas*, 111.

4. Ibid.

5. "Grab-Bag Centennial Negates Virtues."

6. Foshee, "San Antonio, the Centennial, and the Cenotaph," 103; Tinkle, *An American Original*, 158–159.

7. Foshee, "San Antonio, the Centennial, and the Cenotaph," 103.

8. Law Offices of Hertzberg & Kercheville to Dobie, January 6, 1936, Dobie Papers, SWWC; Dobie to Harry Hertzberg, March 11, 1936, Dobie Papers, SWWC.

9. Foshee, "San Antonio, the Centennial, and the Cenotaph," 106.

10. "Radio Address," transcript, Dobie Papers, SWWC.

11. Foshee, "San Antonio, the Centennial, and the Cenotaph," 113.

12. *Handbook of Texas Online*, "Texas Institute of Letters," http://www.tshaonline. org/handbook/online/articles/TT/kqt1.html; Dobie to William Vann, August 1, 1935, Texas Institute of Letters Papers, Southwestern Writers Collection/The Wittliff Collections, Albert B. Alkek Library, Texas State University–San Marcos; hereafter cited as TIL Papers, SWWC.

13. Dobie to William Vann, September 14, 1936, TIL Papers, SWWC.

14. William H. Vann, *Texas Institute of Letters, 1936–1966* (Austin: Encino Press for the Texas Institute of Letters, 1967), 7.

15. *Handbook of Texas Online*, "Texas Institute of Letters."

16. J. Frank Dobie, "A Corner Forever Texas," pamphlet, 4, Dobie Papers, SWWC; Bode, "Pancho and the Patio," 16–17.

17. Bode, "Pancho and the Patio," 16–17; Don Graham, ed., *Literary Austin* (Fort Worth: TCU Press, 2007), 182; Bode, "Pancho and the Patio," 16–17; Douglas and Wharton, "Maverick Professor," 15.

18. Frantz, *The Forty-Acre Follies*, 171; Chandler Robinson, *J. Evetts Haley and the Passing of the Old West* (Austin: Jenkins Pub. Co., 1978), 122; Bode, *A Portrait of Pancho*, 96.

19. Tinkle, *An American Original*, 155.

20. Ibid.

21. Ibid.

22. "Dobie Works Out Traffic Fine."

23. Ibid.

24. Tinkle, *An American Original*, 163; McNutt, "Beyond Regionalism," 239, 240.

25. J. Frank Dobie, *The Flavor of Texas* (Dallas: Dealey and Lowe, 1936), 2, 5, 125.

26. Ibid., 61–62.

27. Ibid., 61–62, 12.

28. Ibid., 7.

29. Michael Lind, *Made in Texas: George W. Bush and the Southern Takeover of American Politics* (New York: Basic Books, 2003), 3; Sprague, "James Evetts Haley and the New Deal," 62, 52.

30. Chandler A. Robinson, *J. Evetts Haley, Cowman-Historian* (El Paso: C. Hertzog, 1967), 12; J. Evetts Haley, *Charles Goodnight, Cowman & Plainsman* (Boston: Houghton Mifflin, 1936), 447.

31. B. Byron Price, *Crafting a Southwestern Masterpiece: J. Evetts Haley and "Charles Goodnight, Cowman & Plainsman"* (Midland, Tex.: Nita Stewart Haley Memorial Library, 1986), 43.

32. Don E. Carleton, *A Breed So Rare: The Life of J. R. Parten, Liberal Texas Oil Man, 1896–1992* (Austin: Texas State Historical Association in cooperation with the Center for American History, University of Texas at Austin, 1998), 168; J. Evetts Haley to Dobie, February 28, 1937, Dobie Papers, HRC.

33. Dobie to J. Evetts Haley, November 30, 1936, Haley Library.

34. J. Frank Dobie, "Museum of Range and Ranch Life in Texas Suggested," *Dallas Morning News*, October 1, 1939.

35. Saldívar, *The Borderlands of Culture*, 88, 91.

36. Ibid., 118.

37. Abernethy, *Texas Folklore Society, Volume 1*, 206.

38. A character modeled on Paredes as the young reporter appears in Hart Stilwell's 1945 novel, *Border City*.

39. Saldívar, *The Borderlands of Culture*, 118.

40. Ibid., 118–119.

41. Ibid., 119.

42. Américo Paredes, *George Washington Gómez: A Mexicotexan Novel* (Houston: Arte Público, 1990), 271.

43. Ibid., 272.

44. Ibid., 274.

45. Américo Paredes, (lecture, Texas State University–San Marcos, May 1994).

CHAPTER 14: THE AUSTIN LIBERALS, 1936–1938

1. Patrick Cox, *Ralph W. Yarborough, the People's Senator* (Austin: University of Texas Press, 2001), 156, xv, 53.

2. Webb, *The Texas Rangers*, 178, 183, 181. For information on Webb's version of Cortina, see pages 175–193.

3. J. Frank Dobie, "Private Stock," typescript, Dobie Papers, HRC.

4. Frantz, *The Forty-Acre Follies*, 177.

5. Walter Prescott Webb, *Divided We Stand: The Crisis of a Frontierless Democracy* (New York: Farrar and Rinehart, 1937), 119.

6. Ibid., 125.

7. Ibid., 92.

8. Ronnie Dugger, ed., *Three Men in Texas: Bedichek, Webb, and Dobie* (Austin: University of Texas Press, 1967), 13–14.

9. Walter Prescott Webb, "Dear Bedichek," in *Three Men in Texas*, 84.

10. Frantz, *The Forty-Acre Follies*, 162.

11. Ibid., 165.

12. Dugger, *Three Men in Texas*, 4; Frantz, *The Forty-Acre Follies*, 163.

CHAPTER 15: *APACHE GOLD VS. PALE HORSE, 1937–1939*

1. Dobie to J. Evetts Haley, December 8, 1937, Haley Library.

2. Rebecca Craver and Adair Margo, eds., *Tom Lea: An Oral History* (El Paso: Texas Western Press, 1995), 58.

3. J. Frank Dobie, *Apache Gold and Yaqui Silver* (Boston: Little, Brown, 1939), 189.

4. Abernethy, *Texas Folklore Society, Volume 1*, 214.

5. Dobie, *Apache Gold and Yaqui Silver*, 203.

6. Ibid., x, xii–xiii.

7. Don Graham, "J. Frank Dobie: A Reappraisal," *Southwestern Historical Quarterly* (July 1988): 13; Tinkle, *An American Original*, 127.

8. *Handbook of Texas Online*, "Porter, Katherine Anne," http://www.tshaonline. org/handbook/online/articles/PP/fpo40.html; Don Graham, "Katherine Anne Porter's Journey from Texas to the World," in Busby, *From Texas to the World and Back*, 3.

9. Clinton Machann and William Bed, eds., *Katherine Anne Porter and Texas: An Uneasy Relationship* (College Station: Texas A&M University Press, 1990), 41, 49.

10. Katherine Anne Porter to William Vann, September 29, 1939, TIL Papers, SWWC.

11. Vann, *Texas Institute of Letters*, 14.

12. Ibid., 15.

13. Sylvia Ann Grider, "Introduction," in *Katherine Anne Porter and Texas*, xvii.

14. Joan Givner as quoted in James Ward Lee, "Porter and Dobie: The Marriage from Hell," in Busby, *From Texas to the World and Back*, 69.

CHAPTER 16: THE LONGHORNS, 1939–1941

1. Roy Bedichek to Dobie, February 23, 1944, Dobie Papers, SWWC.

2. Sandra E. Miller, "Elithe Hamilton Kirkland: The March Toward Perfection" (master's thesis, Texas State University–San Marcos, 1999), 35.

3. J. Frank Dobie, "New Monument to Alamo," *Dallas Morning News*, November 19, 1939.

4. See T. J. Barragy, *Gathering Texas Gold: J. Frank Dobie and the Men Who Saved the Longhorns* (Texas: Cayo del Grullo Press, 2002), 66.

5. J. Frank Dobie, *The Longhorns* (Boston: Little, Brown, 1941), 38.

6. See Barragy, *Gathering Texas Gold*, 8, 149.

7. Ibid., 8.

8. Dobie to Tom Lea, June 9, 1949, Dobie Papers, HRC. For information on the royalty arrangement, see Barragy, *Gathering Texas Gold*, 185.

9. Dobie to Tom Lea, n.d., Dobie Papers, HRC.

10. Dobie, *The Longhorns*, 71; Francis Edward Abernethy, *J. Frank Dobie* (Austin: Steck-Vaughn Co., 1967), 23.

11. "History with Horns," *Time*, March 17, 1941, http://www.time.com/time/magazine/article/0,9171,765324-1,00.html.

CHAPTER 17: TRUE PATRIOTISM AND THE SINGING GOVERNOR, 1940–1941

1. Dobie to Tom Lea, June 26, 1940, Dobie Papers, HRC.

2. J. Frank Dobie, "Out of the Melting Pot Into the Fire," *Dallas Morning News*, June 2, 1940; J. Frank Dobie, "Give Arms to the Allies," *Dallas Morning News*, May 22, 1940.

3. Porterfield, *Last Cavalier*, 432.

4. *Handbook of Texas Online*, "O'Daniel, Wilbert Lee," http://www.tshaonline.org/handbook/online/articles/OO/fo'4.html.

5. The Coen Brothers film *O Brother, Where Art Thou* features a sleazy politician named "Pappy O'Daniel" who is loosely based on the actual O'Daniel.

6. *Handbook of Texas Online*, "O'Daniel, Wilbert Lee."

7. William A. Owens and Lyman Grant, eds., *Letters of Roy Bedichek* (Austin: University of Texas Press, 1985), 227.

8. J. Evetts Haley to Dobie, July 20, 1940, Dobie Papers, HRC; J. Evetts Haley to Dobie, November 15, 1940, Dobie Papers, HRC.

9. Porterfield, *Last Cavalier*, 453.

10. Dobie to Tom Lea, November 27, 1939, Dobie Papers, HRC.

11. Carleton, *A Breed So Rare*, 237; Owens and Grant, *Letters of Roy Bedichek*, xlvii; Dugger, *Our Invaded Universities*, 43.

12. Dobie to J. Evetts Haley, December 1, 1941, Haley Library.

13. Dobie to Tom Lea, September 18, 1940, Dobie Papers, HRC.

14. Roy Bedichek to Dobie, July 31, 1940, Dobie Papers, SWWC.

15. J. Frank Dobie, "My Texas, Patriots and Patriotism," *Dallas Morning News*, September 7, 1941.

16. Ibid.

17. Roy Bedichek to Dobie, September 8, 1941, Dobie Papers, SWWC.

CHAPTER 18: THE LIBERAL HERO, 1941–1943

1. Dobie to Tom Lea, October 27, 1941, Dobie Papers, HRC.

2. Dobie to Sid Richardson, December 10, 1941, Dobie Papers, HRC.

3. "Pappy in Trouble," *Time*, July 27, 1942, http://www.time.com/time/magazine/article/0,9171,802332,00.html.

4. J. Frank Dobie, "O'Daniel and the War," *Dallas Morning News*, July 17, 1942; J. Frank Dobie, "This and That in Texas," *Dallas Morning News*, August 16, 1942.

5. Roy Bedichek to Dobie, August 13, 1942, Dobie Papers, HRC.

6. Dobie to Tom Lea, August 20, 1942, Dobie Papers, HRC.

7. Dobie to Tom Lea, August 26, 1942, Dobie Papers, HRC.

8. Carleton, *A Breed So Rare*, 245.

9. Porterfield, *Last Cavalier*, 453.

10. Carleton, *A Breed So Rare*, 301; "Trouble in Texas," *Time*, November 13, 1944, http://www.time.com/time/magazine/article/0,9171,801579,00.html; Carleton, *A Breed So Rare*, 302.

11. Carleton, *A Breed So Rare*, 302.

12. Ibid.

13. J. Frank Dobie, "Commencement Oration on Texas That Nobody Will Deliver," *Dallas Morning News*, June 1, 1943.

14. Dobie to Tom Lea, July 28, 1942, Dobie Papers, HRC.

15. Porterfield, *Last Cavalier*, 458, 457. A fuller discussion of this controversy appears in Susan R. Richardson, "Reds, Race, and Research: Homer P. Rainey and the Grand Texas Tradition of Political Interference, 1939–1944," *Perspectives on the History of Higher Education* 24 (2005): 125–171.

16. "Killing Freedom Makes Imitation Men, Says Dobie in Academic Controversy," *Austin American-Statesman*, August 1, 1943.

17. Owens and Grant, *Letters of Roy Bedichek*, 213.

CHAPTER 19: A CONTEMPORARY OF HIMSELF, 1943–1946

J. Frank Dobie, "Taking Stock of Trust and Distrust," *Dallas Morning News*, January 3, 1943. Dobie adapted this verse from British poet John Oxenham.

1. *Handbook of Texas Online*, "World War II," http://www.tshaonline.org/handbook/online/articles/WW/npwnj.html.

2. Dobie, "Taking Stock of Trust and Distrust."

3. Ibid.; "Lieutenant Governor Censures President," *Dallas Morning News*, December 30, 1942.

4. "How to Get Arrested," *Time*, October 4, 1943, http://www.time.com/time/magazine/article/0,9171,932140,00.html?promoid=googlep.

258

5. "Dobie War Article Brings Him Name of Long-Haired Brother," *Dallas Morning News*, February 3, 1943.

6. Roy Bedichek to Dobie, February 9, 1943, Dobie Papers, SWWC.

7. Ibid.

8. J. Frank Dobie, "Divided We Stand," *Dallas Morning News*, February 21, 1943.

9. Ibid.

10. Tinkle, *An American Original*, 189; William A. Owens, *Three Friends, Roy Bedichek, J. Frank Dobie, Walter Prescott Webb* (Austin: University of Texas Press, 1975), 138; Porterfield, *Last Cavalier*, 465.

11. Craver and Margo, *Tom Lea*, 62; Graham, *Giant Country*, 110; Porterfield, *Last Cavalier*, 433.

12. Frank H. Wardlaw, "I Have That Honor," *Texas Observer*, July 24, 1964, 32; Richard M. Morehead, "J. Frank Dobie," *Southwestern Historical Quarterly* (July 1988): 118–119.

13. Porterfield, *Last Cavalier*, 456.

14. Memorandum, January 9, 1943, from FBI office SA100–7231, Department of Justice, Federal Bureau of Investigation, J. Frank Dobie files (1942–1964), acquired through the Freedom of Information Act; hereafter cited as Dobie FBI files.

15. Mr. A. Rose, from Mr. G. H. Scatterday, April 13, 1961, Dobie FBI files.

16. Clipping from *The Valley Evening Monitor*, July 6, 1947, Dobie FBI files.

17. David M. Kennedy, *Freedom from Fear: The American People in Depression and War, 1929–1945* (New York: Oxford University Press, 1999), 768.

18. Porterfield, *Last Cavalier*, 458.

19. Roy Bedichek to Dobie, June 22, 1944, Dobie Papers, SWWC.

20. Dobie, "Commencement Oration on Texas That Nobody Will Deliver."

21. "Letters from Readers," *Dallas Morning News*, June 27, 1943.

22. J. Frank Dobie, "Dobie Gets Letters on Inalienable Rights," *Dallas Morning News*, December 10, 1944; J. Frank Dobie, "Signs of Awareness in Texas," *Dallas Morning News*, July 8, 1945.

23. Steven L. Davis, *Texas Literary Outlaws: Six Writers in the Sixties and Beyond* (Fort Worth: TCU Press, 2004), 78.

24. J. Frank Dobie, "Dobie Sees South Thrown into Days Worse Than in Carpet-Bagging with Moore Bill," *Austin American-Statesman*, March 18, 1945.

25. M. A. Jones to Mr. Nichols, August 21, 1947, Dobie FBI files.

26. *Handbook of Texas Online*, "Sweatt, Heman Marion," http://www.tshaonline.org/handbook/online/articles/SS/fsw23.html.

27. Ibid.; Ralph W. Yarborough, *Frank Dobie: Man and Friend* (Washington, D.C.: Potomac Corral, the Westerners, 1968), 16.

28. Roy Bedichek to Dobie, January 16, 1947, as quoted in Owens, *Three Friends*, 234.

29. Porterfield, *Last Cavalier*, 455.

CHAPTER 20: A TEXAN IN ENGLAND, 1943–1946

1. Dobie, *A Texan in England*, 130.
2. Ibid., 18, 102.
3. Roy Bedichek to Dobie, June 22, 1944, Dobie Papers, SWWC.
4. J. Frank Dobie, "British Natural History Displays Remind Dobie of Texas," *Austin American-Statesman*, clippings file, Dobie Papers, SWWC.
5. J. Frank Dobie, "Soldiers in England Air Views on Contrasts in British and U.S. Ways," *Austin American-Statesman*, May 7, 1944; Tinkle, *An American Original*, 179; Dobie, "Commencement Oration on Texas That Nobody Will Deliver."
6. J. Frank Dobie, "No Other Man Has Ever Before Been Regarded by So Many Millions as Their Personal Friend as Roosevelt," *Austin American-Statesman*, April 22, 1945.
7. Tinkle, *An American Original*, 184.
8. Roy Bedichek to Dobie, April 10, 1944, Dobie Papers, SWWC.
9. Ibid., Roy Bedichek to Dobie, April 14, 1944, Dobie Papers, SWWC.
10. Tinkle, *An American Original*, 181, 185.
11. Abernethy, *J. Frank Dobie*, 21.
12. Tinkle, *An American Original*, 185.
13. Ibid., 99. For information on the possibility of adopting a child, see BMD Papers, SWU.
14. Tinkle, *An American Original*, 183, 203.
15. Porterfield, *Last Cavalier*, 458.
16. Susan R. Richardson, "Reds, Race, and Research," 158.
17. Carleton, *A Breed So Rare*, 304, 311.
18. Porterfield, *Last Cavalier*, 459.
19. Carleton, *A Breed So Rare*, 304.
20. "Regents Oust Rainey," *Dallas Morning News*, November 2, 1944.
21. Dugger, *Our Invaded Universities*, 55.
22. Ibid.
23. "Folklorist Abroad," *Time*, May 7, 1945, http://www.time.com/time/magazine/article/0,9171,797528,00.html.
24. Roy Bedichek to Dobie, April 23, 1945, Dobie Papers, HRC.
25. J. Frank Dobie, "Signs of Hatred, Too Common at Dachau, Are Found All over Germany," *Austin American-Statesman*, March 31, 1946.
26. Ibid.
27. J. Frank Dobie, "German Lawyers at Nuernberg Trying Harder to Clear People of Crime Complicity Than Acquit Accused," *Austin American-Statesman*, April 28, 1946.
28. Dobie, "German Lawyers at Nuernberg"; J. Frank Dobie, "A Civilian Goes to Germany," *Dallas Morning News*, February 10, 1946.
29. Tinkle, *An American Original*, 179.
30. Dobie to Tom Lea, April 6, 1946, Dobie Papers, HRC.

31. Tinkle, *An American Original*, 179; Don Graham, James W. Lee, and William T. Pilkington, eds., *The Texas Literary Tradition: Fiction, Folklore, History* (Austin: College of Liberal Arts, University of Texas at Austin, Texas State Historical Association, 1983), 21.

32. Dobie to Tom Lea, December 18, 1946, Dobie Papers, HRC.

33. Owens, *Three Friends*, 179.

34. Ibid., 182.

35. Tinkle, *An American Original*, 192.

CHAPTER 21: TEXAS NEEDS BRAINS, 1946–1947

1. "Bedichek and Dobie," *Texas Observer*, August 24, 1955, 6; Wardlaw, "I Have That Honor," 30.

2. Edmund Heinsohn, "A Question of Implications," *Texas Observer*, July 24, 1964, 23; Frantz, *The Forty-Acre Follies*, 163; Dugger, *Three Men in Texas*, 63.

3. "Bedichek and Dobie," 6–7.

4. Owens, *Three Friends*, 178, 180.

5. Roy Bedichek to Dobie, January 12, 1946, Dobie Papers, SWWC.

6. Dobie to Roy Bedichek, June 12, 1947, Dobie SWWC Papers.

7. J. Frank Dobie, "Texas Needs Brains," *Ranger*, October 1946, 16–17.

8. Ibid., 26–27.

9. Roy Bedichek to Dobie, n.d., Dobie Papers, SWWC.

10. "Politicians Throw Their Haymakers," *Dallas Morning News*, July 24, 1946; "Suggests Negro University Bossed by Rainey and Dobie," *Dallas Morning News*, July 10, 1946.

11. J. Evetts Haley, *The University of Texas and the Issue* (Clarendon, Tex.: Clarendon Press, 1945), 18, 19.

12. J. Frank Dobie, unprocessed box labeled "Piss & Vinegar," Dobie Papers, HRC.

13. "Fight Halts Rainey Rally," *Dallas Morning News*, July 16, 1946.

14. Dobie, "Piss & Vinegar," Dobie Papers, HRC.

15. Frantz, *The Forty-Acre Follies*, 121; "Segregation Ruling Attacked by Haley," *Dallas Morning News*, July 17, 1956; Robinson, *J. Evetts Haley and the Passing of the Old West*, 112.

16. Frantz, *The Forty-Acre Follies*, 121–122.

17. Ibid., 122.

18. Roy Bedichek to Dobie, n.d., Dobie Papers, SWWC.

19. Owens, *Three Friends*, 188.

20. Ibid., 187.

21. J. Frank Dobie, "A Wise and Civilized Book on Nature," review of *Adventures with a Texas Naturalist*, by Roy Bedichek, *Dallas Morning News*, October 5, 1947.

22. McMurtry, *In a Narrow Grave*, 34–35; Greene, *The Fifty Best Books on Texas*, 37.

23. "The Case of Professor Pancho," *Time*, October 13, 1947, http://www.time.com/time/magazine/article/0,9171,933735,00.html.

24. Dwonna Goldstone, "Heman Sweatt and the Racial Segregation of the University of Texas Law School," *The Journal of Blacks in Higher Education* (Winter 2006/2007): 88; J. Frank Dobie, "Dobie Questions Future Tranquility in Texas," *Austin American-Statesman*, February 25, 1945.

25. "The Case of Professor Pancho," http://www.time.com/time/magazine/article/0,9171,933735,00.html.

26. Ibid.

27. "Governor in Favor of Ousting Dobie," *Dallas Morning News*, October 19, 1946.

28. "Dobie Turned Down on Leave Extension," *Dallas Morning News*, September 19, 1947. The *Handbook of Texas* states that the Board of Regents restricted leaves of absence to two years, rather than one year, but the contemporary sources I found, including the *Dallas Morning News*, cited above, indicate that the regents "placed leaves of absence under a one-year limitation rule."

29. See Tinkle, *An American Original*, 200.

30. Bertha McKee Dobie to Edgar Kincaid, Jr., September 28, 1947, BMD Papers, SWU.

31. "Student Group Thanks Dobie," *Dallas Morning News*, September 25, 1947; Bertha McKee Dobie to Edgar Kincaid, Jr., September 28, 1947, BMD Papers, SWU.

## CHAPTER 22: COYOTE WISDOM, 1948–1953

1. Barragy, *Gathering Texas Gold*, 208. For information on the farm in the Lower Rio Grande Valley, see BMD Papers, SWU.

2. J. Frank Dobie, "Let Us Try UNESCO," *Dallas Morning News*, October 6, 1946.

3. J. Frank Dobie, "Man Who Was a Book Seller," *Austin American-Statesman*, October 11, 1959.

4. Owens, *Three Friends*, 186.

5. "Dogwood Dobie," *Dallas Morning News*, April 5, 1953.

6. J. Frank Dobie, "In Eyes of Unadulterated Greed, Human Lives and Human Ideals Said to Count for Nothing," *Austin American-Statesman*, July 22, 1945; Frantz, *The Forty-Acre Follies*, 162.

7. Joe Goulden, "J. Frank Dobie Explains His Convictions on Life," *Dallas Morning News*, November 13, 1960.

8. Dobie, "Texas Needs Brains," 26; Dobie, "Dobie Questions Future Tranquility in Texas."

9. "Texans Cold to Wallace," *Dallas Morning News*, May 8, 1947.

10. "Dobie Declares He Won't Do a 'Doggone Thing' for Wallace," *Dallas Morning News*, April 25, 1948.

11. J. Frank Dobie, *The Voice of the Coyote* (Boston: Little, Brown, 1949), xiii.

12. Ibid., 31, 85, 86.

13. Ibid., xvi.

14. Ibid., xii.

15. "Part of the Life," *Time*, May 16, 1949, http://www.time.com/time/magazine/article/0,9171,853761,00.html; Ivan T. Sanderson, "Of the Prairie Wolf," *New York Times*, June 26, 1949.

CHAPTER 23: ELDER STATESMAN, 1951–1958

1. Tinkle, *An American Original*, 209.

2. Owens, *Three Friends*, 186.

3. Roy Bedichek to "Clara," March 13, 1955, in Dobie files marked "Old Age," Dobie Papers, SWWC; J. Frank Dobie, "No Ancestor Worship," *Austin American-Statesman*, August 11, 1957.

4. J. Frank Dobie, "In New York or Amarillo."

5. Dugger, *Three Men in Texas*, 252.

6. Ibid., 229.

7. "Dobie Unexpurgated," *Texas Observer*, February 15, 1956, 3.

8. Dobie to Ralph Yarborough, January 22, 1954, Dobie Papers, HRC.

9. Yarborough, *Frank Dobie: Man and Friend*, 16.

10. "Advertisement," *Austin American-Statesman*, July 26, 1958.

11. Dobie to Ralph Yarborough, April 18, 1957, Dobie Papers, HRC.

12. *Handbook of Texas Online*, "Yarborough, Ralph Webster," http://www.tshaonline.org/handbook/online/articles/YY/fyags.html.

13. J. Frank Dobie, *The Mustangs* (Boston: Little, Brown, 1952), xi.

14. Ibid., xii.

15. Ibid., 11.

16. Abernethy, *J. Frank Dobie*, 38–39.

17. Yarborough, *Frank Dobie: Man and Friend*, 16.

18. J. Frank Dobie, "Early '20s a Rough Time for Cattlemen," *Austin American-Statesman*, December 21, 1952.

19. Bode, *A Portrait of Pancho*, 30.

20. Dobie, *Some Part of Myself*, 8.

21. J. Frank Dobie, "A Warm Salute to All Libraries," *Austin American-Statesman*, March 16, 1958.

22. J. Frank Dobie, "Every Generation Boasts Its Old-Timers to Add Their Part to Rich Texas Lore," *Austin American-Statesman*, February 2, 1958.

23. J. Frank Dobie, untitled *Austin American-Statesman* article from clipping file, Dobie Papers, SWWC.

24. J. Frank Dobie, "A Deferential Interview," *Texas Observer*, January 10, 1958, 3; Dobie, *Some Part of Myself*, 171; "Frank Dobie Raps Courses in Education," *Dallas Morning News*, June 22, 1960.

25. "Religiosity & Palaver," *Time*, January 13, 1958, http://www.time.com/time/magazine/article/0,9171,862863,00.html; Dobie, *Some Part of Myself*, 170.

26. Dobie to William Vann, January 30, 1959, TIL Papers, SWWC; Dobie to William Vann, May 13, 1959, TIL Papers, SWWC.

27. Mildred B. Keyser, "J. Frank Dobie: Artist-In-Depth" (master's thesis, Texas Western College, 1961), 4.

CHAPTER 24: LITERARY DICTATOR, 1952–1960

1. Accounts of the event were carried in the *Dallas Morning News*. See "Banquet Honors Negro Writer," December 13, 1953; "Significant Publication Party: Austin Event Honors Negro Writer," December 20, 1953; "Prize-Winning Editor Plans Austin Speech," December 9, 1953.
2. "Piss & Vinegar," Dobie Papers, HRC.
3. Ibid.
4. Richard M. Dorson, review of *The Word on the Brazos*, by J. Mason Brewer, *Journal of American Folklore* (1955): 101–102. Although Brewer's decision to retell the folktales in dialect was not controversial at the time, it has made it difficult for contemporary readers to appreciate his works.
5. Wayne Gard, "Aspirants Owe Debt to Dobie," *Dallas Morning News*, May 26, 1959.
6. Ibid.; Fermina Guerra to Dobie, October 11, 1943, Dobie Papers, HRC.
7. Gard, "Aspirants Owe Debt to Dobie."
8. Don Graham, "Reader's Report" for the author's first draft for this book, submitted March 2008; James Ward Lee, "Arbiters of Texas Literary Taste," in *Range Wars: Heated Debates, Sober Reflections, and Other Assessments of Texas Writing*, ed. Craig Clifford and Tom Pilkington (Dallas: Southern Methodist University Press, 1989), 125.
9. Dobie, *Guide to Life and Literature of the Southwest*, 143; J. Frank Dobie, "The Current of Texas Writing," *Dallas Morning News*, October 19, 1947.
10. Richard M. Morehead, "Panelists See Renaissance of Southwestern Literature," *Dallas Morning News*, April 13, 1958.
11. J. Frank Dobie, "Definition of the Southwest Depends on the Definer," *Austin American-Statesman*, clipping file, Dobie Papers, SWWC; Dobie, "The Current of Texas Writing."
12. J. Frank Dobie, "Class of Frontier Rangeman Epitomized," *Austin American-Statesman*, clipping file, Dobie Papers, SWWC; "Frontier Excalibur," *Time*, July 30, 1951, http://www.time.com/time/magazine/article/0,9171,815210,00.html?promoid=googlep.
13. J. Frank Dobie, "Dobie Previews Tom Lea's Novel," *Dallas Morning News*, March 20, 1949.
14. Ibid.
15. Dobie, "The Current of Texas Writing."
16. Dobie, *Guide to Life and Literature of the Southwest*, 181.
17. Ibid.; J. Frank Dobie, review of *Divided We Stand*, by Walter Prescott Webb, *Southwestern Historical Quarterly* (January 1938): 259.

18. Dugger, *Three Men in Texas*, 249.

19. Dobie, *Guide to Life and Literature of the Southwest*, 2.

20. Ibid., 2, 3.

21. Mabel Major, review of *Guide to Life and Literature of the Southwest*, by J. Frank Dobie, *The South-Central Bulletin* (February 1944): 8.

22. Sarah Ragland Jackson, *Texas Woman of Letters, Karle Wilson Baker* (College Station: Texas A&M University Press, 2005), xiii.

23. Dobie, *Guide to Life and Literature of the Southwest*, 180.

24. Lee, "Arbiters of Texas Literary Taste," in *Range Wars*, 125; Dugger, *Three Men in Texas*, 249.

25. Richard Holland, "Guest Editor's Introduction, Special Section on J. Frank Dobie," *Southwestern American Literature* (Spring 1994): 22.

26. J. Frank Dobie, "John Graves, Writing Man," *Austin American-Statesman*, October 9, 1960.

27. Dobie to William Vann, January 30, 1959, TIL Papers, SWWC.

CHAPTER 25: END OF AN ERA, 1955–1959

1. Jane Gracy Bedichek, *The Roy Bedichek Family Letters* (Denton: University of North Texas Press, 1998), 436; Tinkle, *An American Original*, 226; J. Frank Dobie, "Dobie on Bedichek, Ceniza, Joy of Living," *Dallas Morning News*, July 31, 1955.

2. J. Frank Dobie, "About Roy Bedichek and the Great Outdoors," *Austin American-Statesman*, clipping files, Dobie Papers, SWWC.

3. Craver and Margo, *Tom Lea*, 62.

4. Dobie to Tom Lea, December 24, 1955, Dobie Papers, HRC; Dobie to Tom Lea, August 19, 1956, Dobie Papers, HRC.

5. See J. Frank Dobie, "Texas-Mexican Border Broadsides," *Journal of American Folklore* (April–June 1923). Dobie, *The Flavor of Texas*, 221.

6. Américo Paredes, (untitled lecture, Texas State University–San Marcos, May 1994); Saldívar, *The Borderlands of Culture*, 117, 119. For the exchange of letters between Dobie and Paredes, see Paredes correspondence, Dobie Papers, HRC.

7. Américo Paredes, *"With His Pistol in His Hand": A Border Ballad and Its Hero* (Austin: The University of Texas Press, 1958), 22.

8. Ibid., 17.

9. Ibid., 23.

10. Sonia Salinas, "Américo Paredes: Uncovering the Multifaceted Life of the Scholar and the Man" (master's thesis, University of Texas–Pan American, 2005), 23.

11. Ibid.; Saldívar, *The Borderlands of Culture*, 114; Renato Rosaldo, "Politics, Patriarchs, and Laughter," in "The Nature and Context of Minority Discourse," special issue, *Cultural Critique* 6 (Spring 1987): 70.

12. Paredes, *"With His Pistol in His Hand,"* 20; Limón, *Dancing with the Devil*, 215.

13. Saldívar, *The Borderlands of Culture*, 114.

14. Ibid., 117, 119.
15. Dobie to Tom Lea, July 29, 1957, Dobie Papers, HRC.
16. Dobie to Tom Lea, September 1, 1957, Dobie Papers, HRC.
17. Dugger, *Three Men in Texas*, 269.
18. Walter Prescott Webb, "Tom Lea's Powerful Portrait of the King Ranch," *Dallas Morning News*, September 15, 1957.
19. J. Frank Dobie, "A Giant Among Texans," *New York Times Book Review*, September 15, 1957.
20. Ibid.
21. Ibid.
22. Craver and Margo, *Tom Lea*, 112.
23. J. Frank Dobie, "Camping Beneath an Oxygen Tent," *Austin American-Statesman*, October 27, 1957.
24. Ibid.; Audrey Slate, "At Paisano, the Dobie Fellowships, 1967–2005," typescript made available to the author.
25. Dobie, "Camping Beneath an Oxygen Tent."
26. Bertha McKee Dobie, "The Sunday Pieces," 7, typescript of a talk given by Bertha to the Texas Institute of Letters in 1965, BMD Papers, SWU.
27. Tinkle, *An American Original*, 223.
28. Dugger, *Three Men in Texas*, 269; Slate, "At Paisano," 8.
29. Owens and Grant, *Letters of Roy Bedichek*, 519.
30. Dugger, *Three Men in Texas*, 18.
31. Ibid., 83.

CHAPTER 26: ONE TOUCH OF NATURE, PLUS, 1960–1962

1. Tinkle, *An American Original*, 226.
2. As Don Graham has noted, Dobie's tolerance for sexually direct writing did not extend to the new generation of Texas novelists, and he made critical comments in his private copies of novels by Larry McMurtry, Billy Lee Brammer, and Edwin "Bud" Shrake. See Graham, "J. Frank Dobie: A Reappraisal."
3. "Piss & Vinegar," Dobie Papers, HRC.
4. Dobie to Tom Lea, November 28, 1958, Dobie Papers, HRC. For Dobie's essays, see "Piss & Vinegar," Dobie Papers, HRC.
5. Dobie, *The Voice of the Coyote*, 132–133; "Piss & Vinegar," Dobie Papers, HRC.
6. "Piss & Vinegar," Dobie Papers, HRC.
7. Lon Tinkle notes in his biography of Dobie that "both the manuscript and the books Frank assembled for it disappeared soon after Frank's death. There is reason to believe that the manuscript will soon surface, at least for the use of scholars." Tinkle, *An American Original*, 227. Don Graham was the first to come across the previously restricted Dobie material at the Harry H. Ransom Humanities Research Center at the University of Texas at Austin, and he included information

about Dobie's book in his essay "Pen Pals," published in the March 1996 issue of *Texas Monthly* and later reprinted in his book *Giant Country*. For additional information about Dobie's "Piss & Vinegar" papers, see Steven L. Davis, "Eros in Dobie Country," *Southwestern American Literature* (Fall 2006): 49–55.

8. J. Frank Dobie, "Private Stock," typescript, 3, Dobie Papers, HRC; Heinsohn, "A Question of Implications," 23.

9. Owens, *Three Friends*, 307.

10. Dobie, "Private Stock," 3, Dobie Papers, HRC; Frantz, *The Forty-Acre Follies*, 167.

11. Frantz, *The Forty-Acre Follies*, 167.

12. J. Frank Dobie, "Roy Bedichek," *Texas Observer*, June 27, 1959, 1.

13. Ronnie Dugger to Lillian Bedichek, August 4, 1959, Dobie Papers, SWWC.

14. Craver and Margo, *Tom Lea*, 112; Dobie to Tom Lea, June 3, 1958, Dobie Papers, HRC.

15. Craver and Margo, *Tom Lea*, 112.

16. Richard Stewart Kirkendall, *The Harry S. Truman Encyclopedia* (New York: G. K. Hall, 1989), 6.

17. Memorandum from Mr. G. H. Scatterday to Mr. A. Rose concerning J. Frank Dobie, April 13, 1961, Dobie FBI files.

18. Ibid.

19. Ibid.

20. For a study of the FBI's COINTELPRO, see Brian Click, *War at Home: Covert Action Against U.S. Activists and What We Can Do About It* (Boston: South End Press, 1989).

21. J. Edgar Hoover to SAC, San Antonio, April 18, 1961, concerning "J. Frank Dobie, Security Matter," Dobie FBI files.

22. Report on J. Frank Dobie by George W. H. Carlson, May 8, 1961, Bureau File No.: 100–352167, Dobie FBI files.

23. Ibid.

24. Ibid.

25. Ibid.

26. Ibid.

27. Tinkle, *An American Original*, 231.

28. Jack Nelson and Gene Roberts, *The Censors and the Schools* (Boston: Little, Brown, 1963), 121; Paul F. Boller, Jr., *Memoirs of an Obscure Professor and Other Essays* (Fort Worth: Texas Christian University Press, 1992), 25.

29. "Battle Over Books, Subversive or Not," *Dallas Morning News*, November 12, 1961; Nelson and Roberts, *The Censors and the Schools*, 121; Boller, *Memoirs of an Obscure Professor*, 28.

30. Boller, *Memoirs of an Obscure Professor*, 28; Willie Morris, *North Towards Home* (Boston: Houghton Mifflin, 1967), 286.

31. "Critic Says Texts Err, U.S. Not a Democracy," *Dallas Morning News*, November 14, 1961.

32. J. Frank Dobie, "Censors and Satire," *Bacchanal: Student Humor Magazine for the Southwest Conference* (March 1962), clipping file, Dobie Papers, SWWC.

33. Tinkle, *An American Original*, 232.

34. Nelson and Roberts, *The Censors and the Schools*, 142.

35. Ibid.

36. Ibid., 143.

CHAPTER 27: SUNSET, 1962–1964

1. "Witty Dobie Brightens Trip with Wide-Ranging Quips," *Waco Herald-Tribune*, October 29, 1961; Richard M. Morehead, "J. Frank Dobie—Changed Man," *Dallas Morning News*, August 8, 1964, clipping files, Dobie Papers, SWWC.

2. Polk Shelton, Jr., telephone interview with the author, July 30, 2007; Tinkle, *An American Original*, 232.

3. Dugger, *Three Men in Texas*, 99.

4. Dobie, "Private Stock"; J. Frank Dobie, "On the Projected Shadow of Walter P. Webb," *Dallas Morning News*, March 17, 1963.

5. "Dobie Flies Back Home on His 75th Birthday," *Dallas Morning News*, September 27, 1963.

6. J. Frank Dobie, "Mirror, Mirror, on the Wall," *Book Week, New York Herald-Tribune*, April 19, 1964.

7. Lon Tinkle, "NBA's New Prize: Porter, Dobie," *Dallas Morning News*, March 15, 1964.

8. J. Frank Dobie, "Hash and Humanity in the White House," *Austin American-Statesman*, May 17, 1964.

9. Dobie to Tom Lea, June 14, 1964, Dobie Papers, HRC.

10. Frank H. Wardlaw, "Enlightened, Compassionate Citizen of the World," *Austin American-Statesman*, October 25, 1964.

11. Dugger, *Three Men in Texas*, 285.

CHAPTER 28: DOBIE'S LEGACY

1. Richard Holland, "A Corner Forever Texas," in *Corners of Texas, Publication of the Texas Folklore Society, Vol II*, ed. Francis Edward Abernethy (Denton: University of North Texas Press, 1993), 208.

2. Tim O'Leary, "Texas Picked Up on Gardner's Trail," *Press Enterprise* (Riverside, Calif.), July 21, 2002.

3. Mike Cox, "Scattering of Dobie Estate a Sad Legacy for Writer," *Austin American-Statesman*, December 24, 1985.

4. Hart Stilwell, "Listening With the Third Ear," *Texas Observer*, July 24, 1964, 19; Bode, *A Portrait of Pancho*, 55.

5. McMurtry, *In a Narrow Grave*, 46; Larry McMurtry, "Ever a Bridegroom: Reflections on the Failure of Texas Literature," in *Range Wars*, 15; Lee, "Arbiters of Texas Literary Taste," in *Range Wars*, 14, 125–126; Gregory Curtis, "Behind the Lines," *Texas Monthly*, August 1981, 5.

6. Tom Pilkington, "Herding Words: Texas Literature as Trail Drive," in *Range Wars*, 168.

7. *Handbook of Texas Online*, "Paisano Ranch," http://www.tshaonline.org/handbook/online/articles/PP/app1.html.

8. Holland, "A Corner Forever Texas," in *Corners of Texas*, 9.

9. Bill Wittliff, "Interview by Steve Davis," The J. Frank Dobie day symposium at the Southwestern Writers Collection/The Wittliff Collections, Texas State University–San Marcos, April 8, 2006.

10. Holland, "A Corner Forever Texas," in *Corners of Texas*, 9.

11. Dudley Dobie, Jr., email to author, February 12, 2008. Dudley Dobie also provided a tour of the Dobie home, which provided additional information.

12. John Graves, "The Old Guard: Dobie, Webb, Bedichek," in *The Texas Literary Tradition*, 20.

13. Américo Paredes, review of *Legends of Texas* and *Happy Hunting Ground*, *Journal of American Folklore* (April–June 1965): 164.

# SELECTED BIBLIOGRAPHY

BOOKS BY J. FRANK DOBIE, IN CHRONOLOGICAL ORDER

Dobie, J. Frank, ed. *Legends of Texas*. Austin: Texas Folk-Lore Society, 1924.

———, ed. *Publications of the Texas Folk-Lore Society, Number V.* Austin: Texas Folk-Lore Society, 1926.

———. *A Vaquero of the Brush Country, Partly from the Reminiscences of John Young.* Dallas: Southwest Press, 1929.

———. *Coronado's Children: Tales of Lost Mines and Buried Treasures of the Southwest.* Dallas: Southwest Press, 1930.

———, ed. *Tone the Bell Easy, TFS Publication No. X.* Austin: Texas Folk-Lore Society, 1932.

———. *Tongues of the Monte.* Boston: Little, Brown, 1935. (Reprinted in 1942 as *The Mexico I Like.* Dallas: Southern Methodist University Press, 1942.)

———. *The Flavor of Texas.* Dallas: Dealey and Lowe, 1936.

———. *Apache Gold and Yaqui Silver.* Boston: Little, Brown, 1939.

———. *The Longhorns.* Boston: Little, Brown, 1941.

———. *Guide to Life and Literature of the Southwest: With a Few Observations.* Austin: University of Texas Press, 1943.

———. *A Texan in England.* Boston: Little, Brown, 1945.

———. *The Voice of the Coyote.* Boston: Little, Brown, 1949.

———. *The Ben Lilly Legend.* Boston: Little, Brown, 1950.

———. *The Mustangs.* Boston: Little, Brown, 1952.

———. *Tales of Old-Time Texas.* Boston: Little, Brown, 1955.

270

———. *I'll Tell You a Tale*. Boston: Little, Brown, 1960.

———. *Cow People*. Boston: Little, Brown, 1964.

———. *Rattlesnakes*. Boston: Little, Brown, 1965.

———. *Some Part of Myself*. Boston: Little, Brown, 1967.

———. *Out of the Old Rock*. Boston: Little, Brown, 1972.

———. *Prefaces*. Boston: Little, Brown, 1975.

ARTICLES BY J. FRANK DOBIE, IN CHRONOLOGICAL ORDER

Dobie, J. Frank. "The Cowboy and His Songs." *Texas Review* (January 1920): 163–169.

———. "La Canción del Rancho de Los Olmos." *Journal of American Folklore* (April–June 1923): 192–195.

———. "Texas-Mexican Border Broadsides." *Journal of American Folklore* (April–June 1923): 185–191.

———. "Picturesque History of Texas Ranch Is Related with Accuracy and Flavor." Review of *The XIT Ranch and the Early Days of the Llano Estacado*, by J. Evetts Haley. *Dallas Morning News*, April 28, 1929.

———. Review of *Divided We Stand*, by Walter Prescott Webb. *Southwestern Historical Quarterly* (January 1938): 257.

———. "Museum of Range and Ranch Life in Texas Suggested." *Dallas Morning News*, October 1, 1939.

———. "New Monument to Alamo." *Dallas Morning News*, November 19, 1939.

———. "Give Arms to the Allies." *Dallas Morning News*, May 22, 1940.

———. "Out of the Melting Pot into the Fire." *Dallas Morning News*, June 2, 1940.

———. "My Texas, Patriots and Patriotism." *Dallas Morning News*, September 7, 1941.

———. "O'Daniel and the War." *Dallas Morning News*, July 17, 1942.

———. "This and That in Texas." *Dallas Morning News*, August 16, 1942.

———. "Taking Stock of Trust and Distrust." *Dallas Morning News*, January 3, 1943.

———. "Divided We Stand." *Dallas Morning News*, February 21, 1943.

———. "Commencement Oration on Texas That Nobody Will Deliver." *Dallas Morning News*, June 1, 1943.

———. "Soldiers in England Air Views on Contrasts in British and U.S. Ways." *Austin American-Statesman*, May 7, 1944.

———. "Dobie Gets Letters on Inalienable Rights." *Dallas Morning News*, December 10, 1944.

———. "Dobie Questions Future Tranquility in Texas." *Austin American-Statesman*, February 25, 1945.

———. "Dobie Sees South Thrown into Days Worse Than in Carpet-Bagging with Moore Bill." *Austin American-Statesman*, March 18, 1945.

———. "No Other Man Has Ever Before Been Regarded by So Many Millions as Their Personal Friend as Roosevelt." *Austin American-Statesman*, April 22, 1945.

———. "Signs of Awareness in Texas." *Dallas Morning News*, July 8, 1945.

———. "In Eyes of Unadulterated Greed, Human Lives and Human Ideals Said to Count for Nothing." *Austin American-Statesman*, July 22, 1945.

———. "A Civilian Goes to Germany." *Dallas Morning News*, February 10, 1946.

———. "Signs of Hatred, too Common, at Dachau, Are Found All over Germany." *Austin American-Statesman*, March 31, 1946.

———. "German Lawyers at Nuernberg Trying Harder to Clear People of Crime Complicity Than Acquit Accused." *Austin American-Statesman*, April 28, 1946.

———. "Let Us Try UNESCO." *Dallas Morning News*, October 6, 1946.

———. "Texas Needs Brains." *Ranger*, October 1946: 5–7.

———. "A Wise and Civilized Book on Nature." Review of *Adventures with a Texas Naturalist*, by Roy Bedichek. *Dallas Morning News*, October 5, 1947.

———. "The Current of Texas Writing." *Dallas Morning News*, October 19, 1947.

———. "Dobie Previews Tom Lea's Novel." Review of *The Brave Bulls*, by Tom Lea. *Dallas Morning News*, March 20, 1949.

———. "Early '20s a Rough Time for Cattlemen." *Austin American-Statesman*, December 21, 1952.

———. "In New York or Amarillo, 'The People' Live." *Austin American-Statesman*, April 11, 1954.

———. "Dobie on Bedichek, Ceniza, Joy of Living." *Dallas Morning News*, July 31, 1955.

———. "No Ancestor Worship." *Austin American-Statesman*, August 11, 1957.

———. "A Giant Among Texans." Review of *The King Ranch*, by Tom Lea. *New York Times Book Review*, September 15, 1957.

———. "Camping Beneath an Oxygen Tent." *Austin American-Statesman*, October 27, 1957.

———. "Luck Is Just Being Ready for a Chance." *Austin American-Statesman*, November 10, 1957.

———. "A Deferential Interview." *Texas Observer*, January 10, 1958.

———. "Every Generation Boasts Its Old-Timers to Add Their Part to Rich Texas Lore." *Austin American-Statesman*, February 2, 1958.

———. "A Warm Salute to All Libraries." *Austin American-Statesman*, March 16, 1958.

———. "Roy Bedichek." *Texas Observer*, June 27, 1959.

———. "Man Who Was a Book Seller." *Austin American-Statesman*, October 11, 1959.

———. "John Graves, Writing Man." Review of *Goodbye to a River*, by John Graves. *Austin American-Statesman*, October 9, 1960.

———. "Possessed by Books." *Austin American-Statesman*, November 11, 1961.

———. "Censors and Satire." *Bacchanal: Student Humor Magazine for the Southwest Conference*, March 1962.

———. "On the Projected Shadow of Walter P. Webb." *Dallas Morning News*, March 17, 1963.

———. "Mirror, Mirror, on the Wall." *Book Week, New York Herald-Tribune*, April 19, 1964.

———. "Hash and Humanity in the White House." *Austin American-Statesman*, May 17, 1964.

BOOKS, ARTICLES, THESES, DISSERTATIONS

Abernethy, Francis Edward. *J. Frank Dobie*. Austin: Steck-Vaughn Co., 1967.

———. *Texas Folklore Society, Volume 1, 1909–1943*. Denton: University of North Texas Press, 1992.

———. "Texas Folklore Society History, 1909–1997." www.texasfolkloresociety. org/History.htm.

Alexander, Hansen. *Rare Integrity: A Portrait of L. W. Payne*. Austin: Wind River Press, 1986.

Barragy, T. J. *Gathering Texas Gold: J. Frank Dobie and the Men Who Saved the Longhorns*. Texas: Cayo del Grullo Press, 2002.

Bedichek, Jane Gracy. *The Roy Bedichek Family Letters*. Denton: University of North Texas Press, 1998.

Boatright, Mody. "A Mustang in the Groves of Academe." *Texas Observer*, July 24, 1964.

Bode, Winston. "Pancho and the Patio." *The University of Texas: Alcalde*, December 1965.

———. *A Portrait of Pancho*. Austin: Steck-Vaughn Co., 1968.

Boller, Paul F. Jr. *Memoirs of an Obscure Professor and Other Essays*. Fort Worth: Texas Christian University Press, 1992.

Busby, Mark, ed. *From Texas to the World and Back: Essays on the Journeys of Katherine Anne Porter*. Fort Worth: Texas Christian University Press, 2001.

———. "J. Frank Dobie's *A Vaquero of the Brush Country*: A Reevaluation." *Cross Timbers Review* 3.1 (1986).

Byrd, James W. *J. Mason Brewer: Negro Folklorist*. Austin: Steck-Vaughn Co., 1967.

Cabeza de Vaca, Álvar Núñez. *La relación y comentarios*. http://www.library.txstate. edu/swwc/cdv/book/40.html.

Carleton, Don E. *A Breed So Rare: The Life of J. R. Parten, Liberal Texas Oil Man, 1896–1992*. Austin: Texas State Historical Association in cooperation with the Center for American History, University of Texas at Austin, 1998.

Carmack, George. "A Lifetime of Love Between Texas Creeks." *San Antonio Express-News*, September 29, 1973.

Click, Brian. *War at Home: Covert Action Against U.S. Activists and What We Can Do*

*About It.* Boston: South End Press, 1989.

Cox, Mike. "Scattering of Dobie Estate a Sad Legacy for Writer." *Austin American-Statesman*, December 24, 1985.

Cox, Patrick. *Ralph W. Yarborough, the People's Senator.* Austin: University of Texas Press, 2001.

Craver, Rebecca, and Adair Margo, eds. *Tom Lea: An Oral History.* El Paso: Texas Western Press, 1995.

Curtis, Gregory. "Behind the Lines." *Texas Monthly*, August 1981.

Custer, Judson S., ed. *Dobie at Southwestern University: The Beginnings of His Literary Career, 1906–1911.* Austin: Jenkins Pub. Co., 1981.

Davis, Steven L. "Eros in Dobie Country." *Southwestern American Literature* (Fall 2006): 49–55.

———. *Texas Literary Outlaws: Six Writers in the Sixties and Beyond.* Fort Worth: Texas Christian University Press, 2004.

Dorman, Robert L. *Revolt of the Provinces: The Regionalist Movement in America, 1920–1945.* Chapel Hill: University of North Carolina Press, 1993.

Dorson, Richard M. Review of *The Word on the Brazos*, by J. Mason Brewer. *Journal of American Folklore* (1955): 101–102.

Douglas, Jeanne, and Liz Wharton. "Maverick Professor." *Saturday Evening Post*, September 11, 1943.

Duffus, R. L. "Lost Treasure in the Southwest." *New York Times*, February 8, 1931.

Dugger, Ronnie. *Our Invaded Universities: Form, Reform and New Starts.* New York: Norton, 1974.

———, ed. *Three Men in Texas: Bedichek, Webb, and Dobie.* Austin: University of Texas Press, 1967.

Foshee, Page S. "San Antonio, the Centennial, and the Cenotaph: Grounds for Controversy: J. Frank Dobie and Pompeo Coppini." Master's thesis, Texas State University–San Marcos, 1993.

Frantz, Joe B. *The Forty-Acre Follies.* Austin: Texas Monthly Press, 1983.

Gard, Wayne. "Aspirants Owe Debt to Dobie." *Dallas Morning News*, May 26, 1959.

Gilb, Dagoberto, ed. *Hecho en Tejas: An Anthology of Texas Mexican Literature.* Albuquerque: University of New Mexico Press, 2007.

Goldstone, Dwonna. "Heman Sweatt and the Racial Segregation of the University of Texas Law School." *The Journal of Blacks in Higher Education* (Winter 2006/2007).

González, Jovita, and Eve Raleigh. *Caballero: A Historical Novel.* College Station: Texas A&M University Press, 1996.

Goulden, Joe. "J. Frank Dobie Explains His Convictions on Life." *Dallas Morning News*, November 13, 1960.

Graham, Don. *Giant Country: Essays On Texas.* Fort Worth: Texas Christian University Press, 1998.

274

———. "J. Frank Dobie: A Reappraisal." *Southwestern Historical Quarterly* (July 1988): 1–15.

———, ed. *Literary Austin*. Fort Worth: Texas Christian University Press, 2007.

———. "Who Wrote *A Vaquero of the Brush Country*? A Strange Case of Demoted Authorship." *Southwestern American Literature* (Fall 2006): 71–77.

Graham, Don, James W. Lee, and William T. Pilkington, eds. *The Texas Literary Tradition: Fiction, Folklore, History*. Austin: College of Liberal Arts, University of Texas at Austin, Texas State Historical Association, 1983.

Graves, John. "The Old Guard: Dobie, Webb, Bedichek." In *The Texas Literary Tradition: Fiction, Folklore, History*, edited by Don Graham, James W. Lee, and William T. Pilkington, 16–25. Austin: College of Liberal Arts, University of Texas at Austin, Texas State Historical Association, 1983.

Green, George Norris. *The Establishment in Texas Politics: The Primitive Years, 1938–1957*. Westport, Conn.: Greenwood Press, 1979.

Greene, A. C. "The Fifty Best Texas Books." In *Range Wars: Heated Debates, Sober Reflections, and Other Assessments of Texas Writing*, edited by Craig Clifford and Tom Pilkington, 1–12. Dallas: Southern Methodist University Press, 1989.

Greer, Hilton R. "Secretary of Texas Folk-Lore Society Gathers Notable Collection of Legends." *Dallas Morning News*, June 1, 1924.

Haley, J. Evetts. *Charles Goodnight, Cowman & Plainsman*. Boston: Houghton Mifflin, 1936.

———. *The University of Texas and the Issue*. Clarendon, Tex.: Clarendon Press, 1945.

Handbook of Texas Online: http://www.tsha.utexas.edu/handbook/online/.

Heinsohn, Edmund. "A Question of Implications." *Texas Observer*, July 24, 1964.

Hill, Kevin, and Jim Stewart. "Greetings from Frank Dobie." In *2001: A Texas Folklore Odyssey*, edited by Francis Edward Abernethy and Shannon R. Thompson, 101–104. Denton: University of North Texas Press, 2001.

Holland, Richard. "A Corner Forever Texas." In *Corners of Texas, Publication of the Texas Folklore Society, Vol II*, edited by Francis Edward Abernethy, 3–29. Denton: University of North Texas Press, 1993.

———. "Guest Editor's Introduction, Special Section on J. Frank Dobie." *Southwestern American Literature* (Spring 1994): 21–23.

Hudson, Wilson. "Love and Life of Freedom." *Texas Observer*, July 24, 1964.

Jackson, Sarah Ragland. *Texas Woman of Letters, Karle Wilson Baker*. College Station: Texas A&M University Press, 2005.

Johnson, Benjamin Heber. *Revolution in Texas: How a Forgotten Rebellion and Its Bloody Suppression Turned Mexicans into Americans*. New Haven: Yale University Press, 2003.

Kennedy, David M. *Freedom from Fear: The American People in Depression and War, 1929–1945*. New York: Oxford University Press, 1999.

Keyser, Mildred B. "J. Frank Dobie: Artist-In-Depth." Master's thesis, Texas Western College, 1961.

Kirkendall, Richard Stewart. *The Harry S. Truman Encyclopedia*. New York: G. K. Hall, 1989.

Lee, James Ward. "Arbiters of Texas Literary Taste." In *Range Wars: Heated Debates, Sober Reflections, and Other Assessments of Texas Writing*, edited by Craig Clifford and Tom Pilkington, 123–136. Dallas: Southern Methodist University Press, 1989.

———. "Porter and Dobie: The Marriage from Hell." In *From Texas to the World and Back: Essays on the Journeys of Katherine Anne Porter*, edited by Mark Busby, 66–77. Fort Worth: Texas Christian University Press, 2001.

Limón, José. *Dancing with the Devil: Society and Cultural Poetics in Mexican-American South Texas*. Madison: University of Wisconsin Press, 1994.

Lind, Michael. *Made in Texas: George W. Bush and the Southern Takeover of American Politics*. New York: Basic Books, 2003.

Machann, Clinton, and William Bed, eds. *Katherine Anne Porter and Texas: An Uneasy Relationship*. College Station: Texas A&M University Press, 1990.

Major, Mabel. Review of *Guide to Life and Literature of the Southwest*, by J. Frank Dobie. *The South-Central Bulletin* (February 1944): 8.

McCutcheon, J. Forrest. "James Frank Dobie—Texan: An Appreciation." Privately printed, 1932.

McMurtry, Larry. *In a Narrow Grave*. Austin: Encino Press, 1968.

McNutt, James. "Beyond Regionalism: Texas Folklorists and the Emergence of a Post-Regional Consciousness." Ph.D. diss., University of Texas at Austin, 1982.

Miller, Nathan. *New World Coming: The 1920s and the Making of Modern America*. New York: Scribner, 2003.

Miller, Sandra E. "Elithe Hamilton Kirkland: The March Toward Perfection." Master's thesis, Texas State University–San Marcos, 1999.

Montejano, David. *Anglos and Mexicans in the Making of Texas, 1836–1986*. Austin: University of Texas Press, 1987.

Morehead, Richard M. "J. Frank Dobie." *Southwestern Historical Quarterly* (July 1988): 118–124.

———. "J. Frank Dobie—Changed Man." *Dallas Morning News*, August 8, 1964.

———. "Panelists See Renaissance of Southwestern Literature." *Dallas Morning News*, April 13, 1958.

Morris, Roy Jr., and Roy Morris. *Ambrose Bierce: Alone in Bad Company*. New York: Oxford University Press, 1999.

Morris, Willie. *North Towards Home*. Boston: Houghton Mifflin, 1967.

Nelson, Jack, and Gene Roberts. *The Censors and the Schools*. Boston: Little, Brown, 1963.

O'Leary, Tim. "Texas Picked Up on Gardner's Trail." *Press Enterprise* (Riverside, Calif.), July 21, 2002.

276    Owens, William A., and Lyman Grant, eds. *Letters of Roy Bedichek.* Austin: University of Texas Press, 1985.

Owens, William A. *Three Friends, Roy Bedichek, J. Frank Dobie, Walter Prescott Webb.* Austin: University of Texas Press, 1975.

Paredes, Américo. *George Washington Gómez: A Mexicotexan Novel.* Houston: Arte Público, 1990.

———. Review of *Legends of Texas* and *Happy Hunting Ground. Journal of American Folklore* (April–June 1965): 163–164.

———. *A Texas-Mexican Cancionero: Folksongs of the Lower Border.* Urbana: University of Illinois Press, 1976.

———. *"With His Pistol in His Hand": A Border Ballad and Its Hero.* Austin: University of Texas Press, 1958.

Pilkington, Tom. "Herding Words: Texas Literature as Trail Drive." In *Range Wars: Heated Debates, Sober Reflections, and Other Assessments of Texas Writing,* edited by Craig Clifford and Tom Pilkington, 155–172. Dallas: Southern Methodist University Press, 1989.

———. "J. Frank Dobie's Reputation and Influence: A Brief Overview." *Southwestern American Literature* (Fall 2006).

Porterfield, Nolan. *Last Cavalier: The Life and Times of John A. Lomax, 1867–1948.* Urbana: University of Illinois Press, 1996.

Price, B. Byron. *Crafting a Southwestern Masterpiece: J. Evetts Haley and "Charles Goodnight, Cowman & Plainsman."* Midland, Tex.: Nita Stewart Haley Memorial Library, 1986.

Ragsdale, Kenneth B. *The Year America Discovered Texas: Centennial '36.* College Station: Texas A&M University Press, 1987.

Richardson, Susan R. "Reds, Race, and Research: Homer P. Rainey and the Grand Texas Tradition of Political Interference, 1939–1944." *Perspectives on the History of Higher Education* 24 (2005).

Richardson, Vivian. "J. Frank Dobie Digs for Texas Legends." *Frontier Times* (1926): 38–40.

Robinson, Chandler A. *J. Evetts Haley, Cowman-Historian.* El Paso: C. Hertzog, 1967.

———. *J. Evetts Haley and the Passing of the Old West.* Austin: Jenkins Pub. Co., 1978.

Rosaldo, Renato. "Politics, Patriarchs, and Laughter." Special issue, *Cultural Critique* 6 (Spring 1987).

Rudnick, Lois Palken. *Utopian Vistas: The Mabel Dodge Luhan House and the American Counterculture.* Albuquerque: University of New Mexico Press, 1996.

Saldívar, Ramón. *The Borderlands of Culture: Américo Paredes and the Transnational Imaginary.* Durham: Duke University Press, 2006.

Salinas, Sonia. "Americo Paredes: Uncovering the Multifaceted Life of the Scholar and the Man." Master's thesis, University of Texas–Pan American, 2005.

Sanderson, Ivan T. "Of the Prairie Wolf." *New York Times*, June 26, 1949.

Slate, Audrey. "At Paisano, The Dobie Fellowships, 1967–2005." Typescript made available to the author.

Smith, Henry. "In His Most Recent Book Frank Dobie Uses Past Experience as Divining Rod to Discover the Spirit of Mexican Life." *Dallas Morning News*, October 20, 1935.

Sprague, Stacey. "James Evetts Haley and the New Deal: Laying the Foundations for the Modern Republican Party in Texas." Master's thesis, University of North Texas, 2004.

Steiner, Michael C. "Regionalism in the Great Depression." *The Geographic Review* (October 1983).

Stilwell, Hart. "Listening with the Third Ear." *Texas Observer*, July 24, 1964.

Stone, Paul Clois. "J. Frank Dobie and the American Folklore Movement: A Reappraisal." Ph.D. diss., Yale University, 1995.

———. "Whatever Happened to J. Frank Dobie?" *Southwestern American Literature* (Fall 2006): 65–70.

Supple, Catherine, and James Supple. "J. Frank Dobie at Columbia University, 1913–1914: His Letters and Diary." *Southwestern American Literature* (Fall 2006): 9–35.

Supple, James. *J. Frank Dobie's Columbia University Days Revisited*. Master's thesis, Texas State University–San Marcos, 2003.

*Time* magazine archives online: http://www.time.com/time.

Tinkle, Lon. *An American Original: The Life of J. Frank Dobie*. Boston: Little, Brown, 1978.

———. "NBA's New Prize: Porter, Dobie." *Dallas Morning News*, March 15, 1964.

———. "Time to Reconsider Our Regionalism." *Dallas Morning News*, August 22, 1948.

Vann, William H. *Texas Institute of Letters, 1936–1966*. Austin: Encino Press for the Texas Institute of Letters, 1967.

Wardlaw, Frank H. "Enlightened, Compassionate Citizen of the World." *Austin American-Statesman*, October 25, 1964.

———. "I Have That Honor." *Texas Observer*, July 24, 1964.

Warren, Bill. "Books." *Austin American-Statesman*, June 27, 1971.

Webb, Walter Prescott. *Divided We Stand: The Crisis of a Frontierless Democracy*. New York: Farrar and Rinehart, 1937.

———. *The Great Plains*. Boston: Ginn and Co., 1931.

———. *The Texas Rangers: A Century of Frontier Defense*. Boston: Houghton Mifflin, 1935.

———. "Tom Lea's Powerful Portrait of the King Ranch." *Dallas Morning News*, September 15, 1957.

Yarborough, Ralph W. *Frank Dobie: Man and Friend*. Washington, D.C.: Potomac Corral, The Westerners, 1968.

278  ARCHIVAL AND OTHER PRIMARY SOURCES

Bertha McKee Dobie Papers, A. Frank Smith, Jr. Library Center, Southwestern University, Georgetown, Texas.

Department of Justice, Federal Bureau of Investigation, J. Frank Dobie files (1942–1964), acquired through the Freedom of Information Act.

J. Evetts Haley Papers, Haley Memorial Library & History Center, Midland, Texas.

J. Frank Dobie Papers, Harry H. Ransom Humanities Research Center, University of Texas at Austin.

J. Frank Dobie Papers, Southwestern Writers Collection/The Wittliff Collections, Albert B. Alkek Library, Texas State University–San Marcos.

Lyndon Baines Johnson Library and Museum, University of Texas at Austin.

Miller Center of Public Affairs, University of Virginia.

Texas Institute of Letters Papers, Southwestern Writers Collection, Albert B. Alkek Library, Texas State University–San Marcos.

Bill Wittliff, "Interview by Steve Davis," the J. Frank Dobie day symposium at the Southwestern Writers Collection/The Wittliff Collections, Texas State University–San Marcos, April 8, 2006.

Note: Numbers in *italics* refer to figures.

Abernethy, Francis Edward, 66, 122
Adams, Andy 15, 25, 91
Alamo, 25, 112–114, 148, 149, 200
*Alcalde*, 54
Allred, Jimmy, 98, 114, 124, 144
Alonzo, Armando, 78
Álvarez Bravo, Manual, 69
American Folklore Society, 61, 66, 198
*American Mercury*, 68–69, 186
Anaya, Rudolfo, 70
Anderson, Clinton, 225
*Arizona Highways*, 191
*Atlantic Monthly*, 186
Austin, Mary, 70, 72, 91, 204
*Austin American*, 40, 43
*Austin American-Statesman*, 234
*Austin Statesman*, 117

Baker, Karle Wilson, 204
Balzac, Honoré de, 221
Barton Springs, *173*, *175*, 206, 216, 236–237
Bass, Rick, 179
Bean, Peter Ellis, 118
Beatles, the, 230

Bedichek, Lillian, 216, 224
Bedichek, Roy, *127*, 129–130, 139, 145, 146,
    148–149, 151, 153, 154, 156, 159–160,
    162, 164, 166, 168, 170, 171–174, *175*,
    176, 178–179, 186, 190–191, 206, *207*,
    214–217, 223–225, 231, 235–236, *237*
Benton, Thomas Hart, 86
Bierce, Ambrose, 28
Blakely, Bill, *192*
Boas, Franz, 31, 32, 34, 39, 60–61
Boatright, Mody, 124, 211
Bode, Winston, 235
Bosque, Genardo del, 17–18, 40
Bowie, Jim, 6, 112, 140, 201
Brewer, J. Mason, 7, *93*, 95, 133, 197–198
Brown, Milton, 144
Brown, Pat, 4
*Brown v. Board of Education*, 161, 228
Bullington, Orville, 147, 151–152, 159, 168

Cabeza de Vaca, Álvar Núñez, 11–12, 91
Callaway, Morgan, 38, 47, 54
Carter, Hodding, 197
Cather, Willa, 70, 91, 92, 228

280

Centennial, 6, 109–114, 116, 118, 131, 208
Cherry Springs Ranch, 191, 215–216
Chittenden, Larry, 111
Cisneros, Sandra, 236
Clemens, Samuel, 20, 61, 85
Coker, Willie Belle, 238
Columbia University, 29–33, 36, 38, 61, 69,
      147, 191, 235
Congress of Racial Equality, 159
Coppini, Pompeo, 112–114, 116
Coronado, Francisco Vasquez de, 79
Cortez, Gregorio, 208–210
Cortez, Santos, 56–57, 58, 191
Cortina, Juan, 13, 77, 126
*Country Gentleman*, 64–65, 68
Cox, Mike, 235
Crane, Stephen, 25
Crockett, Davy, 91, 140, 176, 195
Cunningham, Eugene, 204
Cunningham, Minnie Fisher, 166
Curtis, Gregory, 236

*Daily Texan*, 192
*Dallas Morning News*, 46, 69, 98, 108, 139,
      154, 157–158, 177, 187, 201, 214
Davenport, Mrs. O. H., 197
Davis, Mollie E. Moore, 25
Dealey, Ted, 158
Díaz, Porfirio, 28
Dies, Martin Jr., 168
Dobie, Bertha McKee, 4, 23, 24–26, 28–29,
      33, 35–42, 44–49, 55–56, 59, 63, 67–69,
      72, 85–86, 89, 99, 105, 106, 116, 124,
      166–167, 170, 174, 177, 180, 186, 191,
      213–216, 220, 223–225, 232, 234–235;
      and courtship with Dobie, 24–26, 28–
      29, 33–40, 42; as Dobie's editor, 88, 104,
      135, 215, 223; and gardening, 85, 88–90,
      104; writings of, 68–69, 90, 102, 104
Dobie, Dick (father), 15–19, 140
Dobie, Dudley, Jr., 238–239
Dobie, Ella Byler (mother), 15–19, 40, 41,
      166, 190
Dobie, J. Frank: and African Americans,
      7, 8, 31, 95–96, 125–126, 133–134, 159–

162, 176, 197–198, 240–241; childhood
      of, 12, 14–21; college years of, 21–36;
      early writings of, 23–25, 33, 35, 39, 42,
      46, 54; in England, 163–167, 169–170;
      FBI investigation of, 4, 158–159, 161,
      179, 225–228; literary criticisms of,
      107–108, 110, 134–135, 142, 169–170,
      188–189, 193–194, 200, 233, 235–236,
      239–240; and marital relations, 42, 48–
      49, 55–56, 63, 166–167, 170; and Mexi-
      can Americans, 17–18, 44, 56, 72–74,
      77–78, 104–105, 121–123, 198, 208–212,
      214, 236, 240; and Mexico, 28, 39, 44,
      101–108; newspaper column of, 120,
      139–140, 143, 149–151, 154–160, 164,
      166, 171, 176, 178–179, 183, 190–191,
      195, 198, 200–202, 205–206, 215, 226,
      229; photographs of, 2, 7, 23, 41, 47, 65,
      79, 87, 103, 107, 111, 115, 125, 153, 165,
      175, 184–185, 199, 203, 207, 220, 233, 237;
      and politics, 6, 7, 35, 99, 112, 118–120,
      124–126, 128–130, 144–162, 165–169,
      174–177, 179–180, 187–188, 191–192,
      225–229; teaching career of, 27–28,
      37–42, 47, 53, 59, 63–64, 67, 75–76,
      90–92, 100, 115, 116, 146, 151–154,
      158–162, 175–176, 179–180, 183, 227,
      234–236, 238–239; and World War I
      service, 45–49
Dobie, J. Frank, works of: *Apache Gold and
      Yaqui Silver*, 131–136; *Coronado's Chil-
      dren*, 78–81, 85, 94, 95–96, 97, 131–132;
      *Cow People*, 231, 233; *The Flavor of Texas*,
      118–119, 208; *Guide To Life And Litera-
      ture of The Southwest*, 92, 203–204; *Leg-
      ends of Texas*, 64–67, 68; *The Longhorns*,
      4, 140–142, 148; *The Mustangs*, 186, 193–
      194, 231; *A Texan in England*, 169–170;
      *Tongues of the Monte*, 106–108, 110, 126,
      131, 134; *A Vaquero of the Brush Country*,
      76–79, 102; *The Voice of the Coyote*, 178,
      188–189, 222
Dobie, Jim (uncle), 40, 54–55, 57–58, 59,
      140, 235
Dobie, Saza, 238–239

Dobie-Paisano Fellowship, 236
Dodge, Mabel, 34, 70
Dos Passos, John, 153–154, 167, 177
Doubleday, Doran, and Company, 101
Dugger, Ronnie, 224

Einstein, Albert, 228
Eliot, T. S., 34
Encino Press, 237
Evans, Walker, 87

Farm Security Administration, 87
Faulk, John Henry, 91, *125*, 126, 166
Faulkner, William, 76, 200, 228
Federal Bureau of Investigation, 4, 158–
    159, 161, 179, 225–228
Ferguson, Jim "Pa," 94, 129, 146
Flipper, Henry O., 133–134
Foote, Horton, 205
Frantz, Joe, 126, 129, 187, 224
Frost, Robert, 86, 186

Gaddis, Isabel, 167
*Galveston Daily Tribune*, 37
Gard, Wayne, 198
Gardner, Erle Stanley, 234
Gipson, Fred, 91, 202
Gish, Lillian, 69
Givner, Joan, 136
Goldman, Emma, 34
González, Jovita, 7, *71*, 72–74, 95, 167, 198
Goodacre, Glenna, 236
Goodnight, Charles, 91, 97, 119
Goodwyn, Frank, 202
Graham, Don, 135, 200
Graves, John, 205, 239–240
Greene, A. C., 179, 202
Grey, Zane, 76, 223
Grider, Sylvia Ann, 136
Guerra, Fermina, 200

Haley, J. Evetts, 96, 97, 98–99, 116, 119–
    120, 124, 145–149, 157–158, 176–177,
    228–229
Harrigan, Stephen, 236
Harrison, Dan, 147

Harry H. Ransom Humanities Research
    Center, 234–235, 238
Heinsohn, Edmund, 223–224
Hemingway, Ernest, 88, 200, 228
Henderson, Alice Stillwell, 27
Henry, O., 25, 85
Hillerman, Tony, 70
*Holiday*, 186
*Holland's*, 68, 104
Hoover, J. Edgar, 159, 161, 226–228
House Un-American Activities Commit-
    tee, 168
Houston, Andrew Jackson, 147–148
Houston, Sam, 112, 147–148, 149, 195, 222
Hudson, Wilson, 174
Hughes, Langston, 228
Hurston, Zora Neale, 62
Huston-Tillotson University, 95
Huxley, Aldous, 70
Hyer, R. S., 21, 22, 28

Indiana University, 133, 195
Internal Security Act of 1950, 225–226
Irving, Washington, 62

Jeffersonian Democrats, 119, 147
John Birch Society, 119, 177, 230
Johnson, Lady Bird, 4, 232, 236
Johnson, Lyndon Baines, 3, 4, 148, 177,
    188, 192, 232, *233*, 236
Johnston, Ralph, 236
Jones, Anson, 111–112
*Journal of American Folklore*, 32, 39, 60–61,
    65–66, 212
Jung, Carl, 70

Kahlo, Frida, 69
Kennedy, John F., 228, 231
Kidd, Rodney, 129
Kincaid, Edgar, 48
Kincaid, Edgar, Jr., 234, 238
King, Richard, 13, 19
King Ranch, 19, 44, 105, 206–208, 212–214
Kirkland, Elithe Hamilton, 200
Kleberg, Richard, 157

La Farge, Oliver, 70, 91
Lange, Dorthea, 87
Laval, Pierre, 179
Lawrence, D. H., 70, 221
Lea, Sarah, 225
Lea, Tom, 132, 142–143, 146, 148, 150–151,
    171, 201–202, 203, 206–208, 212, 213,
    214–215
Leadbelly, 87
Lee, James Ward, 200, 204, 235
Lee, Russell, 87
Lewis, Sinclair, 34
Lindbergh, Charles, 148, 149
Little, Brown and Company, 142
Lomax, John A., 53–54, 55, 57–59, 64, 87,
    129, 157–158, 190, 240
Los Olmos Ranch, 55–59, 191, 235
Lost Tayopa Mine, 101, 131–133
Luhan, Mabel Dodge, 34, 70
Luhan, Tony, 70

Marshall, Thurgood, 161
McCarthy, Cormac, 240
McCarthy, Joseph, 192, 193, 196, 228
McCutcheon, J. Forrest, 88
McMurtry, Larry, 6, 110, 178, 205, 235,
    238, 240
McNeil, Marshall, 4
McNutt, James, 77, 104
Mencken, H. L., 69
Michener, James A., 239
Millay, Edna St. Vincent, 69
Miller, Henry, 221
Mireles, Edmund, 73–74
Mitchell, Margaret, 86
Mitchum, Robert, 201
Modernism, 33–35, 69–70, 200
Montaigne, Michel de, 48
Moreland, Patrick D., 114, 135
Morgan, George, 147
Morris, Willie, 192
Murrow, Edward R., 186

National Association of the Advancement
    of Colored People, 159, 179

National Geographic, 169, 171
Newsom, Rollo K., 66
New York Herald-Tribune, 68, 85, 104, 141,
    231
New York Literary Guild, 81
New York Times, 81, 108, 142, 212–214
Ney, Elisabet, 112
Nichols, John, 70
Norman-Butler, Belinda, 167

O'Connor, Kate, 4, 157
O'Daniel, W. Lee "Pappy," 144, 145,
    146–151, 155
Odum, Howard, 75–76
O'Keeffe, Georgia, 70
Olmos, Edward James, 211
O'Neill, Eugene, 34

Painter, Theophilus Schickel, 179–180
Paisano Ranch, 216, 231, 236
Paredes, Américo, 4, 120, 121, 122–123,
    208, 209, 210–212, 214, 240
Parten, J. R., 146
Payne, Leonidas, 59–60, 67
Pegues, Albert, 21, 29
Perry, George Sessions, 201
Picasso, Pablo, 34
Plan of San Diego, 44–45
Porter, Katherine Anne, 69, 71, 85, 135–
    136, 191, 200, 232
Porter, William Sydney, 25, 85
Pulitzer, Joseph, 30

Quinn, Anthony, 201

Rainey, Homer P., 146, 152, 153, 167–169,
    172, 176–178, 228
Ramirez, José Antonio, 13, 57
Ramirez, José Victoriano, 13, 57
Ransom, Harry, 234–235
Rayburn, Sam, 166
Reed, John, 34
Reuther, Walter, 4
Richardson, Sid, 141–142, 150, 157
Rivera, Diego, 69

Rogers, Will, 86
Roosevelt, Eleanor, 144
Roosevelt, Franklin Delano, 7, 87, 98–99,
    109, 128, 144–145, 147–150, 152–153,
    155–156, 159, 188
Roosevelt, Theodore, 54
Ruggles, C. B., 102, 131
Russell, Charles, 192

Sacco and Vanzetti, 69
*San Antonio Express*, 26, 129, 141
Sandburg, Carl, 64, 86, 186, 228
Sanford, Winifred, 69
Sanger, Margaret, 34
Santa Anna, 80, 147
*Saturday Evening Post*, 98, 141, 169–170, 186
*Saturday Review of Literature*, 65
Scarborough, Dorothy, 69
Schlesinger, Arthur, 186
Shelton, Polk, Jr., 230
Sheppard, Morris, 147
Shivers, Allan, 192, 195
Shockley, Martin, 194
Shrake, Bud, 240
Silko, Leslie Marmon, 70
Silva, Chelo, 122
Simms, William Gilmore, 28
Sinclair, Upton, 34
Smith, Henry Nash, 102, 108
Smith, John Lee, 155–157
Southern Methodist University, 47, 110,
    114, 229
Southwestern University, 21–24, 26, 28–29,
    191
Southwestern Writers Collection, 238
Southwest Press, 79–80, 90, 92, 100
*Southwest Review*, 91, 186
Stark, Lutcher, 146, 152, 169
Steinbeck, John, 86, 228
Stevenson, Coke, 151, 155, 169, 179–180,
    188
Stilwell, Hart, 202
Stone, Paul, 32
Stravinsky, Igor, 34
Strickland, D. F., 152, 168, 169

Sweatt, Heman, 161, 179

Taylor, E. H., 64
Texans for America, 228
Texas Folklore Society, 7, 39, 59–61, 64–67,
    72–73, 91, 95–96, 97, 121–122, 125, 141,
    171, 191, 211–212
Texas Institute of Letters, 114, 116, 135–
    136, 170, 191, 194, 196, 198, 202, 205,
    229, 232
*Texas Observer*, 192, 224, 235
Texas Rangers, 13, 45, 56, 94, 105, 126,
    210–211
*Texas Review*, 54
*Texas Spectator*, 187, 202
Texas Tech University, 67
Thackeray, William, 167
Thompson, Stith, 133
Thoreau, Henry David, 117
Thorp, Jack, 204
Tinkle, Lon, 167, 201
Tolson, Clyde, 226
Trent, William Porterfield, 32
Trinity University, 121
Truman, Harry, 3, 4, 187, *233*
Twain, Mark, 20, 61, 85

United Nations, 186
University of Texas at Austin, 3, 4, 37–42,
    46–47, 53–54, 59, 63, 67–68, 72, 75–76,
    92, 96, 98, 102, 104, 110, 112–113,
    115–116, 119–120, 124–125, 128–129,
    146–147, 151–154, 161–162, 167–169,
    175, 177, 179–180, 192, 196, 204, 210–
    212, 227, 228, 234, 236, 238–239

Vann, William, 135–136, 196, 205
Villa, Pancho, 28, 45
Villon, François, 223

Wallace, Big Foot, 41, 118, 164
Wallace, Henry, 187–188
Wardlaw, Frank, 204–205, 210–211
Warren, Earl, 228
Washington, Booker T., 160

Webb, Terrell Maverick, 231
Webb, Walter Prescott, 39, *93*, 94, 98,
    126, 127, 128, 152, 154, 156, 168, 174,
    178, 191, 202, 204, 209–211, 214, 217,
    223–224, 225, 231, 236, *237*
Wilkie, Wendell, 145
Wills, Bob, 144
Wilson, Woodrow, 43
Wister, Owen, 25
Wittliff, Bill, 237–238

Wittliff, Sally, 237–238
Wood, Grant, 86
Works Progress Administration, 87

XIT ranch, 97–98

*Yale Review*, 186
Yarborough, Opal, 124, 180
Yarborough, Ralph, 124, 180, 192–193, 224
Young, John, 27, 76–78, 102

Milton Keynes UK
Ingram Content Group UK Ltd.
UKHW011605230624
444424UK00014B/166